Societal Contexts of Child Development

Societal Contexts of Child Development

PATHWAYS OF INFLUENCE AND
IMPLICATIONS FOR PRACTICE AND POLICY

Edited by
Elizabeth T. Gershoff,
Rashmita S. Mistry,
and
Danielle A. Crosby

OXFORD
UNIVERSITY PRESS

OXFORD
UNIVERSITY PRESS

Oxford University Press is a department of the University of Oxford.
It furthers the University's objective of excellence in research, scholarship,
and education by publishing worldwide.

Oxford   New York

Auckland   Cape Town   Dar es Salaam   Hong Kong   Karachi
Kuala Lumpur   Madrid   Melbourne   Mexico City   Nairobi
New Delhi   Shanghai   Taipei   Toronto

With offices in

Argentina   Austria   Brazil   Chile   Czech Republic   France   Greece
Guatemala   Hungary   Italy   Japan   Poland   Portugal   Singapore
South Korea   Switzerland   Thailand   Turkey   Ukraine   Vietnam

Oxford is a registered trademark of Oxford University Press
in the UK and certain other countries.

Published in the United States of America by
Oxford University Press
198 Madison Avenue, New York, NY 10016

Library of Congress Cataloging-in-Publication Data
Societal contexts of child development : pathways of influence and implications
for practice and policy / edited by Elizabeth T. Gershoff, Rashmita S. Mistry, and
Danielle A. Crosby.
pages cm
Includes index.
ISBN 978-0-19-994391-3
1. Child development.   2. Child psychology.   3. Children—Social conditions.
I. Gershoff, Elizabeth T.   II. Mistry, Rashmita, 1968–   III. Crosby, Danielle A.
HQ767.9.S666 2014
305.231—dc23
2013022440

1 3 5 7 9 8 6 4 2
Printed in the United States of America
on acid-free paper

This volume is dedicated to Dr. Aletha C. Huston, whose substantial contributions to the field of developmental science served as its inspiration. For more than 50 years, her scholarship through both basic and applied research has sought to understand what changes in the social, cultural, economic, and political landscape have meant for the lives of children. Across multiple aspects of her personal and professional life, Aletha has worked diligently to foster interdisciplinary collaboration, strengthen the connections between research and policy, and promote the well-being of children and families. With wisdom, generosity, and grace, she has nurtured, challenged, and inspired her many students and colleagues (including the contributors to this volume), and we are sincerely grateful for her leadership, mentorship, and friendship.

CONTENTS

{ ACKNOWLEDGMENTS }

Most of the chapters in this volume were presented at a festschrift conference in honor of Dr. Aletha Huston, Priscilla Pond Flawn Regents Professor Emerita of Child Development at the University of Texas at Austin, held on May 10, 2011, at the University of Texas at Austin. We are grateful to several organizations and their leaders for their financial support of this conference, namely the Society for Research in Child Development (Dr. Lonnie Sherrod), the William T. Grant Foundation (Dr. Robert Granger), the Population Research Center at the University of Texas at Austin (Dr. Mark Hayward), and the School of Human Ecology at the University of Texas at Austin (Dr. Sheldon Ekland-Olson). We also extend sincere thanks to Dr. Marci Gleason who assisted in the organization of the festschrift and to Dr. Kelly Purtell and Holly Sexton at the University of Texas at Austin for their generous assistance in helping prepare the manuscript for publication. Rashmita Mistry acknowledges the generous support of the Department of Education at the University of California at Los Angeles for supporting her time working on the festschrift and this volume. Finally, we would like to thank Sarah Harrington, Andrea Zekus, and their colleagues at Oxford University Press for their assistance in shepherding this volume through the publication process.

—Elizabeth T. Gershoff, Rashmita S. Mistry, and Danielle A. Crosby

{ ABOUT THE EDITORS }

Elizabeth T. Gershoff, Ph.D., is an Associate Professor of Human Development and Family Sciences at the University of Texas at Austin. Dr. Gershoff's research focuses on the impacts of parenting, poverty, community violence, neighborhoods, and school contexts on child and youth development over time.

Rashmita A. Mistry, Ph.D., is an Associate Professor of Education at the University of California, Los Angeles. Dr. Mistry's research examines the consequences of poverty and economic stress on family and child well-being, children's reasoning about social class and inequality, and the design and evaluation of elementary and middle school curricula focused on social and economic inequality.

Danielle A. Crosby, Ph.D., is an Associate Professor of Human Development and Family Studies at the University of North Carolina at Greensboro. Dr. Crosby studies the environments, programs, and policies that impact young children's development in the context of social and economic disadvantage.

{ CONTRIBUTORS }

Aprile D. Benner, Ph.D.
Assistant Professor
Human Development and Family
  Sciences and the Population
  Research Center
University of Texas at Austin
Austin, Texas

Rebecca S. Bigler, Ph.D.
Professor
Department of Psychology and
  Center for Women's and Gender
  Studies
University of Texas at Austin
Austin, Texas

Margaret Burchinal, Ph.D.
Senior Scientist
Director, Data Management and
  Analysis Center
Frank Porter Graham Child
  Development Institute
University of North Carolina
Chapel Hill, North Carolina

Sandra L. Calvert, Ph.D.
Professor
Department of Psychology
Director
Children's Digital Media Center
Georgetown University
Washington, District of Columbia

K. Alison Clarke-Stewart, Ph.D.
Research Professor and Professor
  Emerita of Psychology and Social
  Behavior
University of California at Irvine
Irvine, California

Danielle A. Crosby, Ph.D.
Associate Professor
Department of Human Development
  and Family Studies
School of Health and Human
  Sciences
University of North Carolina at
  Greensboro
Greensboro, North Carolina

Robert Crosnoe, Ph.D.
Elsie and Stanley E. (Skinny) Adams,
  Sr. Centennial Professor in
  Liberal Arts
Department of Sociology and the
  Population Research Center
University of Texas at Austin
Austin, Texas

Greg J. Duncan, Ph.D.
Distinguished Professor
School of Education
University of California at Irvine
Irvine, California

Jacquelynne S. Eccles, Ph.D.
McKeachie-Pintrich Distinguished
    University Professor of Psychology
    and Education
Department of Psychology
University of Michigan
Ann Arbor, Michigan

Elizabeth T. Gershoff, Ph.D.
Associate Professor
Human Development and Family
    Sciences and the Population
    Research Center
University of Texas at Austin
Austin, Texas

Cynthia García Coll, Ph.D.
Charles Pitts Robinson and John
    Palmer Barstow Professor
Professor of Education, Psychology
    and Pediatrics
Department of Education
Brown University
Providence, Rhode Island

Camila Godoy
Graduate Student
Department of Psychology
Suffolk University
Boston, Massachusetts

Robert C. Granger, Ed.D.
President
William T. Grant Foundation
New York, New York

Cecily R. Hardaway, Ph.D.
Postdoctoral Fellow
Department of Psychiatry
Interdisciplinary Alcohol Research
    Training Program
University of Pittsburgh School of
    Medicine
Pittsburgh, Pennsylvania

Lacey J. Hilliard, Ph.D.
Postdoctoral Fellow
Institute for Applied Research in
    Youth Development
Tufts University
Medford, Massachusetts

Aletha C. Huston, Ph.D.
Priscilla Pond Flawn Regents
    Professor Emerita of Child
    Development
Human Development and Family
    Sciences
University of Texas at Austin
Austin, Texas

Jennifer A. Kotler, Ph.D.
Vice President for Domestic
    Research
Sesame Workshop
New York, New York

Tama Leventhal, Ph.D.
Associate Professor
Eliot-Pearson Department of Child
    Development
Tufts University
Medford, Massachusetts

Lynn S. Liben, Ph.D.
Distinguished Professor
Departments of Psychology, Human
    Development and Family Studies,
    and Curriculum and Instruction
Pennsylvania State University
University Park, Pennsylvania

Amy K. Marks, Ph.D.
Assistant Professor
Director of Undergraduate and
    Graduate Studies
Department of Psychology
Suffolk University
Boston, Massachusetts

Vonnie McLoyd, Ph.D.
Ewart A. C. Thomas Collegiate
    Professor
Chair, Developmental Psychology
    Program
Department of Psychology
University of Michigan
Ann Arbor, Michigan

Rashmita S. Mistry, Ph.D.
Associate Professor
Human Development and Psychology
    Division, Department of Education
University of California at Los
    Angeles
Los Angeles, California

Ana María Nieto, Ed.M.
Graduate Student
Harvard Graduate School of
    Education
Harvard University
Boson, Massachusetts

Marion O'Brien, Ph.D.
Professor
Department of Human Development
    and Family Studies
School of Human Environmental
    Sciences
University of North Carolina at
    Greensboro
Greensboro, North Carolina

Nina Smith, Ph.D.
Postdoctoral Research Associate
African and African American
    Studies
Duke University
Durham, North Carolina

Rosemarie T. Truglio, Ph.D.
Senior Vice President for Education
    and Research
Sesame Workshop
New York, New York

Vivian Tseng, Ph.D.
Vice President for Programs
William T. Grant Foundation
New York, New York

Deborah Lowe Vandell, Ph.D.
Founding Dean
School of Education
University of California at Irvine
Irvine, California

Ellen A. Wartella, Ph.D.
Sheikh Hamad bin Khalifa Al-Thani
    Professor of Communication
Professor of Psychology and Professor
    of Human Development and
    Social Policy
School of Communication
Northwestern University
Evanston, Illinois

Jennifer M. Weaver, Ph.D.
Assistant Professor
Department of Psychology
Boise State University
Boise, Idaho

Thomas S. Weisner, Ph.D.
Distinguished Professor of
    Anthropology
Departments of Psychiatry and
    Anthropology
Center for Culture and Health, Semel
    Institute
University of California at Los Angeles
Los Angeles, California

Brian L. Wilcox, Ph.D.
Professor of Psychology
Director, Center on Children,
    Families and the Law
University of Nebraska
Lincoln, Nebraska
Senior Program Associate
William T. Grant Foundation
New York, New York

Hirokazu Yoshikawa, Ph.D.
Walter H. Gale Professor of
  Education and
  Academic Dean
Harvard Graduate School of
  Education
Harvard University
Boston, Massachusetts

Martha Zaslow, Ph.D.
Director
Office for Policy and
  Communications, Society for
  Research in Child Development
Senior Scholar
Child Trends
Washington, District of Columbia

Contextualizing Child Development

Elizabeth T. Gershoff, Rashmita S. Mistry, and Danielle A. Crosby

In the early part of the past century, the nascent field of child development research focused on describing and charting individual development over time across the physical, cognitive, and social domains, and on understanding the processes of child socialization, particularly within the context of parent–child relationships. These two themes continue to characterize the majority of developmental research; however, over the past several decades they have been joined by a growing appreciation that contexts beyond the home environment also influence the course and quality of children's development (Huston & Ripke, 2010; Shonkoff & Phillips, 2000).

This approach to understanding the role of contexts in children's development has its theoretical grounding in Bronfenbrenner's ecological (and later, bioecological) theory (Bronfenbrenner, 1979; Bronfenbrenner & Morris, 2006). Bronfenbrenner and others maintained that human development cannot be understood without adequate attention paid to the multiple and overlapping contexts within which it takes place (Sameroff, 2010). From this perspective, development is conceived of as a product of interactions with and reactions to the multiple systems or contexts in which children are embedded. Furthermore, the relations between children and the ecological systems they inhabit are not unidirectional; children are understood to affect systems in a reciprocal, or transactional, manner (Huston & Bentley, 2010; Sameroff, 2010).

The increased interest among social scientists in multiple levels of influence on development has occurred alongside two other major advancements in developmental science. The first of these is an appreciation of the importance of interdisciplinary research to truly understand the ecological systems surrounding individual child development. Disciplines vary not only in their topics of inquiry but also in their methods and levels of analysis, and, as a result, interdisciplinary approaches allow for a more comprehensive understanding of the developmental phenomena under study (Huston, 2008).

A second major trend has been a growing interest in what is termed "applied developmental science" (Lerner & Fisher, 2000), a branch of developmental science concerned with scholarship that promotes, rather than just understands, positive development. Applied developmental research is conducted with the explicit goal of improving the lives of children and their families. This goal is sometimes achieved through evaluations of the effectiveness of actual interventions but at other times is met through basic research that can be used to inform evidence-based interventions down the line. In many cases, applied developmental research explicitly or implicitly aims to improve children's lives by informing social policies (Huston, 2008).

What We Mean by Context

Contexts are often thought of as merely the physical environments that children experience directly through what they can see, hear, touch, smell, and taste. Although we acknowledge that the physical world is extremely impactful on children's growth, health, and development (see Evans & Wachs' [2010] volume on chaotic environments and child development), in this volume, we conceive of contexts more broadly, defining *contexts* as *the physical, social, cultural, and political environments that determine the type and quality of opportunities, interactions, and experiences children will have in their day-to-day lives*

Our primary focus is on the contexts beyond the home environment, although all of the contexts discussed in this volume impact home environments and the family relationships within them.

Organization of This Volume

These trends in developmental science, namely, an appreciation of contextual influences on development, a push toward interdisciplinary approaches, and an encouragement of applied research, have slowly pervaded research on children's development, yet there have been few attempts made to take stock of what has been gained by the addition of these three new perspectives to the study of child development. The current volume aims to do just this. Informed by bioecological theory, the chapters in this volume summarize how individual child development is influenced by the social, cultural, economic, and political contexts in which children and families are embedded.

The volume takes an inherently interdisciplinary approach to understanding the influences that contexts have on the lives of children. Different disciplines bring distinct theories, methods, and variables of interest to the study of specific contexts; thus viewing the same topic from two or more disciplinary lenses can provide a richer understanding of it. In this volume, chapter authors are prominent social scientists and recognized experts on their respective topics, but they also represent a diverse set of disciplines, including psychology, sociology, education, economics, human development, anthropology, public policy, and communication studies. This book thereby provides an opportunity for scholars and students to benefit from the combined expertise of multiple disciplines.

The volume is distinctive in that it is committed to advancing both basic and applied developmental science. To do so, the book devotes two chapters to each context. The first chapter in each pair presents a review of extant research on a topic from a basic research perspective, discussing the prominent theoretical and methodological approaches that guide research in that area and highlighting key mechanisms of influence. The second chapter in each section takes an applied research perspective, examining and documenting how basic research can be, has been, or should be used to improve and enhance the everyday lives and developmental outcomes of children and their families through the shaping of opportunities, interventions, or social policies. Importantly, the chapters were not created in isolation; authors cross-reference each other's chapters and defer to coverage of certain topics in each other's chapters, thereby minimizing substantive overlap while ensuring complementary and comprehensive coverage of each context.

It is our hope that this volume will be of interest to and will inform the work of three major audiences, namely, researchers seeking to quickly familiarize themselves with the state of research on these societal contexts, students in advanced undergraduate and graduate courses that take an ecological approach to studying child development, and nonacademic researchers, policy makers, and practitioners whose focus is on improving children's lives through improving their contexts.

Content of This Volume

We focus in this volume on contexts outside the social environment of the family. We include both proximal contexts, which children experience directly, and distal contexts, which exert their influence indirectly. In some instances, contexts are closely tied to the physical environment in which children spend their time, such as schools, neighborhoods, or child care settings. In other instances, contexts are not defined by a particular physical space but instead are manifest as social or cultural beliefs and experiences (as is the case for gender roles) or as social opportunities that are created or restricted as a function of a family's social or economic status (as is the case for poverty).

The chapters in this volume provide state-of-the-science reviews of the theory, methodology, and research findings relevant to each of seven contexts of child development: gender roles, child care and early childhood education, culture and immigration, poverty, neighborhoods and schools, media, and public programs and public policy. We chose these contexts because they represent key influences on development beyond the boundaries of home and family, because they have received a large amount of research attention in recent years, and because each has been affected by major social and political trends over the past several decades. Six contexts are covered in paired basic and applied research chapters grouped into sections. The seventh context—public programs and policies—is inherently applied and thus is covered in only one chapter. The book ends with an epilogue by a prominent child development researcher, Aletha Huston, who has been at the forefront of studying many of the contexts included in this volume.

What follows is a brief description of the rationale for each of the chosen contexts and of the content of the paired chapters in each section.

GENDER AS A SHAPING CONTEXT

In the 1960s and 1970s, the social movement known as the Women's Movement (or Sexual Revolution) dramatically changed public attitudes about women's social roles, especially regarding the acceptability of work outside the home and the pursuit of higher education. These changes led to increases in the number of women enrolled at institutions of higher education and, indeed, in the number of universities that admitted women. An integral part of this social movement was a focus on society's role in shaping social attitudes about gender and, in turn, the gender development of children.

As Liben, Bigler, and Hilliard recount in Chapter 1, most of the early theoretical and empirical work on gender development was directed toward understanding universals. Underlying this work were the beliefs that differentiated gender roles facilitated societal tasks (e.g., through efficient division of labor) and that an important marker of healthy individual development was the acquisition of culturally defined, "appropriate" gender roles. As investigators began to identify the full range of constructs and content areas relevant to sex typing, as well as some of the collateral consequences of gender-differentiated behaviors and socialization, more attention was directed toward identifying and explaining variability rather than universality in gender development. Liben and colleagues review theoretical models that describe pathways by which gender-differentiated outcomes develop (Liben & Bigler, 2002) and identify environmental and individual factors that exacerbate or diminish the impact of gender divisions (Bigler & Liben, 2007). In addition, they describe empirical research demonstrating the power of environmental structure on gender attitudes and behaviors, and they close by discussing illustrative policy implications of this body of work (e.g., implications for single-sex schooling).

In Chapter 2, Eccles applies this basic research on gender roles to better understand the real-world problem of the underrepresentation of women in STEM fields (science, technology, engineering, and mathematics). By affecting the values associated with particular career fields (e.g., helping people) and girls' and women's expected efficacy in particular fields and occupations, gender roles affect the subjects girls study in school, the majors they undertake in college, and the careers they pursue as adult women, over and above their actual academic abilities. As Eccles notes, interventions that change girls' beliefs about the utility and applicability of STEM careers hold promise for increasing the number of women in STEM fields.

CHILD CARE: AN EARLY CONTEXTUAL OPPORTUNITY

Prior to the 1970s, children under the age of 6 spent most, if not all, of their time in the care and company of family members in a home setting, primarily with their mothers. Accordingly, for much of the 20th century, research on early development in context focused almost exclusively on the mother–child relationship and the home environment. Over the past 40 years, however, child care provided by someone other than a parent has come to play an essential role in modern family life and is considered a normative developmental experience. The primary impetus for this shift has been the dramatic increase in women's workforce participation as a result of changing social norms (as discussed in the previous section), expanded educational and occupational opportunities for women, and more general economic trends. In the United States and elsewhere, a majority of households now rely heavily, and sometimes exclusively, on women's earnings. The most significant employment changes have occurred for mothers of young children; in 1970, 27% of U.S. mothers of preschoolers were in the labor force (Casper & Bianchi, 2002) compared to more than 70% today (Bureau of Labor Statistics, 2011).

Research to date has given us a broad outline of how women's work and child care are linked to child outcomes and family functioning. Early concerns about potentially serious negative consequences associated with the separation of young children from their mothers have been shown to be unfounded, and, in fact, high-quality child care appears to provide substantial benefits for children and their parents. Questions about the ways in which changing lifestyles relate to child and family well-being remain central to developmental science. To date, the underlying processes by which child care affects children are not thoroughly understood, nor have our national policies been fully responsive to the changing lives of families.

The chapters in this section begin with the premise that, to be effective, child care programs and policies must serve the dual purpose of supporting parents' employment efforts and promoting children's development. In Chapter 3, O'Brien and her colleagues explore the connections between parents' work lives, child care, and child and family well-being, presenting illustrative results from the National Institute of Child Health and Development (NICHD) Study of Early Child Care and Youth Development (on which most of the authors are investigators). Findings are discussed in terms of their implications for public policy and suggest an unfinished research agenda. In Chapter 4, Zaslow, Crosby, and Smith consider recent changes to the early care and education (ECE) policy landscape and evidence of their impact on child well-being. They observe that, despite important advancements in understanding how ECE environments relate to children's development and a significant expansion of public investments in early childhood programs, many children who stand to benefit from high-quality ECE experiences currently do not have consistent access to them. To more fully realize the potential of ECE, Zaslow and colleagues argue that the next generation of policies (and the research seeking to inform them) will need to attend equally to issues of quality and access. Along with highlighting emerging issues in each area, they discuss the need for continued movement toward a more unified field, one in which research and policy acknowledge the dual functions of ECE as a support for working families and an opportunity for developmental enrichment, and seek more integrated approaches.

CULTURAL CONTEXTS AND IMMIGRANT FAMILIES

The past 50 years have seen a dramatic increase in the number of immigrant children in the United States. Approximately 25% of all children under the age of 18—more than 16 million in all—have at least one parent who was born outside the United States (Hernandez, Denton, & Macartney, 2008). By 2015, immigrant children are projected to comprise 30% of the school-based population (Capps, Fix, Murray, Ost, Passel, & Herwantoro, 2004). Given the rapid racial and ethnic diversification of the child population in the United States, theories of child development need to better reflect the complexity and diversity of the contexts within which children are developing (García Coll, Crnic, Lamberty, Wasik et al., 1996).

In Chapter 5, Marks, Godoy, and García Coll describe the challenges endemic to growing up as an immigrant child in a majority American cultural context, including social and economic barriers. The challenges immigrant children and youth face are compounded by the fact that they are faced with mastering additional developmental tasks that nonimmigrant children are not, including being bilingual and developing multiethnic and multicultural identities. However, they also emphasize that many immigrant youth are resilient to these challenges and achieve successful developmental outcomes in spite of them. Acknowledging such challenges, Nieto and Yoshikawa, in Chapter 6, argue that efforts to improve the lives of immigrant children will be most effective if they focus on contexts outside the family, for instance, by strengthening social networks and developing political capital in immigrant communities. The authors further suggest that research and intervention efforts will be successful only if they view immigrant communities and families as competent, knowledgeable, and able to inform program and policies.

CHILD POVERTY AS A LIMITING CONTEXT OF DEVELOPMENT

Over the course of the past 50 years, child poverty rates have stubbornly hovered around 20%. According to the most recent data from 2011, 15.5 million children and adolescents—more than 1 in 5 of all children living in the U.S. (21.4%)—lived in families with incomes below the federal poverty line (FPL; $22,113 for a four-person household; DeNavas-Walt, Proctor, & Smith, 2012). Children from racial or ethnic minority groups are disproportionately more likely than other children to experience poverty, as are children from immigrant families, children younger than age 6, and those living in rural communities. Poverty affects children by restricting their opportunities, degrading the physical conditions of their lives, and forcing children to live in disadvantaged neighborhoods and attend underresourced schools. Research on child poverty has clearly indicated that living in poverty places children at elevated risk for school failure, physical and mental health problems, delinquency, and reduced lifetime earnings and productivity (Huston & Bentley, 2010; McLoyd, Aikens, & Burton, 2006).

The two chapters in this section summarize and extend what is known about child poverty and how its negative impacts can be alleviated. McLoyd, Mistry, and Hardaway (Chapter 7) explicate the processes by which poverty influences children's social-emotional and academic functioning, discuss some of the inherent strengths and limitations of the current body of research, and propose some novel and interesting directions for future research in this area, including greater attention to the out-of-home social contexts that can mitigate these processes. In their contribution, Weisner and Duncan (Chapter 8) discuss the New Hope Project, an antipoverty demonstration intervention experiment, and detail how it did and did not manage to successfully intervene in the lives of low-income children and families (Duncan, Huston, & Weisner, 2007). The authors also discuss the implications of the New Hope findings for future research and social policy initiatives.

SCHOOLS AND NEIGHBORHOODS: THE MICROCOSMS OF CHILDHOOD

As settings where American children spend most of their out-of-home time, neighborhoods and schools are two of the most important social contexts for children (Duncan & Raudenbush, 1999) and are thus logical places to examine how contexts matter for children's development. Over the past 50 years of social science research, a confluence of investigators from disparate fields, including sociology (e.g., Jencks & Mayer, 1990) and psychology (e.g., Bronfenbrenner & Morris, 2006), has argued for and presented evidence of neighborhood effects on children and youth. Research in subsequent decades has documented the developmental impacts of neighborhood social contexts (Leventhal & Brooks-Gunn, 2000; Sampson, Raudenbush, & Earls, 1997).

The past 50 years have also seen increasing attention paid to schools as contexts of child development, beginning with the highly influential Coleman report (Coleman et al., 1966). Given that the goal of education is to increase students' knowledge, as well as their preparedness for jobs and for lives as citizens, it is not surprising that the majority of school-based research has focused on children's academic learning. However, there is growing appreciation that the social environments of schools can have as great an impact on children's achievement and developmental trajectories as the academic environment of schools (Crosnoe, 2011).

The two chapters in this section focus on the social aspects of neighborhood and school contexts. The chapter by Gershoff and Benner (Chapter 9) summarizes what is known about how the social organization of neighborhoods and schools affect children's social and behavioral adjustment, as well as their academic achievement. In Chapter 10, Crosnoe and Leventhal discuss the implications of this body of work for intervention efforts aimed at changing neighborhoods and schools to improve children's developmental trajectories, especially for those at greatest risk for experiencing educational failure and poor life outcomes.

DEVELOPMENT IN THE CONTEXT OF OMNIPRESENT MEDIA

Children of the 21st century live and develop in a world of electronic media, a trend that has escalated considerably over the past 50 years. In the first 6 years of life, children are now exposed to an average of 2 hours of screen media per day (Rideout & Hamel, 2006), which increases to 7.5 hours of media exposure per day for school-aged children (Rideout, Foehr, & Roberts, 2010). The past several decades of research on children's media has demonstrated that children can and do learn from television, computer games, and the Internet, although the lessons they learn and the skills they develop are not always the ones parents would prioritize.

The two chapters in this section explore the ways in which electronic and social media affect children's development. In Chapter 11, Calvert and Wartella provide a comprehensive summary of research on children's media, including its usage, formal features, and impacts on children's physical, social, and cognitive development. Truglio and Kotler, in the second chapter of this section (Chapter 12), take an in-depth look at one of the most beloved children's television programs, *Sesame Street*, and assess its success (and limitations) in promoting young children's early educational and psychosocial development, especially for children from low-income families.

PROGRAMS AND POLICIES AS CONTEXTUAL OPPORTUNITIES FOR IMPROVING CHILDREN'S LIVES

In recent years, child development scholars have been increasingly encouraged to connect their research findings to public policy as a means of affecting practices in the daily settings that shape development (Huston, 2008). Given the important influence that contexts have on children's lives, and the number of children influenced by a given context, policy and program interventions at the contextual level have the potential to be cost-effective and impactful means of improving children's lives. Granger, Tseng, and Wilcox (Chapter 13) argue that the most expedient path between research and improved outcomes for children is not between research and policy but rather between research and the programs that serve children and families directly. Granger and colleagues describe efforts sponsored by the William T. Grant Foundation to learn how public agencies at the state and local level acquire, interpret, and use research evidence to improve daily life for children and their families. They make recommendations for how to improve the research–practice connection, including by targeting administrators and program managers, developing a better understanding of the needs and constraints of these decision makers, creating new forms of research–practice partnerships, and communicating with opinion leaders in practitioners' networks.

THE RISE OF CONTEXTS IN UNDERSTANDING DEVELOPMENT: A REFLECTION

With such disparate contexts and differing levels of influence, it can be difficult to assimilate the work on each of the contexts of this book. We are fortunate to end this volume with an Epilogue by Aletha Huston, a preeminent scholar in the field of child development who is Past President of the Society for Research in Child Development and of the Consortium of Social Science Associations. Dr. Huston has won numerous research awards, including the Urie Bronfenbrenner Award for Lifetime Contributions to Developmental Psychology, and the SRCD award for contributions to Child Development and Public Policy. Huston's own research over the past 50 years has encompassed most of the social contexts featured in this book, including gender, child care, poverty, media, and policy, and has been disseminated in more than 200 publications. She brings this experience to bear in her reflection on the current status and future directions of research on the contexts of child development.

Conclusion

The chapters in this volume provide a foundation for the next generation of basic and applied scholars interested in how the contexts in which children live, learn, and interact with others affect their development. It is our hope that this volume will inspire both current and future researchers to "contextualize" their research findings and, in so doing, increase our understanding of how contexts can enrich, or restrict, what children experience in their everyday lives. In addition, we hope this collection of work further encourages policy makers and practitioners to seek out and make decisions that are informed by social science research.

References

Bigler, R. S., & Liben, L. S. (2007). Developmental intergroup theory: Explaining and reducing children's social stereotyping and prejudice. *Current Directions in Psychological Science, 16,* 162–166.

Bronfenbrenner, U. (1979). *The Ecology of Human Development.* Cambridge, MA: Harvard University Press.

Bronfenbrenner, U., & Morris, P. (2006). The bioecological model of human development. In R. M. Lerner & W. Damon (Eds.), *Theoretical models of human development.* Vol. 1 of the *Handbook of child psychology* (5th ed., pp. 793–828). New York: Wiley.

Bureau of Labor Statistics. (2011). *Employment characteristics of families—2010.* Washington, DC: United States Department of Labor. Retrieved from http://www.bls.gov/news.release/archives/famee_03242011.htm

Casper, L. M., & Bianchi, S. M. (2002). *Continuity and change in the American family.* Thousand Oaks, CA: Sage.

Capps, R., Fix, M., Murray, J., Ost, J., Passel, J. S., & Herwantoro, S. (2004). *The new demography of America's schools: Immigration and the No Child Left Behind Act.* Washington, DC: Urban Institute.

Coleman, J. S., Campbell, E. Q., Hobson, C. J., McPartland, J., Mood, A. M., Weinfeld, F. D., & York, R. L. (1966). *Equality of educational opportunity.* Washington, DC: U. S. Government Printing Office.

Crosnoe, R. (2011). *Fitting in, standing out: Navigating the social challenges of high school to get an education.* New York: Cambridge University Press.

DeNavas-Walt, C., Proctor, B. D., & Smith, J. C. (2012). *Income, poverty, and health insurance coverage in the United States: 2011.* U.S. Census Bureau, Current Population Reports (P60-243). Washington, DC: U.S. Government Printing Office.

Duncan, G. J., & Raudenbush, S. W. (1999). Assessing the effects of context in studies of child and youth development. *Educational Psychologist, 34,* 29–41.

Duncan, G. J., Huston, A. C., & Weisner, T. (2007). *Higher ground: New Hope for the working poor and their children.* New York: Sage.

Evans, G. W., & Wachs, T. D. (Eds.). (2010). *Chaos and its influence on children's development.* Washington, DC: American Psychological Association.

García Coll, C., Crnic, K., Lamberty, G., Wasik, B. H., Jenkins, R., Garcia, H. V., & McAdoo, H. P. (1996). An integrative model for the study of developmental competencies in minority children. *Child Development, 67,* 1891–1914.

Hernandez, D. J., Denton, N. A., & MacCartney, S. E. (2008). Children in immigrant families: Looking to America's future. *Social Policy Report, 22,* 3–22.

Huston, A. C. (2008). From research to policy and back. *Child Development, 79,* 1–12.

Huston, A. C., & Bentley, A. B. (2010). Human development in societal context. *Annual Review of Psychology, 61,* 411–437.

Huston, A. C., & Ripke, M. N. (Eds.). (2010). *Developmental contexts in middle childhood: Bridges to adolescence and adulthood.* New York: Cambridge University Press.

Jencks, C., & Mayer, S. (1990). The social consequences of growing up in a poor neighborhood. In L. Lynn & Mc-Geary (Eds.), *Inner-city poverty in the United States* (pp. 111–186). Washington, DC: National Academy Press.

Lerner, R. M., & Fisher, C. B. (2000). Toward a science for and of the people: Promoting civil society through the application of developmental science. *Child Development, 71*, 11–20.

Leventhal, T., & Brooks-Gunn, J. (2000). The neighborhoods they live in: The effects of neighborhood residence on child and adolescent outcomes. *Psychological Bulletin, 126*, 309–337.

Liben, L. S., & Bigler, R. S. (2002). The developmental course of gender differentiation: Conceptualizing, measuring, and evaluating constructs and pathways. *Monographs of the Society for Research in Child Development, 67* (2, Serial No. 269, pp. 1–187).

McLoyd, V., Aikens, N., & Burton, L. (2006). Childhood poverty, policy, and practice. In W. Damon, R. Lerner, K. A. Renninger, & I. Sigel (Eds.), *Handbook of child psychology: child psychology in practice* (pp. 700–775). Thousand Oaks, CA: Sage.

Rideout, V., & Hamel, E. (2006). *The media family: Electronic media in the lives of infants, toddlers, preschoolers and their parents.* Menlo Park, CA: Kaiser Family Foundation.

Rideout, V., Foehr, U. G., & Roberts, D. F. (2010). Generation M2: Media in the lives of 8-18-year-olds. *A Kaiser Family Foundation Study, January* 2010. Retrieved from http://www.kff.org/entmedia/mh012010pkg.cfm

Sameroff, A. (2010), A unified theory of development: A dialectic integration of nature and nurture. *Child Development, 81*, 6–22.

Sampson, R. J., Raudenbush, S. W., & Earls, F. (1997). Neighborhoods and violent crime: A multilevel study of collective efficacy. *Science, 277*, 918–924.

Shonkoff, J. P., & Phillips, D. A. (2000). *From neurons to neighborhoods: The science of early childhood development.* Washington, DC: National Academy Press.

Gender as a Shaping Context

{ 1 }

Gender Development

FROM UNIVERSALITY TO INDIVIDUALITY

Lynn S. Liben, Rebecca S. Bigler, and Lacey J. Hilliard

Overview

Psychologists, educators, politicians, journalists, and the proverbial person on the street have long used biological sex to organize observations and actions, as when school data or salary statistics are reported separately for males and females, scout troops enroll either boys or girls, and political messages are targeted to men or women.

Early theoretical and empirical work in developmental psychology implicitly (and often explicitly) began from the premise that differences between boys and girls were "normal" in two senses. One was normality in the statistical sense: in varied arenas (e.g., activity preferences, personality traits, and cognitive profiles), central tendencies and modal profiles differed between girls and boys. Second was normality in the evaluative sense: girls were expected to develop traditional feminine self-identities, interests, and behaviors; boys were expected to develop masculine counterparts. Such outcomes made for happy, healthy, fulfilled lives and maintained the established social order.

The field of gender development—the study of the acquisition, maintenance, and modification of qualities, beliefs, or behaviors that are (or are believed to be) associated differentially with males and females—has changed dramatically over the past half century.[1] In this chapter, we first discuss how theoretical perspectives on children's gender development have shifted from universal to individual accounts, and from unidirectional to transactional accounts. We then discuss findings and policy implications of our program of research, which emphasizes children's agency in the process of gender development.

From Historical to Contemporary Perspectives

EARLY DEPICTIONS OF GENDER DEVELOPMENT

Illustrative of early work built on the premise of the normality of gender differentiation is David Lynn's (1969) book, *Parental and Sex-Role Identification*. In the course of defining his focal construct and identifying the desiderata for its measurement, he conveyed the positive valence of traditional gender divisions:

> Sex-role identification refers to internalization of aspects of the role considered appropriate to a given sex, and to unconscious reactions characteristic of that role. An adequate measure of sex-role identification is difficult to devise. What is required is an instrument or procedure that elicits unconscious reactions: i.e., the subject will remain unaware of the implications of his responses and therefore not seek to give socially desirable ones. In addition, of course, males and females should clearly differ in their responses. (p. 16)

The argument that sex differentiation at this time was viewed as normative is also evident in the definition Mischel (1970) gave for sex-typing in his chapter on this topic for the third edition of *Carmichael's Manual of Child Psychology*. There, he wrote that one of the most direct strategies for studying psychological differences between the sexes

> has been to search for those social behavior patterns that seem to be most clearly sex-typed. Sex-typed behaviors may be defined as those that are less expected and sanctioned when performed by one sex, and, in contrast, are considered to be more appropriate when manifested by the other sex. (p. 4)

PLURALISTIC VIEWS OF GENDER OUTCOMES

During the following decades, an alternative perspective on the valence of sex-typing emerged, as illustrated by the opening sentence of the sex-typing chapter that appeared in the subsequent (fourth) edition of the *Carmichael Manual* (now entitled the *Handbook of Child Psychology*), this one written by Aletha Huston (1983):

> Ten years ago, when the last edition of this volume appeared, sex-typing was considered a desirable goal of socialization by most psychologists, educators, and parents. In the interim, that assumption has been reversed with the explicit rejection by many people of traditional sex-typing as a goal of socialization and with the espousal of non-sex-typed rearing for both boys and girls.... At a more subtle level, many advocates of the new view argue that sex-typed roles restrict personal fulfillment for *both* males and females by limiting the options that each can pursue. (p. 388)

Huston's observation identified a changed perspective on the second of the two meanings of "normal" discussed earlier—the evaluative dimension. That is, although a portion of both professionals and the lay public continued to view individuals' conformity to traditional gender distinctions as desirable, many others rejected the assumption that adherence to traditional gender norms is necessarily a path to positive development, instead arguing that cultural gender norms and stereotypes constrain individuals' thinking and personal outcomes (Bem, 1993; Leaper, 2000; Liben & Bigler, 2008).

Although there have thus been striking variations in opinions across historical eras and scholars about the cost–benefit ratio of individuals' adherence to traditional gender differentiation, what has been more universal is the descriptive goal of identifying the ways in which boys and girls differ. To achieve this goal in a more thorough and detailed manner than previous work had allowed, Huston (1983) designed an organizing matrix that crossed four kinds of sex-typing constructs ("Concepts or beliefs; Identity or self-perception; Preferences, attitudes, values (for self or others); [and] Behavioral enactment, adoption," p. 390) with five content areas ("Biological gender; Activities and interests; Personal-social attributes; Gender-based social relationships; [and] Stylistic and symbolic content," pp. 390–391). This matrix not only provided Huston with a way to structure her own review of existing work, it also provided a template for the subsequent two *Handbook* reviews of gender (Ruble & Martin, 1998; Ruble, Martin, & Berenbaum, 2006).

MECHANISMS OF GENDER DIFFERENTIATION

While continuing to catalogue the full range of sex differences, scholars were also attempting to identify mechanisms that could account for their creation and maintenance. Early social scientists often looked to the environment for explanations. For example, Lynn (1969) repeatedly emphasized the powerful role of cultural traditions, noting, for example, the contrast between the "desirable" gender profiles found within U.S. culture and those found in the New Guinea tribes studied by Margaret Mead (1935). The most dramatic contrast he reported was from members of the Tchambuli tribe who:

> in many ways reverse the roles we [in the United States] consider typical for each sex. The women are brisk, unadorned, managing, industrious, and aggressive. The men are submissive and fearful, subordinate to and dependent on their wives. It is they who are emotionally responsive to the children, more like mothers than fathers in our culture. The men are decorative and adorned. They carve, paint, practice dance steps, and gossip.... The Tchambuli interpret these sex-roles, which we consider reversed, to be the biologically natural ones. (p. 21)

Experiential mechanisms were also favored by social learning theorists who investigated environmental factors at the micro level of individual learning histories. Mischel (1966), for example, focused on how learning processes of imitation and selective reinforcement applied in the domain of gender. Illustratively, he studied children's differential imitation of models of their own (rather than of the other) sex, and he studied ways that environmental contingencies (rewards or punishments) differed depending on whether children enacted behaviors culturally approved for their own versus the other sex.

Not surprisingly, given the long history of attention to both nature and nurture in developmental psychology, scholars of gender development have also explored the role of biological mechanisms in sex differentiation (e.g., Wittig & Petersen, 1979), and behavior geneticists have studied the heritability of human traits that show sex differences (e.g., Iervolino, Hines, Golombok, Rust, & Plomin, 2005). Others have urged that, rather than identifying independent roles of nature and nurture, the goal should be to understand these influences at their intersection (Overton, 2011). From this transactional or relational perspective, both nature and nurture give (and receive) meaning to (and from) the other (Sameroff, 2010).

Our approach to gender development—the focus of the remainder of this chapter—is similarly rooted in a transactional, relational, or constructivist perspective. In this approach, children are seen not as passive recipients of the gendered messages in the surrounding social environment nor of their endogenous biology but rather as active agents who use their biological predispositions, experiential histories, reasoning skills, interests, and so on to construct gender-related meaning and behaviors. Our research on gender development, described next, follows this tradition by emphasizing the role of child agency. We first discuss empirical work identifying how and when these constructive gender processes operate and then discuss how these findings may inform educational interventions and policy decisions beyond the walls of the academy.

Child Agency in Gender Development

OVERVIEW

We now turn to reviewing empirical work that demonstrates how children's own qualities affect the process of gender development. We focus on how constructive mechanisms affect the way in which gendered information encountered in the environment is (a) encoded and recalled; (b) interpreted, explained, and extended; and (c) used by children in self-related actions and beliefs. Underlying all our work is the constructive proposition that the processing of gender-related information is controlled by children's gender schemata, defined as "cognitive structures that organize an individual's gender-related knowledge, beliefs, attitudes, and preferences" (Liben & Signorella, 1993, p. 141).

PROCESSING THE INFORMATION GIVEN

In the early 1980s, ideas from cognitive psychology and cognitive development began to inform the study of gender development. For example, based on Piaget's constructive view of memory, positing that memories reflect children's underlying conceptual understanding of the world (Piaget & Inhelder, 1973), and Bartlett's (1932) notion of schematic memory, holding that story and picture recall reflect cultural traditions, Liben and Signorella (1980) tested the hypothesis that children's existing gender schemata would affect their encoding and recall of new gender-related information.

In this work, first- and second-graders first looked at 60 cards, each showing a man or woman performing a job or activity that is culturally stereotyped as either masculine (e.g., dentist), feminine (e.g., nurse), or neutral (e.g., riding a bicycle). After a delay, children were asked to look at a new deck of cards, some with identical drawings, and some with drawings that reversed the sex of the character. Children were asked to decide if each card was exactly like one they had seen earlier ("old") or if the card was new or changed in some way ("new"). Finally, children were given a test of their gender attitudes to distinguish those with relatively strong versus weak endorsement of cultural gender stereotypes.

Children were worse at recognizing old drawings that had initially been stereotype-inconsistent than at recognizing those that had initially been stereotype consistent, an effect primarily accounted for by items initially shown with a man engaged in a traditionally feminine job. This finding is consistent with earlier research showing that men assuming traditionally feminine roles is a greater cultural transgression than the reverse (e.g., Taynor & Deaux, 1975) and that children learn male stereotypes earlier (Williams, Bennett, & Best, 1975). Particularly telling with respect to the importance of children's own agency was the finding that the pattern of differential memory just described was evident in the highly stereotyped children only.

Further support for the importance of the individual child's level of stereotyping comes from subsequent work by Signorella and Liben (1984) that varied task difficulty. Kindergarten, second-, and fourth-grade children first completed a gender-attitude measure to categorize them into high- or low-stereotyped groups. About a month later, they received a free recall memory task. Cards were as described earlier (i.e., traditional, nontraditional, and neutral), but now children were asked to name as many pictures as they could remember. Another sample of children was given an easier version of the task (i.e., fewer pictures per trial). The findings showed that when memory tasks were harder, highly stereotyped children found it particularly difficult to remember nontraditional pictures.

Additional insight into the effects of children's gender attitudes on memory was gained by examining the *ways* in which children recalled the pictures. Children with more- (rather than less-) stereotyped attitudes were nearly twice as likely to recall nontraditional pictures in ways that transformed the pictures into being traditional, either by reversing the sex of the character (e.g., remembering a male secretary as a female secretary) or by changing the activity (e.g., recalling the male secretary as a typewriter repairman).

To learn more about the quality of children's distortions or interpretations of the memory stimuli, children were asked after the recall task if they had used labels or names to aid them in remembering the pictures. If so, they were asked to look at each picture and provide the name or label they had used. If not, they were asked to go through the deck again and provide a label for each picture. Irrespective of gender attitudes, children were able to label the pictures, and, although some drawings were not interpreted as intended, these reinterpretations were rare and did not differ between children who were more- versus less-stereotyped.

Signorella and Liben (1984) also examined the link between recall and labels. About 40% of the labeling reinterpretations matched terms used during the recall task (e.g., using the term "dental hygienist" both when labeling and recalling the picture intended to show a woman dentist). Responses like these suggest that many reinterpretations occurred at initial encoding rather than later in memory. The incidence of matched terms did not differ between more- and less-stereotyped children. The remaining labels differed from the way the drawing was recalled (e.g., labeling the picture as a "woman dentist" after recalling it as "dental hygien-ist"). This response type suggests an effect of gender schemata on memory itself, and these were significantly more common among more-stereotyped children.

To learn more about whether children's difficulty in remembering nontraditional stimuli might be explained by difficulty in interpreting nontraditional materials in the first place, Liben and Signorella (1993) manipulated whether children (kindergarten-ers through third-graders) were supplied with labels (e.g., "dentist") while pictures were first shown. After the free recall task, children were shown each card again and asked to identify each with a name. For the label condition, this task assessed whether the child had attended to the labels he or she had been given earlier; for the no-label condition, this task assessed how children interpreted the pictures on their own.

Responses were scored according to (a) whether the picture was labeled as the researchers intended, and, if changed, whether it transformed traditionality (e.g., labeling the woman dentist as a dental hygienist), and (b) whether the worker's sex was mentioned, and, if so, whether it differed from the depicted sex (i.e., a sex-of-character error). Labels that neither of two independent coders could link to any drawing were coded as intrusions.

Findings showed that label group children were more likely than nonlabel group children to identify pictures as the experimenter had intended. The former group thus necessarily gave fewer reinterpretations. However, even in this label group, children transformed nontraditional pictures into traditional ones signifi-cantly more often than they did the reverse. Additionally, although the two groups differed in how they named pictures on the labeling task, they showed similar pat-terns of performance on the recall task, with both groups showing worse memory for nontraditional pictures.

Having repeatedly found that research using correlational designs showed significant associations between gender schemata and memory, we turned to experimental designs to test the hypothesis that gender attitudes are *causally* related to gender memory. In one study with children ranging from about 6.5 to 11.5 years (Bigler & Liben, 1990), participants were first given a measure of their gender attitudes. Scores on this measure were used to form two intervention groups that had comparable numbers of boys and girls with roughly equivalent pretest gender attitude scores. Both groups then participated in a week-long program of daily, 20-minute classroom lessons in which two occupations were taught each day. Of the ten occupations covered in all, half were traditionally masculine and half traditionally feminine.

In the experimental condition, classroom lessons were designed to increase children's gender-egalitarian beliefs about occupational roles. These children were taught rules for deciding who could perform occupations that were based on the potential workers' interests and skills (e.g., to become a firefighter, "a person must like to fight fires and learn how to drive a fire truck") rather than on their biological sex. As a class, children were given practice problems about each of the taught occupations and asked to respond aloud so that they could be corrected if they attempted to justify their answers with reference to gender or if they distorted the job in some way. For example, in one lesson, children were taught what construction workers must do. They were then told that "Ann loves to build things" and that "Ann knows how to drive a bulldozer" and asked, "Could Ann be a construction worker?" and "How do you know?" Children's responses showed that not all children easily learned the intended lessons. For example, in the scenario just described, one child responded "No, because Ann is a girl" and another responded, "Yes, because he [*sic*] followed the rules." In such cases, the experimenter corrected the child, explained why, and posed a new practice problem. In the control condition lessons addressed the same jobs, but the focus was on job training and activities rather than on workers' gender.

Following the interventions, children were given another test of their gender attitudes in which they were asked who they thought should do various occupations and given response options of "only men," "only women," or "both men and women." The measure included occupations that had been explicitly discussed during the lessons, as well as other gender-stereotyped occupations that had not been discussed in class.

On each of the next 12 school days, children heard a story involving a culturally masculine or feminine occupation, half depicted traditionally and half not (e.g., a male vs. female dentist, counterbalanced across children). Children were then asked to recall each story in ways that forced them to use gender pronouns to refer to the person in the target occupation. Children were virtually errorless when referring to traditional depictions, but erred on nontraditional depictions. Critically, the incidence of errors varied by experimental condition: children whose beliefs had become more gender egalitarian from the experimental lessons showed significantly better memory for nontraditional stories than did children whose gender beliefs had remained unchanged by lessons.

Later research (Bigler & Liben, 1992) demonstrated that classroom instruction for 5- to 10-year-old children can also be effective when lessons target a more general logical skill hypothesized to be relevant to gender stereotypes. The logical skill taught in this study was multiple classification—the ability to classify the same thing in more than one way simultaneously. Skill in multiple classification was hypothesized to be relevant because it could support the child's understanding that a particular person is simultaneously both a woman and an engineer. (The same logical skill is not needed to process a male engineer because, within our current U.S. culture, maleness is automatically entailed in being an engineer.) Given this reasoning, some children were taught to classify pictures of objects or people along two dimensions simultaneously using a 2 × 2 matrix, for example, learning to sort cards into rows by sex (women in the top row, men in the bottom) and into columns by activity (people riding bicycles in the left column and people on the phone in the right).

In addition to replicating the effectiveness of occupational rule training found earlier (Bigler & Liben, 1990), data showed that children who had acquired multiple classification skills via training with either objects or people had better memory for nontraditional stories. Children who were trained to sort people (rather than objects) also showed significantly less-stereotyped gender attitudes.

GOING BEYOND THE INFORMATION GIVEN

Gender schemata affect not only memory, but also the meanings, interpretations, and extensions children take from what they see. An illustration comes from a study of children's judgments about novel occupations (Liben, Bigler, & Krogh, 2001). Younger and older children (6 and 11 years) were told about 12 novel jobs such as higglers (people who sell things from carts on the street) and tenics (people who create handicapped parking spaces). Children also saw four pictures of workers performing each job, either all men or all women, counterbalanced across children (e.g., some saw all female higglers and all male tenics and others saw the inverse). For each job, children then used 5-point scales to rate the difficulty of learning the job, difficulty of doing the job, importance of the job, and pay scale for the job. Responses were combined to yield a composite status score for each job.

The 11-year-olds rated jobs depicted with men as higher in status than they rated the very same jobs depicted with women. Thus, children drew different inferences about jobs depending on whether the jobs appeared to be masculine or feminine. This effect was not found among the 6-year-olds. It is unlikely these younger children lacked beliefs about differential status, however, because these children (like older children) rated familiar masculine jobs as higher in status than familiar feminine jobs. Younger children may simply have needed additional cues to notice the consistency of workers' sex (e.g., accompanying the pictures with a comment such as, "higglers are usually women").

Another way in which children go beyond the information given is with respect to self-conceptions and personal interests. In early work in this area, Martin and Halverson (1981) proposed gender schema theory (GST), positing that children's gender beliefs have a strong influence on children's own activities and further development. For example, a girl who encounters a doll and judges it to be self-relevant (and thus worthy of further processing) would use her cultural knowledge that "dolls are for girls" and her self-knowledge that "I am a girl" to decide that the doll is "for me." A parallel process would lead her to decide that a toy truck is "not for me." Repeated and extended encounters and decisions like these gradually shape girls' and boys' interests and behaviors in ways that increasingly exaggerate the distinctions between them.

In work that built on this schematic processing approach, Liben and Bigler (2002) posited that, in addition to a process like the one proposed in GST, in which the child's cultural beliefs about gender are applied to the self (referred to by Liben & Bigler as the "attitudinal pathway"), there is a second important pathway—the "personal pathway." Here, children's personal interests (or lack of interests) provide the basis for constructing gender beliefs or stereotypes. So, for example, a boy who finds ballet dancing unappealing might claim that ballet is an activity that only girls should do, whereas a boy who finds dancing appealing (as in the plot line of the movie, *Billy Eliot*) would come to view ballet as for boys as well as for girls. Empirical data consistent with this personal pathway model were reported by Liben and Bigler (2002): boys who had rated themselves with a greater number of traditionally feminine traits at the start of grade 6 then went on (over the following 2 years) to develop more gender-egalitarian attitudes about traits than did boys who had initially used fewer traditionally feminine traits in their self-descriptions.

CREATING GENDERED LENSES TO VIEW THE INFORMATION GIVEN

Theoretical accounts of gender development originating during the first half of the 20th century assumed, explicitly or implicitly, the inevitability of individuals' attention to and use of gender as a social category (Kohlberg, 1966). Rather than accept this premise, we have sought to understand the constructive process by which children come to attend to and think about gender. Bigler and Liben (2006, 2007) proposed developmental intergroup theory (DIT), which addresses the formation of social stereotypes and prejudices, including those pertaining to gender. According to the theory, there are potentially limitless ways to classify individuals, and it is the interaction of environmental and child characteristics that leads gender to be psychologically salient for most children.

One such interaction outlined by DIT concerns children's tendencies to focus on perceptually salient or highly visible attributes in person-perception tasks (Livesley & Bromley, 1973). As a consequence of this child characteristic, features such as skin color and secondary sex characteristics are poised to become the bases for social groups and stereotypes. Importantly, though, human qualities of all kinds can be made more or less perceptually salient. For example, gang membership is not inherently physically distinct, but can be made so by clothing or tattoos. Similarly, although biological sex has some distinguishing physical qualities, most cultures exaggerate the perceptual discriminability of gender, for example, by socializing males and females to wear different hairstyles, clothing, and accessories. Such distinctions assist infants and children in discriminating between males and females (see Arthur, Bigler, Liben, Gelman, & Ruble, 2008; Blakemore, Berenbaum, & Liben, 2009). Thus, children's tendency to focus on perceptually distinct characteristics interacts with the degree to which cultures function to make gender highly salient.

A second major tenet of DIT is that children develop stereotypes and prejudices on the basis of those characteristics that adults mark behaviorally as important, for example, by their use of language and strategies for environmental organization. Bigler's (1995) study of teachers' use of gender in the classroom supports the theory. In that study, teachers in an experimental condition were asked to use gender to label children (aged 6 to 11) and to organize their classroom activities. For example, teachers used gender to assign children to desks and to form lines (e.g., to go out for recess). In contrast, teachers in a control condition ignored students' gender. At post-test, children in the experimental condition, especially those with limited skills in classification (see earlier discussion of multiple classification and Bigler & Liben, 1992), showed elevated levels of gender stereotyping relative to children in the control condition.

Hilliard and Liben (2010) extended this line of work to show that preschool teachers' labeling and use of gender affects not only children's gender flexibility but also their peer preferences and behaviors. Both prior to and following a 2-week classroom manipulation similar to that just described, preschoolers were assessed for their endorsement of cultural gender stereotypes and for their play preferences, and they were observed during free play periods. The findings showed that between pre- and post-tests, children in the experimental (but not control) classes expressed significantly increased gender stereotyping, reported significantly reduced interest in playing with classmates of the other sex, and—in free play—interacted significantly less with other-sex peers.

Beyond the Gender Lab: Educational and Policy Implications

Outside of academia, laypersons' views of the desirability of gender differentiation have also changed over the years. Pressure for greater egalitarianism came from diverse sources: second-wave feminists sought greater equity in the workplace and home (Brownmiller, 1999); workforce analysts argued that the nation's critical needs in science, technology, engineering, and math (STEM) could be better met if more women were attracted to these fields (see Eccles, Chapter 2); and risk assessors warned of finding ways to avoid lawsuits related to gender-based bully-ing (Gender Public Advocacy Coalition, 2005). In this final section of our chapter, we address some of the ways in which theoretical and empirical work on children's agency in gender development has important implications for the world beyond academia, focusing, first, on implications for educational curricula and, second, on implications for broader educational policies.

IMPLICATIONS FOR EDUCATIONAL CURRICULA

Many educational organizations and programs target the development of gender egalitarian beliefs among children (e.g., *Teaching Tolerance; Free to Be . . . You and Me; Expanding Your Horizons*). Research on the constructive processes discussed earlier has clear implications for making predictions and recommendations about the efficacy of such programs. One implication of work on gender-schematic pro-cessing is that programs that rely primarily on symbolic models of counterstereo-typic behavior are likely to be ineffective because children will distort and forget models that are inconsistent with their views. This issue is likely to be especially problematic among children whose attitudes are the most sex-typed prior to the intervention (Liben & Bigler, 1987).

Consistent with this interpretation are data described earlier from Bigler and Liben (1990, 1992) showing that although children were exposed to equal numbers of gender stereotypic and counterstereotypic stories, children's constructive processes skewed what they encoded or remembered from their experience. To the extent that children remember more stereotypic than counterstereotypic stories, their construc-tive processes transform the world they encounter so that their experiences function to reinforce rather than challenge their gender-stereotyped attitudes. Consistent with this analysis, the effects of modeling-based intervention programs have been very minimal. Indeed, although counterintuitive at first blush—but fully consistent with constructive theoretical perspectives—modeling-based programs are sometimes found to increase rather than reduce gender stereotyping (Liben & Bigler, 1987).

The power of constructive processing makes it clear that, rather than relying on passive information processing, interventions must monitor how children are processing information and include strategies that engage and hence modify children's schemata, attitudes, and behaviors. Illustrative of this active approach, Lamb, Bigler, Liben, and Green (2009) taught children (aged 5–10) to respond to sexism in one of two ways. In the practice condition, children learned to recognize and actively respond to various forms of sexism (e.g., gender-based exclusion and sex-typing of traits and skills). These children learned a specific retort each day (e.g., "You can't say that girls can't play!" and "I disagree! Sexism is silly to me!"). By practicing each day's retort in short skits they created, children were encour-aged to actively translate material into self-relevant contexts. Children in the nar-rative condition learned the same retorts, but they learned them only passively, via age-appropriate stories.

Tests of the effectiveness of the intervention included assessing, first, children's self-reported responses to hypothetical situations that described peers' sexist acts and, second, children's behavioral responses to an actual sexist encounter. For the latter, each child was asked to carry a counterstereotypic item (purse for boys, tool belt for girls) to the school office under the guise of returning a misplaced item to its owner. While en route, a confederate child stopped the participant with a sexist remark, "Purses [tool belts] are for girls [boys]!" Children's responses were recorded by a hidden observer. At pre-test, children rarely challenged peers' sexist remarks when presented within hypothetical scenarios. At post-test, children's challenges to peers' sexism, in both the hypothetical scenarios and the actual school context were significantly more common in the practice than in the narrative condition.

Although many teachers provide counterstereotypic models in their classrooms and curricula (e.g., inviting women scientists to visit), they also often engage in behaviors that may appear harmless but that increase gender stereotyping among their pupils. Bigler's (1995) and Hilliard and Liben's (2010) research on children's responses to their teachers' use of gender to label and organize students has clear implications for pedagogical practice. Because children construct stereotypes about those social categories that adults label and use, teachers should avoid the routine use of gender to label and organize children (e.g., "Good morning, boys and girls") and should instead treat their students as individuals ("Good morning, Susan") or as a whole ("Good morning, class").

IMPLICATIONS FOR NATIONAL POLICY

Constructivist research on children's gender development also has implications for national policy on single-sex schooling, an increasingly popular trend in the United States. In 2006, Congress amended the original 1972 Title IX regulations as part of the No Child Left Behind Act (NCLBA), easing extant restrictions on sex-segregated education (U.S. Department of Education, 2006). Specifically, the act approved federal funding for innovative education programs, including single-sex schools and single-sex programs within coeducational schools. As a result, hundreds of single-sex programs were started nationwide (Klein & Sesma, 2011).

The change in policy was implemented despite a lack of empirical evidence that single-sex schooling results in achievement outcomes superior to coeducational schooling. Two major reviews of the single-sex education literature have been conducted. The American Association of University Women (AAUW) released a report in 1998 that concluded that there is no credible evidence that single-sex education works better than coeducation for either sex (Morse, 1998). A few years later, in 2005, the American Institutes for Research prepared a review of the literature on single-sex education and similarly concluded that there was relatively little unequivocal evidence for the superiority of single-sex schooling (Mael, Alonso, Gibson, Rogers, & Smith, 2005).

Despite the overarching weakness of the effects, some commentators have argued that single-sex classrooms provide environments in which children can learn without being distracted by gender stereotypes (e.g., peer expectations to conform to stereotypes). Other commentators have argued that single-sex class-rooms and schools can be effective by capitalizing on sex differences in learn-ing and cognition (Sax, 2005). In response to these claims, Halpern et al. (2011) argued, first, that the majority of scientific studies examining brain and behav-ioral function by sex have found insignificant to small differences in adults and even smaller differences in children, and, second, that single-sex classrooms and schools are likely to promote gender stereotyping among children. Drawing on the work by Bigler (1995) and Hilliard and Liben (2010) described earlier, Halpern et al. argued that authority figures' use of biological sex to assign chil-dren to schools or to separate classrooms within coeducational schools is likely to lead children to assume that the sexes differ in important, essential, and multifac-eted ways. Such assumptions are likely to exacerbate gender segregation which, in turn, exacerbates increasingly differentiated interests and modes of interaction (Fabes, Martin, & Hanish, 2003).

Conclusion

Knowledge of gender development has expanded markedly across the past century, made possible, in part, by the evolution of increasingly sophisticated theoretical views of the role of gender in shaping individuals' lives and societies. Overall, con-ceptions of gender development have moved from an emphasis on the universal ways in which males and females differ, to understanding complex and multifac-eted ways in which individuals differ both within and across groups categorized by biological sex. Simultaneously, the emphasis of research has shifted from identify-ing environmental or biological factors operating in isolation, to an emphasis on transactional, constructive processes through which children's unique proclivities, environments, and maturation contribute to the shaping of gender. Our own work has been shaped by—and, we hope, has helped to shape—these evolving frame-works. Our goals include contributing not only to academic scholarship, but also to recommending and influencing practices that can enable children to explore and express their interests and skills, absent constraining assumptions about the universality of gender development.

Notes

1. Some scholars use "sex" for biologically based phenomena and "gender" for socially based phenomena. Given our endorsement of the belief that biological and societal factors cannot be split but are instead transactional or relational (Overton, 2011; Sameroff, 2010), we use the terms interchangeably.

References

Arthur, A. E., Bigler, R. S., Liben, L. S., Gelman, S. A., & Ruble, D. N. (2008). Gender ste-reotyping and prejudice in young children: A developmental intergroup perspective. In S. R. Levy & M. Killen (Eds.), *Intergroup attitudes and relations in childhood through adulthood* (pp. 66–86). Oxford, UK: Oxford University Press.

Bartlett, F. C. (1932). *Remembering: A study in experimental and social psychology.* Cambridge, UK: Cambridge University Press.

Bem, S. (1993). Gender schema theory and its implications for child development: raising gender-aschematic children in a gender-schematic society. *Signs, 8,* 598–616.

Bigler, R. S. (1995). The role of classification skill in moderating environmental influences on children's gender stereotyping: A study of the functional use of gender in the class-room. *Child Development, 66,* 1072–1087.

Bigler, R. S., & Liben, L. S. (1990). The role of attitudes and intervention in gender-sche-matic processing. *Child Development, 61,* 1440–1452.

Bigler, R. S., & Liben, L. S. (1992). Cognitive mechanisms in children's gender stereotyp-ing: Theoretical and educational implications of a cognitive-based intervention. *Child Development, 63,* 1351–1363.

Bigler, R. S., & Liben, L. S. (2006). A developmental intergroup theory of social stereotypes and prejudice. In R. V. Kail (Ed.), *Advances in child development and behavior* (vol. 34, pp. 39–89). San Diego, CA: Elsevier.

Bigler, R. S., & Liben, L. S. (2007). Developmental intergroup theory: Explaining and reduc-ing children's social stereotyping and prejudice. *Current Directions in Psychological Science, 16,* 162–166

Blakemore, J. E. O., Berenbaum, S. A., & Liben, L. S. (2009). *Gender development.* New York: Taylor & Francis.

Brownmiller, S. (1999). *In our time: Memoir of a revolution.* New York: Dial Press Expanding Your Horizons. Retrieved from http://www.expandingyourhorizons.org/

Fabes, R. A., Martin, C. L., & Hanish, L. D. (2003). Young children's play qualities in same-, other-, and mixed-sex peer groups. *Child Development, 74,* 921–932.

Free to Be . . . You and Me. Educational books, films, and music. Retrieved from http://www.freetobefoundation.org/merchandise.htm

Gender Public Advocacy Coalition. (2005). Sticks and stones break bones—and words hurt too: Bullied Kansas teen wins $250K in lawsuit against school district. Retrieved from http://www.gpac.org

Halpern, D. F., Eliot, L., Bigler, R. S., Fabes, R. A., Hanish, L. D., Hyde, J., et al. (2011). The pseudoscience of single-sex schooling. *Science, 333,* 1706–1707.

Hilliard, L. J., & Liben, L. S. (2010). Differing levels of gender salience in preschool class-rooms: Effects on children's gender attitudes and intergroup bias. *Child Development, 81,* 1787–1798.

Huston, A. C. (1983). Sex-typing. In E. M. Hetherington (Ed.), *Handbook of child psychol-ogy. vol. 4* (4th ed., pp. 387–468). New York: Wiley.

Iervolino, A. C., Hines, J., Golombok, S. E., Rust, J., & Plomin, R. (2005). Genetic and environmental influences on sex-typed behavior during the preschool years. *Child Development, 76,* 826–840.

Klein, S., & Sesma, E. (2011). *What are we learning from the 2006-7 Office for Civil Rights survey question about public schools with single-sex academic classes? An exploratory study.* Arlington, VA: Feminist Majority Foundation.

Kohlberg, L. (1966). A cognitive-developmental analysis of children's sex-role concepts and attitudes. In E. E. Maccoby (Ed.), *The development of sex differences*. Stanford, CA: Stanford University Press.

Lamb, L., Bigler, R. S., Liben, L. S., & Green, V. A. (2009). Teaching children to confront peers' sexist remarks: Implications for theories of gender development and educational practice. *Sex Roles, 61*, 361–382.

Leaper, C. (2000). The social construction and socialization of gender during development. In P. H. Miller and E. K. Scholnick (Eds.), *Toward a feminist developmental psychology* (pp. 127–152). New York: Routledge.

Liben, L. S., & Bigler, R. S. (1987). Reformulating children's gender schemata. In L. S. Liben & M. L. Signorella (Eds.), *New directions for child development: Children's gender schemata* (pp. 89–105). San Francisco, CA: Jossey-Bass.

Liben, L. S., & Bigler, R. S. (2002). The developmental course of gender differentiation: Conceptualizing, measuring, and evaluating constructs and pathways. *Monographs of the Society for Research in Child Development, 67* (2, Serial No. 269, pp. v–147, 179–185).

Liben, L. S., & Bigler, R. S. (2008). Developmental gender differentiation: Pathways in conforming and nonconforming outcomes. *Journal of Gay & Lesbian Mental Health, 12*, 95–119.

Liben, L. S., Bigler, R. S., & Krogh, H. R. (2001). Pink and blue collar jobs: Children's judgments of job status and job aspirations in relation to sex of worker. *Journal of Experimental Child Psychology, 79*, 346–363.

Liben, L. S., & Signorella, M. L. (1980). Gender-related schemata and constructive memory in children. *Child Development, 51*, 11–18.

Liben, L. S., & Signorella, M. L. (1993). Gender schematic processing in children: The role of initial interpretations of stimuli. *Developmental Psychology, 29*, 141–149.

Livesley, W. J., & Bromley, D. B. (1973). *Person perception in childhood and adolescence.* New York: Wiley.

Lynn, D. B. (1969). *Parental and sex-role identification: A theoretical formulation.* Berkeley, CA: McCutchan Publishing.

Mael, F., Alonso, A., Gibson, D., Rogers, K., & Smith, M. (2005). *Single-sex versus coeducational schooling: A systematic review.* Washington, DC: American Institutes for Research. Prepared for the U.S. Department of Education.

Martin, C. L., & Halverson, C. F. (1981). A schematic processing model of sex typing and stereotyping in children. *Child Development, 52*, 1119–1134.

Mead, M. (1935). *Sex and temperament in three primitive societies.* New York: McGraw-Hill.

Mischel, W. (1966). A social learning view of sex differences in behavior. In E. E. Maccoby (Ed.), *The development of sex differences* (pp. 56–81). Stanford, CA: Stanford University Press.

Mischel, W. (1970). Sex-typing and socialization. In P. H. Mussen (Ed.), *Carmichael's manual of child psychology* (3rd ed., vol. 2, pp. 3–72). New York: Wiley.

Morse, S. (Ed.). (1998). *Separated by sex: A critical look at single-sex education for girls.* The American Association of University Women Educational Foundation: Washington, DC.

Overton, W. F. (2011). Relational developmental systems and quantitative behavior genetics: Alternative or parallel methodologies? *Research in Human Development, 8*, 258–263.

Piaget, J., & Inhelder, B. (1973). *Memory and intelligence.* New York: Basic Books.

Ruble, D. N., & Martin, C. L. (1998). Gender development. In W. Damon & N. Eisenberg (Eds.), *Handbook of child psychology: Vol. 3. Social, emotional, and personality development* (5th ed., pp. 933–1016). Hoboken, NJ: John Wiley & Sons.

Ruble, D. N., Martin, C. L., & Berenbaum, S. A. (2006). Gender development. In N. Eisenberg (Ed.), *Handbook of child psychology: Vol. 3. Social, emotional, and personality development.* (6th ed., pp. 858–932). Hoboken, NJ: Wiley.

Sameroff, A. J. (2010). A unified theory of development: A dialectic integration of nature and nurture. *Child Development, 81,* 6–22.

Sax, L. (2005). *Why gender matters.* New York: Doubleday.

Signorella, M. L., & Liben, L. S. (1984). Recall and reconstruction of gender-related pictures: Effects of attitude, task difficulty, and age. *Child Development, 55,* 393–405.

Taynor, J., & Deaux, K. (1975). Equity and perceived sex differences: Role behavior as defined by the task, the mode, and the actor. *Journal of Personality and Social Psychology, 32,* 381–390.

Teaching Tolerance Organization. Gender expression lessons. Retrieved from http://www.tolerance.org/activity/gender-expression

U.S. Department of Education, 34 Code of Federal Regulations, Part 106, 1034 (2006); www2.ed.gov/legislation/FedRegister/finrule/2006-4/102506a.html

Williams, J. E., Bennett, S. M., & Best, D. L. (1975). Awareness and expression of sex stereotypes in young children. *Developmental Psychology, 11,* 635–642.

Wittig, M. A., & Petersen, A. C. (Eds.). (1979). *Sex-related differences in cognitive functioning.* New York: Academic Press.

Gender and Achievement Choices

Jacquelynne S. Eccles

In 2007, the president of Harvard, Larry Summers, gave a controversial speech about the relatively low numbers of women researchers in the fields of science, engineering, and math. I found the resulting debate in the media and in scientific journals particularly interesting because I have been studying exactly this issue for the past 40 years. I began my research career in the late 1970s, with a grant from the then National Institute of Education, specifically focused on the relatively low numbers of women at the most advanced levels of mathematics-related professions. A great deal of research was done on this topic at that time and considerable funds were put into designing and testing a wide variety of intervention programs to increase female participation in mathematics-related careers, such as engineering and physical science. Great progress was made, moving the average enrollment of women in bachelor's degree programs in engineering from a little more than 3% to approximately 18% by the 1990s. Interestingly, both then and now, women have always been well represented in mathematics majors at the bachelor's-degree level itself, which turns out to be one of the least sex-typed undergraduate college majors. Furthermore, for at least the past 15 years, women have been very well represented in both undergraduate and master's-levels programs in the biological and medical sciences, as well as in M.D. programs. Nevertheless, women continue to be underrepresented in programs in physical science and engineering and on the university and college faculties in all of the natural sciences, engineering, and mathematics. Why?

As noted, my colleagues and I have studied the psychological and social factors influencing course enrollment decisions, college major selection, career aspirations, and career choices for the past 40 years. I began this work with a particular interest in the psychological and social factors that might underlie the gender differences in educational and vocational choices, particularly in the fields of mathematics, physical science, and engineering. My early thinking in this area was heavily influenced by the seminally important work on gender and achievement by Aletha Huston (then Aletha H. Stein). Four of Huston's most influential empirical studies on gender and achievement motivation came out while I was in graduate school at the University of California, Los Angeles (UCLA) (Stein, 1971; Stein, Pohly, & Mueller, 1971; Stein & Smithells, 1968, 1969). In these articles, Huston and her colleagues documented the sex-typing of different areas of achievement, particularly athletics, social skills, and reading, and showed that these stereotypes increase with age. Interestingly, in these studies, although the perception of arithmetic as masculine becomes more marked with increasing age, arithmetic was the least gender-typed subject area at all ages. In contrast, reading, art, and social skills were seen as feminine whereas athletic, spatial, and mechanical skills were seen as masculine (see also Liben, Bigler, & Hilliard, Chapter 1, this volume). Furthermore, Huston and her colleagues showed that the sex-typing of each skill/subject area predicted gender differences in children's and adolescents' own expectations for success, attainment value, minimal self-performance standards, and actual performance. These articles were followed by Stein and Bailey's 1973 *Psychological Bulletin* article, "The Socialization of Achievement Orientation in Females" and later by Huston's seminal chapter on gender for the *Handbook of Child Psychology* (Huston, 1983). For my generation, Huston's work on gender and achievement was at the center of our intellectual space.

Building on Huston's work and integrating thinking from expectancy-value theories of behavioral choices, my colleagues and I developed a comprehensive theoretical model of achievement-related choices (Eccles [Parsons] et al., 1983; see Figure 2.1 for the most recent version of the Eccles expectancy-value model of achievement-related choices [EVM]). We hypothesized that the kinds of educational and vocational decisions that might underlie gender differences in participation in physical science and engineering would be most directly influenced by individuals' expectations for success and the importance or value that individuals attach to the various options they see as available. We then hypothesized how these quite domain-specific self- and task-related beliefs might be influenced by cultural

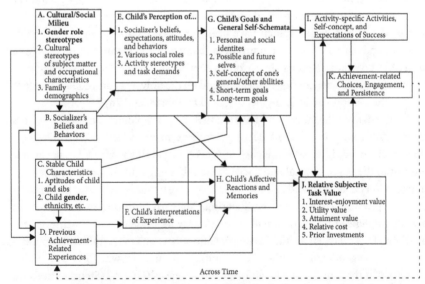

FIGURE 2.1 *Eccles et al. expectancy value model (EVM) of achievement related choices.*

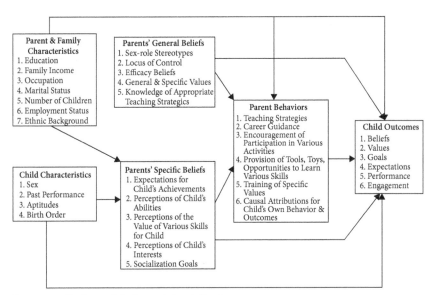

FIGURE 2.2 *Eccles model of parental socialization.*

norms, experiences, aptitudes, and more general personal beliefs (see Eccles, 1994; Eccles [Parsons] et al., 1983; Eccles Wigfield, & Schiefele, 1998). In the early 1980s, we specified a model of parental influences on the development of the psychological components of Figure 2.1 (see Figure 2.2 for latest version) to guide our studies of the socialization of both individual and gender differences in achievement choices. We have used both of these models as guides to our program of research ever since. In this chapter, I provide a brief summary of some of our findings.

Gender and the Eccles Expectancy-Value Model

For example, consider decisions related to selecting a college major. According to the EVM (Figure 2.1), people should be most likely to choose a major that they think they can master and that has high task value for them. Expectations for success (domain-specific beliefs about one's personal efficacy to master the task), in turn, depend on both the confidence that individuals have in their various intellectual abilities and the individuals' estimations of the difficulty of the various options they are considering. We also predicted that these self- and task-related beliefs were shaped over time by both experiences with the related school subjects and activities, and individuals' subjective interpretation of these experiences (e.g., does the person think that her or his prior successes reflect high ability or lots of hard work? And, if the latter, will it take even more work to continue to be successful?). As I discuss in more detail in the section on socialization, gender-role socialization and commonly held stereotypes about gender differences in "natural talents" for various subject areas are likely to lead females and males to have different estimates of their own personal efficacies for physical science and engineering. It is quite likely that females will receive less support for developing a strong sense of their talent for these fields from their parents, teachers, and peers than will males.

Likewise, the Eccles EVM specifies that the subjective task value of various majors is influenced by several factors. For example, does the person enjoy doing the related school work? Is this major seen as instrumental in meeting the individual's long- or short-range goals? Have the individual's parents, counselors, friends, or romantic partners encouraged or discouraged the individual from selecting this major? Does taking the major interfere with other more valued options because of the amount of work needed to be successful, either in the major or in the future professions linked to the major? Again, as discussed in more detail in the section on socialization, it is quite likely that males will receive more support for developing a strong interest in physical science and engineering from their parents, teachers, and peers than will females. In addition, it is absolutely the case that all young people will see more examples of males engaged in these occupations than females. Consequently, according to our model, the likelihood of even considering these occupations as appropriate is much lower for females than for males.

As we developed our model in the mid-1970s, it became clear to us that the theoretical grounding for understanding the nature of subjective task value was much less well-developed than the theoretical grounding for understanding the nature of expectations for success. Consequently, we elaborated our notion of subjective task value to help fill this void. Drawing on work associated with achievement motivation (including Huston's early work, as well as the early work of Virginia Crandall and her colleagues), intrinsic versus extrinsic motivation, self-psychology, identity formation, economics, and organization psychology, we hypothesized that subjective task value was composed of at least four components: interest value (the enjoyment one gets from engaging in the task or activity), utility value (the instrumental value of the task or activity for helping to fulfill another short- or long-range goal), attainment value (the link between the task and one's sense of self and identity—a term used by Huston in her early work), and cost (defined in terms of either what may be given up by making a specific choice or the negative experiences associated with a particular choice).

Because I believe that the last three of these are particularly relevant for understanding gender differences in educational and occupational choices, I elaborate on these further now. My colleagues and I have argued that the socialization processes linked to gender roles are likely to influence both short- and long-terms goals and the characteristics and values most closely linked to core identities (e.g., Eccles, 1993, 1994; Jacobs & Eccles, 1992). For example, gender-role socialization is likely to lead to gender differences in the kinds of work one would like to do as an adult: females should be more likely than males to want to work at occupations that help others and fit well into their family role plans; males should be more likely than females to want future occupations that pay very well and provide opportunities to become famous (see Eccles et al. [1998] and Ruble & Martin [1998] for reviews of evidence supporting these hypotheses; see Eccles & Vida [2003] for empirical support). There is also evidence that males are somewhat more interested than females in activities and jobs related to manipulating physical objects and abstract concepts, whereas females are more interested in activities and jobs related to people and social interactions. These differences are likely to influence the types of jobs that appeal to male and female adolescents as they engage in the process of making related educational decisions. If so, then the utility value and attainment value of various high school courses and college majors should differ on average by gender, precisely because these courses and majors are linked directly to adult occupational choices.

Similarly, the perceived cost of different high school courses and college majors should vary by gender due to the relative importance attached to various options. The cost may also vary by gender due to average level differences in such emotional costs as math anxiety and the fear of rejection for making nontraditional choices (see Eccles et al., 1998).

Three features of our approach that are not well captured by the static model depicted in Figures 2.1 and 2.2 are particularly important for understanding gender differences in the types of educational and occupational choices represented in this book: first, we are interested in both conscious and nonconscious achievement-related behavioral choices. Although the language we use to describe the various components makes it seem that we are talking about quite conscious processes, this is not our intention. We believe that the conscious and nonconscious choices people make about how to spend their time and effort lead, over time, to marked differences between groups and individuals in life-long achievement-related patterns. We also believe, however, that these choices are heavily influenced by socialization pressures and cultural norms (see Liben et al., Chapter 1).

Second, we are interested in what becomes part of an individual's perception of viable options. Although individuals choose from among several options, they do not actively consider the full range of objectively available options. Many options may never be considered because the individual is either unaware of their existence or has little opportunity or encouragement to really consider a wide range of alternatives. Other options may not be seriously considered because the individual has inaccurate information regarding either the option itself or the individual's potential for achieving that option. For example, young people often have inaccurate information regarding the full range of activities associated with various career choices or inaccurate information regarding the financial assistance available for advanced educational training. Yet they make decisions about which occupations to pursue and then select courses in high school that they believe are important for getting into college and majoring in the subject most directly linked to their career aspirations. Too often, these choices are based on either inaccurate or insufficient information. Finally, many options may not be seriously considered because the individual does not believe that a particular choice fits well with his or her gender role or other social role schemas. Again, inaccurate information about what occupations are actually like can lead to premature elimination of quite viable career options. For example, a young woman with excellent math skills may reject the possibility of becoming an engineer or a computer scientist because she has a limited view of what engineers and computer scientists actually do. She may stereotype engineers as nerds or as folks who focus on mechanical tasks with little direct human relevance, when, in fact, many engineers work directly on problems related to pressing human needs. If so, she may well select herself, or be encouraged to select herself, out of a profession that she might both enjoy and find quite compatible with her life goals and values. As a culture, we do a very poor job of providing information to our children and adolescents about various occupations. As a consequence, they must rely on media portrayals and happenstance career counseling from their parents, mentors, and friends. Such portrayals are often quite gender and ethnically stereotyped (see Liben et al., Chapter 1).

Third, we assume that educational and occupational decisions are made within a complex social reality. For example, the decision to major in biology rather than computer science or engineering is made within the context of a complex social reality that presents each individual with a wide variety of choices, each of which has both immediate and long-range consequences that map in complex ways onto the full range of determinants of subjective task value. Furthermore, many options have both positive and negative components. For example, the decision to enroll in an advanced math course in high school is typically made in the context of other important daily life decisions—long-term life decisions such as whether to take an advanced English course to study literature one enjoys, or to take a second foreign language course to aid in one's future travel plans, or to take a course with one's best friend or romantic partner in order to have an intellectual activity to share, or to take less demanding courses in order to spend more time enjoying the social aspects of one's senior year. Similarly, the decision to major in computer science or engineering versus something else is made in the context of a wide variety of options and life demands during the college years. The critical issues, in our view, are the relative personal value of each option and the individual's assessment of his or her relative abilities and potentials at the time the decision is being made. In addition, having narrowed the field to those options at which one feels confident about succeeding, we assume that people will then choose the options with the highest personal value. Thus, it is the hierarchy of subjective task values and expectations for success that matter rather than the absolute values of both of these belief systems that are attached to the various options under consideration. This feature of our approach makes within-person comparisons much more relevant to understanding individual's decisions than between-group mean level comparisons. Unfortunately, very little work has taken such a pattern-centered approach.

Consider two high school students: Mary and Beth. Both young women enjoy mathematics and physical science and have always done very well in these subjects, as well as in their other school subjects. Both have been identified as gifted in mathematics and have been offered the opportunity to participate in an accelerated math program at the local college during their senior year. Beth hopes to major in communications when she gets to college and has also been offered the opportunity to work part-time at the local TV news station doing odd jobs and some copy editing. Mary hopes to major in computer science in college and plans a career as a research scientist designing educational software. Taking the accelerated math course involves driving to and from the college. Since the course is scheduled for the last period of the day, it will take the last two periods of the day, as well as 1 hour of after-school time to take the course. What will the young women do? In all likelihood, Mary will enroll in the program because she both likes math and thinks that the effort required to master the material is important for her long-range career goals. Beth's decision is more complex. She may want to take the class but may also think that the time required is too costly, especially given her alternative opportunity to do an apprenticeship at the local TV station. Whether she takes the college course or not will depend, in part, on the advice she gets from her counselors, family, and friends. If they stress the importance of the math course, then its subjective worth is likely to increase. If the subjective worth of the course increases sufficiently to outweigh its subjective cost, then Beth will likely take the course despite its cost in time and effort. Studying these types of subtle processes is difficult with individual- and group-difference–oriented variable-centered approaches.

In summary, my colleagues and I assume that educational, occupational choices (as well as other achievement-related leisure time choices) are guided by: (a) individuals' expectations for success with (sense of personal efficacy at) the various options, as well as their sense of competence for various tasks; (b) the relation of the options to their short- and long-range goals, to their core personal and social identities, and to their basic psychological needs; (c) individuals' culturally based role schemas linked to gender, social class, and ethnic group; and (d) the potential cost of investing time in one activity rather than another. We assume that all of these psychological variables are influenced by individuals' histories as mediated by their interpretation of these experiences, by cultural norms, and by the behaviors and goals of one's socializers and peers.

Furthermore, we have spent the past 40 years amassing evidence to support each of these hypotheses. The findings related to gender differences in the pursuit of careers in physical science and engineering are quite robust (see Eccles [1993, 1994] and Eccles et al. [1998] for reviews). Here, I give just one example of our most recent findings. The analyses I report were done using data from the Michigan Study of Adolescent Life Transitions (MSALT). This longitudinal study is being conducted by me, Bonnie Barber, and many wonderful graduate students, postdoctoral scholars, and new faculty collaborators, including, most recently, Ming-Te Wang and Barbara Schneider (see our web site www.rcgd.isr. umich.edu/garp under the MSALT project and articles folders). It began in 1982 with a sample of approximately 3,000 sixth-graders in 12 different school districts in Southeastern Michigan; these districts served primarily working- and middle-class small-city communities. The sample is predominantly White but does include about 150 African-American adolescents. We have now followed approximately 1,500 of these adolescents well into their early and middle adulthood years using standard survey-type methods (we are currently collecting a new wave of data on them at age 40). All of the survey instruments reported here have been used in a variety of studies and have well-established reliabilities and good predictive and face validity. All are available on our web site.

First, we looked at the psychological predictors of enrollment in both the honor's mathematics track in high school and high school physics. We found no gender differences in enrollment in high school math courses until the 12th grade, when young women were slightly less likely than young men to enroll in a second-semester advanced math course. We used path analysis to determine whether this gender difference was mediated by constructs directly linked to expectations for success (specifically, the students' self-concept of their math ability) and subjective task value (specifically, how much they enjoyed doing math, the subjective importance of doing well in math, and the usefulness of math courses) while controlling for the students' scores on the Differential Aptitude Test (DAT; Updegraff, Eccles, Barber, & O'Brien, 1996). As predicted, the gender difference in course-taking at grade 12 was completely mediated by these beliefs collected while the students were in either the 10th or 11th grade. But even more importantly from my perspective, the gender difference was totally mediated by perceived importance/utility. Interestingly, neither 10th-grade enjoyment/interest nor self-concept of ability predicted the number of math courses taken once the DAT scores were included in the analyses. The gender difference in self-concept of math ability, however, did mediate the gender differences in taking high school physics courses, although to a lesser extent than did the gender difference in the perceived importance/utility value of math. These results clearly demonstrate the predictive importance of constructs linked to subjective task value in explaining both individual and gender differences in high school STEM-related course taking. We were particularly struck by the strength of the importance/utility construct. Recall the example I gave about the two young women deciding whether to take the college math course, in which I stressed the perceived importance of the course for the young women's future plans. These data support that emphasis. At this point in these students' lives, they must begin to choose between elective courses. These findings suggest that they weigh the utility of the course for their future educational and vocational goals heavily in making these choices, and that gender differences in these course decisions are primarily due to perceived utility rather than either aptitude differences or differences in a sense of personal efficacy to succeed at mathematics. We found exactly the same pattern of results for gender differences in the number of high school physical science courses.

We next looked at the mediators of gender differences in career aspirations, given their apparent role in course decisions. Here, we used four sets of beliefs and values more directly related to career choices: (1) values regarding work, future success, relationships, and leadership (*lifestyle values*); (2) specific job characteristics adolescents may desire in their future occupational settings (*valued job characteristics*); (3) estimates of future success in different categories of occupations (*expected efficacy in jobs*); and (4) self-ratings of job-relevant skills (*self-perception of skills*) (see Eccles, Barber, & Jozefowicz [1999] for details on these scales and their psychometric properties). *Occupational aspirations* were assessed using the following open-ended probe: "If you could have any job you wanted, what job would you like to have when you are 30?" Analyses revealed fairly stereotypic gender differences: the young men aspired to science/math-related occupations, male-typed skilled labor occupations, and protective service jobs more than did the young women. Conversely, these young women aspired to human service jobs, health professions, and female-typed skilled labor more than did their male peers. However, the largest number of both males and females aspired to business/law occupations (31% and 30%, respectively).

We next analyzed which values, job characteristics, skills, and efficacy expectations best discriminated between adolescents who aspired to each of nine occupational categories (see Eccles et al. [1999] for full details). These analyses controlled for mathematical ability. Here, I summarize the results for only two occupational categories: Ph.D. or M.D. level health careers and M.S. or Ph.D. level physical science/engineering/math-related careers. First, as predicted by our model, both females and males who aspired to the health careers were more likely to expect to do well in health-related occupations and placed higher value on people/society-oriented job characteristics than did those who did not aspire to health careers. The young women who aspired to these careers also rated their ability to succeed in science-related careers quite high as well. The young women, on average, were more likely to aspire to the health-related careers primarily because they placed higher value on a people/society-oriented job than did their male peers.

An even more interesting set of results emerged for the science/engineering/math-related careers. Both the young women and men who aspired to these types of careers were more likely than their peers to expect to do well in science-related fields and to value math and computer job tasks. The young men who aspired to science-related careers also had higher ratings of their computer and machinery skills and lower expectancies for doing well in business/law occupations than did their male peers who did not aspire to these careers. Interestingly, the young women who aspired to these types of careers placed much lower value on people/society-oriented job characteristics than did their female colleagues who did not aspire to these careers. This last effect was not evident for the young men.

These results are interesting for several reasons. First, they support the Eccles et al. model of achievement-related choices (Eccles [Parsons] et al., 1983): for both males and females, occupational aspirations are mediated primarily by both expectancy beliefs and subjective task values. In addition, both approach-related (i.e., I expect to do well in science, therefore I will choose a science career) and avoidance-related (i.e., I do not value people/society-oriented job tasks, therefore I will aspire to something else) beliefs predict the occupational choices for both males and females.

Second, there are intriguing gender and occupational category differences in the discriminating characteristics. For instance, expecting to do well in science-related occupations discriminates females who choose science-related or health careers from those who do not aspire to such careers. This is not true of males for whom only science-related expectancies discriminate between those males who choose science careers and those who do not. With regard to the females who choose science-related or health careers, it is important to point out that the value of people/society job characteristics also discriminates between those females who aspire to health or science/math careers and those who do not. However, it discriminates in opposite directions for these two career options. That is, females who aspire to health careers place high value on people/society-oriented job characteristics; in contrast, females who aspire to physical science-related careers place unusually low value on the people/society-oriented aspects of jobs. Considering the fact that both groups of women expect to do well in science-related careers, it follows that one of the critical components influencing females' decisions to go into a science- versus a health-related field is not science-related efficacy but the value these females place on having a job associated with people and humanistic concerns. Thus, if we want to increase the number of females who consider entering physical science and engineering careers, it will be important to help them see that these careers provide opportunities to fulfill their humanistic and people-oriented values and life goals; such interventions are likely to be as successful, if not more successful than interventions designed to raise females' perceptions of their math-related abilities.

We have done comparable analyses on these young people's actual college majors and jobs at age 25 (Eccles & Vida, 2003). Again, we sought to determine which beliefs and values distinguished those women and men who completed a physical science or engineering degree and who went into physical science and engineering careers from those who did not, controlling for actual mathematical ability. We found exactly the same pattern: as predicted by our model, both men and women who go into these professions have high expectations to succeed in these fields and place high subjective task value on doing the types of tasks inherent in these professions. But even more important, both the men and women who go into these fields place unusually low value on having a job that directly benefits other people or society. Although this effect is true for both men and women, the young women in this sample are much more likely than the young men to want jobs that provide direct benefits to society.

Finally, Ming-Te Wang and I compared the men and women in this sample who went into the traditional STEM fields (physical science, math, computers, and engineers) with those men and women who went into the health, biology, and medical sciences. We used the same measures in Eccles and Vida (2003) (actual mathematical and numerical abilities, math and English ability self-concepts and values, a desire to go into a field in which one directly helps other people or society, and careerism) and added indicators of a desire for a job that fits well with one's family and parental responsibilities, thus allowing a good work–family balance, as well as desiring a job that lets one work with mechanical devices. As we expected, at age 20, these females rated the importance of a job that helps others and a job that allows for a good work–family balance higher than did their male peers; the reverse was true for the importance of a job allowing one to work with mechanical devices.

First, the fact that men were more likely to go into any STEM field than women was completely explained by the fact the men have higher math ability self-concepts, a greater desire to work with things, and a lesser desire to work with people than do women, after controlling for actual competence in math and reading. As one would expect, both men and women with higher DAT math scores and more high school math courses were more likely to go into STEM fields. Finally, higher family income and education also predicted entry into STEM fields.

We next directly compared the men and women who went into the more biological and medical STEM fields to the men and women who went into the physical, computer, and engineering sciences. The gender difference in choice between these two types of STEM careers was mediated by the greater desire of women for a career that helps others. This job value predicted going into the medical/biological sciences rather than the engineering and physical sciences.

Finally, we reran both of these analyses within sex. Interestingly, wanting to have a family-friendly job drove women away from the full set of STEM professions but had no impact on men's decision to enter STEM fields. In contrast, wanting a job that allows one to work with mechanical things attracted men to the full set of STEM professions but had no impact on women's decisions to enter STEM fields. Also in contrast, neither of these beliefs discriminated between selecting between the two types of STEM fields.

Thus, our analyses suggest that the main source of gender differences in entry into these types of occupations is not gender differences in either math aptitude or a sense of personal efficacy to succeed at these occupations; rather, it is a gender difference in the value placed on different types of occupations. Furthermore, our results suggest that these differences begin influencing educational decisions quite early in life. Finally, my own opinion is that these differences reflect, at least to some extent, inaccurate stereotypes about physical science and engineering that lead some young women and men to reject these careers for the wrong reasons. Many jobs in these fields do provide opportunities for individuals to fulfill humanistic and helping people/society values. If we want to increase the number of females who aspire to and then actually go into these fields, we need to provide them with better information about the nature of these occupations, so that they can make better-informed decisions regarding the full range of occupations they might consider as they try to pick a career that fits well with their personal values and identity, as well as with their short- and long-term goals.

Socialization of Gendered Achievement Choices in the Family

The second part of our research has focused on the role of experiences in the home and at school in shaping the types of gender differences in self- and task-related beliefs just discussed. Our work in this area has been guided by the theoretical model illustrated in Figure 2.2. Most of this work has been conducted most recently with Pamela Davis-Kean, Jennifer Fredricks, Rena Harold, Janis Jacobs, and Sandi Simpkins and is based on both MSALT data and a second longitudinal study—The Childhood and Beyond Study (see our web site under the CAB project). This project involved approximately 1,000 elementary school children (three cohorts, initially in kindergarten, first grade, and third grade) and their parents living in small urban areas in southeastern Michigan. We followed these children and their families annually for 4 years, beginning in 1988. Given my limited space, I can only give a brief overview of our findings.

First, using a variety of longitudinal modeling techniques, we have been able to demonstrate the basic links summarized in Figure 2.2. Many parents do endorse gender-stereotypic beliefs about general gender differences in abilities and interest in these various skills and activities; parents' gender role stereotypes predict their perceptions of their own children's math, sport, and English abilities and interests even after independent assessments of their children's actual abilities in these three domains have been controlled (Eccles, 1993; Eccles et al., 1999; Eccles, Freedman-Doan, Frome, & Yoon, 2000; Eccles & Jacobs, 1986; Eccles et al., 1993; Frome & Eccles, 1998; Jacobs & Eccles, 1992; Neuenschwander, Vida, Garrett, & Eccles, 2007), leading them, on average, to underestimate their daughters' math and athletic abilities. In turn, parents' estimates of their children's abilities in different skills predict developmental changes in their children's own estimates of their abilities in these skills, as well as the children's expectations for success in these different skill areas, to a greater extent than do actual indicators of performance (Jacobs & Eccles, 1992; Schnabel, Alfeld, Eccles, Köller, & Baumert, 2002; Simpkins, Davis-Kean, & Eccles, 2005), leading to the kinds of gender differences in the children's own beliefs and task values discussed earlier in this chapter.

Second, on average, parents provide their daughters and sons with gender role stereotypic types of toys and activity opportunities, even in academic subject areas (Eccles et al., 1993). Thus, for example, parents read more with their daughters than with their sons (Eccles & Harold, 1996). They also provide their sons with more math, computer-related, and athletic activities and books (Fredricks & Eccles, 2005; Jacobs, Davis-Kean, Bleeker, Eccles, & Malanchuk, 2005; Jacobs, Vernon, & Eccles, 2005) beginning at a very young age. Interestingly, they also provide their daughters with more opportunities to learn to play musical instruments during the elementary school years (Eccles, 1993; Eccles & Harold, 1993; Jacobs, Vernon et al., 2005). Not surprisingly, these differential patterns of experiences mediate, to some but not fully, the emergence of gender differences in children's confidence in their own abilities, their interests in participating in different activities, and, at least in sports and music, their actual competence (Jacobs, Vernon et al., 2005). Not surprisingly, the extent to which each of these facts holds true is more marked when parents endorse the traditional gender role stereotypes associated with both ability and interest in these different skills areas (Jacobs & Eccles, 1992).

Third, on average, parents make different causal attributions for their daughter's and son's successes in mathematics: they attribute girls' successes more to hard work than natural ability, and they attribute boys' successes equally to both. As a result, effort is seen as more influential and ability as less influential for girls than for boys (Yee & Eccles, 1988). Furthermore, the more parents attribute their child's math successes to effort rather than ability, the more their child's estimates of their own ability in math decline over time.

Interestingly, the better parents think their child is in English, independent of how good they think their child is in math, the lower their child's confidence in their math abilities (Eccles, 2006). Not surprisingly, parents of daughters, on average, rate their child's English abilities higher than their math abilities. Thus, daughters' math ability self-concepts can be undermined by their parents in several ways, including (a) the direct impact of distortions in their views of their daughters' math abilities in a stereotypic direction, (b) the indirect distortions in their views of their daughters' math ability due to their stereotypic estimations of their daughter's English abilities, (c) the ways in which parents attribute their children's successes and failures at various activities, and (d) the impact of their stereotypes on the kinds of activities they provide for their daughters and sons on the kinds of skills their children get exposed to and get to practice.

There are two important experimental and quasi-experimental studies that illustrate the policy implications of these findings. In the first, Jacobs and Eccles (1985) investigated the impact of 1980 media coverage of the Benbow and Stanley (1980) *Science* article showing the expected gender difference in the performance of gifted children on the PSAT exam. At that time, Eccles and her colleagues were in the middle of collecting longitudinal data on parents' perceptions of their children's math and English abilities. They had already collected the first wave of data in 1979. The second wave of data was collected after the media coverage of this article had been completed. Jacobs and Eccles (1985) found that the mothers who reported reading about this study showed a decline in their perceptions of their own daughters' math abilities. Thus, they had incorporated the Benbow and Stanley findings into their views of their own child, perhaps because the findings were consistent with the cultural stereotype and thus exacerbated the mothers' gender stereotypic distortion of their views of their own daughters. Interestingly, fathers who reported having read about the article showed an increase in both their view of their daughters' math abilities and their endorsement of the cultural stereotype about males generally being better than females at math. Clearly, in this case, reports of scientific results can influence parents' own gender stereotypes, as well as their perceptions of their own children's math ability.

The second study is still in process. It is being conducted by Judith Harackiewicz, Janet Hyde, and their colleagues (Harackiewicz, Rozek, Hulleman, & Hyde, 2012). They developed an intervention that provides parents with information on the utility value of math and science for future high-quality careers. In a randomized intervention, they are showing that the children of parents who received these materials are more likely to take additional math and science courses in high school. This finding is particularly true for daughters of mothers with a college education. Apparently, one can successfully intervene with parents of daughters (as well as sons) to increase the likelihood of daughters and sons both taking more math and science courses and considering careers in the STEM fields.

Conclusion

In summary, my and my colleagues' research, as well as similar research by other scholars, has provided clear evidence that gender role-related personal and social processes explain, at least in part, the gender differences we see in the educational and career choices of youth in many Western countries. Furthermore, interventions have been created that can help ameliorate these processes, with the result that both girls/women and boys/men are able to make less gender-role stereotypic choices for their own lives.

Acknowledgments

Aletha Huston's early research laid the groundwork for much of what I have summarized in this chapter. I am very grateful for her influence on the work that my colleagues and I have done over the past 40 years.

References

Benbow, C. P., & Stanley, J. C. (1980). Sex differences in mathematical ability: Fact or artifact? *Science, 210,* 1262–1264.

Eccles, J. S. (1993). School and family effects on the ontogeny of children's interests, self-perceptions, and activity choice. In J. Jacobs (Ed.), *Nebraska Symposium on motivation, 1992: Developmental perspectives on motivation* (pp. 145–208). Lincoln: University of Nebraska Press.

Eccles, J. S. (1994). Understanding women's educational and occupational choices: Applying the Eccles et al. model of achievement-related choices. *Psychology of Women Quarterly, 18,* 585–609.

Eccles, J. S. (2006). Families, schools, and developing achievement-related motivations and engagement. In J. E. Grusec & P. D. Hastings (Eds.), *Handbook of socialization: Theory and research* (pp. 665–691). New York: Guilford Press.

Eccles (Parsons), J., Adler, T. F., Futterman, R., Goff, S. B., Kaczala, C. M., Meece, J. L., & Midgley, C. (1983). Expectations, values and academic behaviors. In J. T. Spence (Ed.), *Perspective on achievement and achievement motivation* (pp.75–146). San Francisco: W. H. Freeman.

Eccles, J. S., Barber, B., & Jozefowicz, D. (1999). Linking gender to education, occupation, and recreational choices: Applying the Eccles et al. model of achievement-related choices. In W. B. Swann, J. H. Langlois, & L. A. Gilbert (Eds.), *Sexism and stereotypes in modern society: The gender science of Janet Taylor Spence* (pp. 153–192). Washington, DC: APA Press.

Eccles, J. S., Freedman-Doan, C., Frome, P., Yoon, K. S. (2000). Gender-role socialization in the family: A longitudinal approach. In T. Eckes and H. M. Trautner (Eds.), *The developmental social psychology of gender* (pp. 333–360). Mahwah, NJ: Erlbaum.

Eccles, J. S., & Harold, R. D. (1993). Parent-school involvement during the early adolescent years. *Teachers' College Record, 94,* 568–587.

Eccles, J., & Harold, R. (1996). Family involvement in children's and adolescents' schooling. In A. Booth, & J. Dunn (Eds.), *Family-school links: How do they affect educational outcomes* (pp. 3–34). Hillsdale, NJ: Lawrence Erlbaum Associates.

Eccles, J. S., & Jacobs, J. E. (1986). Social forces shape math attitudes and performance. *Signs: Journal of Women in Culture and Society, 11* (2), 367–380.

Eccles, J. S., Jacobs, J., Harold, R., Yoon, K. S., Arbreton, A., & Freedman-Doan, C. (1993). Parents and gender role socialization during the middle childhood and adolescent years. In S. Oskamp & M. Costanza (Eds.), *Gender issues in contemporary society* (pp. 59–83). Newbury Park, CA: Sage Publications.

Eccles, J. S., & Vida, M. (March, 2003). *Predicting gender and individual differences in college major, career aspirations, and career choice.* Paper presented at the biennial meeting of the Society for Research on Child Development, Tampa, FL.

Eccles, J. S., Wigfield, A., & Schiefele, U. (1998). Motivation to succeed. In W. Damon (series ed.) and N. Eisenberg (vol. ed.), *Handbook of child psychology* (5th ed., Vol. III, pp. 1017–1095). New York: Wiley.

Fredricks, J., & Eccles, J. S. (2005). Family socialization, gender, and sport motivation and involvement. *Journal of Sport & Exercise Psychology, 27,* 3–31.

Frome, P., & Eccles, J. S. (1998). Parental influence on children's achievement-related perceptions. *Journal of Personality and Social Psychology, 74,* 435–452.

Harackiewicz, J. M., Rozek, C. R., Hulleman, C. S., & Hyde, J. S. (2012). Helping parents to motivate adolescents in mathematics and science: An experimental test of a utility-value intervention. *Psychological Science, 23,* 899–906. doi: 10.1177/0956797611435530

Huston, A. C. (1983). Sex-typing. In E. M. Hetherington (Ed.), *Handbook of child psychology. vol. 4.* (4th ed., pp. 387–468). New York: Wiley.

Jacobs, J. E., Davis-Kean, P., Bleeker, M., Eccles, J. S., & Malanchuk, O. (2005). "I can, but I don't want to": The impact of parents, interests and activities on gender differences in math. In A. Gallager and J. Kaufman (Eds.), *Gender differences in mathematics* (pp. 246–263). New York: Cambridge University Press.

Jacobs, J. E., & Eccles, J. S. (1985). Gender differences in math ability: The impact of media reports on parents. *Educational Researcher, 14,* 20–25.

Jacobs, J. E., & Eccles, J. S. (1992). The impact of mothers' gender-role stereotypic beliefs on mothers' and children's ability perceptions. *Journal of Personality and Social Psychology, 63,* 932–944.

Jacobs, J. E., Vernon, M. K., & Eccles, J. S. (2005). Activity choices in middle childhood: The roles of gender, self-beliefs, and parents' influence. In J. L. Mahoney, R. W. Larson, & J. S. Eccles (Eds.), *Organized activities as contexts of development: Extracurricular activities, after-school and community programs* (pp. 235–254). Mahwah, NJ: Erlbaum.

Neuenschwander, M. P., Vida, M., Garrett, J. L., & Eccles, J. S. (2007). Parents' expectations and students' achievement in two western nations. *International Journal of Behavioral Development, 31*(6), 594–602.

Ruble, D. N., & Martin, C. L. (1998). Gender development. In W. Damon (series ed.) & N. Eisenberg (vol. ed.), *Handbook of child psychology: Vol. 3. social, emotional, and personality development* (5th ed., pp. 933–1016). New York: John Wiley & Sons Inc.

Schnabel, K. U., Alfeld, C., Eccles, J. S., Köller, O., & Baumert, J. (2002). Parental influence on students' educational choices in the U.S.A. and Germany: Different ramification—same effect? *Journal of Vocational Behavior, 60*, 178–198.

Simpkins, S. D., Davis-Kean, P. E., & Eccles, J. S. (2005). Parents' socializing behavior and children's participation in math, science, and computer out-of-school activities. *Applied Developmental Science, 9*(1), 14–30.

Stein, A. H. (1971). The effects of sex-role standards for achievement and sex-role preference on three determinants of achievement motivation. *Developmental Psychology, 4*, 219–231.

Stein, A. H., & Bailey, M. M. (1973). The socialization of achievement orientation in females. *Psychological Bulletin, 80*, 345–366.

Stein, A. H., Pohly, S. R., Mueller, E. (1971). The influence of masculine, feminine, and neutral tasks on children's achievement behavior, expectations of success, and attainment value. *Child Development, 42*, 195–207.

Stein, A. H., & Smithells, J. (1968). *The sex-role standards about achievement held by Negro and White children from father-present and father-absent homes.* Unpublished manuscript. Cornell University, Ithaca, NY.

Stein, A. H., & Smithells, J. (1969). Age and sex differences in children's sex-role standards about achievement. *Developmental Psychology, 1*, 252–259.

Updegraff, K. A., Eccles, J. S., Barber, B. L., & O'Brien, K. M. (1996). Course enrollment as self-regulatory behavior: Who takes optional high school math courses? *Learning and Individual Differences, 8*, 239–259.

Yee, D., & Eccles, J. S. (1988). Parent perceptions and attributions for children's math achievement. *Sex Roles, 19*, 317–333.

Child Care

AN EARLY CONTEXTUAL OPPORTUNITY

{ 3 }

Women's Work and Child Care

PERSPECTIVES AND PROSPECTS

Marion O'Brien, Jennifer M. Weaver, Margaret Burchinal,
K. Alison Clarke-Stewart, and Deborah Lowe Vandell

Child care emerged as a topic of interest to developmental psychologists in the
1970s, when it became clear that the entry of large numbers of mothers into the
workforce was a trend unlikely to be reversed. In most of the literature, the term
child care refers to regularly scheduled care provided by someone other than the
child's mother; the context of care may be a center, the caregiver's home, or the
child's own home. The first descriptive studies comparing the social, emotional,
and cognitive functioning of children in child care with those cared for at home
by their mothers reported either no differences between the groups (Doyle,
1975; Moyles & Wolins, 1971) or positive relations with child care (Robinson &
Robinson, 1971). These findings did not satisfy all developmental psychologists,
however. Based largely on attachment theory and clinical reports of severe social-
emotional deficits in children who were separated from their mothers and placed
in substitute care settings or institutions (e.g., Bowlby, 1958, 1969; Yarrow, 1961),
concern was raised that nonmaternal child care was a potentially "depriving" environment similar to institutional care. From this viewpoint, child care was seen as
likely to have long-term negative effects on children's development. As a result,
much child care research published in the late 1970s and 1980s was framed from a
deficit perspective. Still, the overall picture that emerged from this early work was
one showing few of the predicted negative effects (see review in Clarke-Stewart &
Allhusen [2005]). Children cared for by someone other than their mothers were
not more likely than other children to show insecure attachment to their mothers,
and their development in social and cognitive domains did not differ from children cared for at home.

Beginning in the 1990s, research into maternal employment and child care
became more sophisticated in its conceptualization and design, recognizing the
complexities of family life and children's developmental paths, as well as the variations in type, quantity, and quality of child care. In this chapter, we briefly describe
the current state of knowledge about child care and its relation to children's

concurrent functioning and longer term outcomes. Following this summary, we suggest some potentially fruitful avenues for future research.

Children and Families in Context: Women's Work and Child Care

A majority of U.S. mothers of young children are employed outside the home— 64% of those with children under the age of 6 and 57% among mothers of infants (U.S. Department of Labor, 2012). Almost all U.S. children receive some form of regular child care prior to school entry. Thus, the context of family life for the typical U.S. parent includes juggling work and household responsibilities and, when children are young, making arrangements for child care and paying for that care. For the typical U.S. child, beginning in infancy, spending some time away from home in a setting that often includes other unrelated children is a part of daily life. Thus, maternal employment and child care have been the focus of much research into families and children's development.

MATERNAL EMPLOYMENT

Surprisingly little research has been done to describe differences in family life and mothers' well-being when mothers work. Research from an economic and sociological perspective has tended to focus on the lost resource to children when mothers are employed outside the home and therefore to emphasize that employed mothers spend less time with their children than do nonemployed mothers (e.g., Bianchi, Robinson, & Milkie, 2006; Coleman, 1988). Developmental psychologists who examine time use tend to focus more on "quality time," usually considered active involvement and interaction with a child, rather than physical presence. Researchers have found few differences in parenting quality between working and nonworking mothers, with differences sometimes favoring employed mothers (Booth, Clarke-Stewart, Vandell, McCartney, & Owen, 2002; Huston & Aronson, 2005).

Considerable evidence links maternal employment with positive personal well-being. Mothers who are employed report fewer depressive symptoms (Buehler & O'Brien, 2011; Coley, Lohman, Votruba-Drzal, Pittman, & Chase-Lansdale, 2007), although Brooks-Gunn, Han, and Waldfogel (2010) found long-term increases in depressive symptoms in mothers employed during their child's infancy. In addition, although they may spend somewhat less time with their children, mothers who are employed are equally sensitive and more likely to provide a stimulating learning environment at home (Buehler, O'Brien & Walls, 2011; Huston & Aronson, 2005). Given these correlates of employment, it is perhaps not surprising that there appear to be few or no concurrent or long-term disadvantages to children associated with maternal employment. Recent meta-analytic reviews of the maternal employment literature focusing on child outcomes confirm the findings of few differences in children of employed versus nonemployed mothers (Goldberg, Prause, Lucas-Thompson, & Himsel, 2008; Lucas-Thompson, Goldberg, & Prause, 2010).

CHILD CARE

Given the reality that most mothers of young children are employed, the question for most families becomes one of selecting a reliable and affordable option for child care. Before age 3, many children are cared for in home settings, either by caregivers commonly referred to as family day-care providers, or by relatives. Center-based care, either privately operated or publicly funded, is the most common option for children of preschool age.

Concerns about potential negative effects of child care for infants contributed to the decision in the late 1980s by the National Institutes of Child Health and Human Development (NICHD) to support research into infant child care through a large-scale multisite study that ultimately became the NICHD Study of Early Child Care and Youth Development (SECCYD; NICHD Early Child Care Research Network [ECCRN], 2001). The idea was that questions about child care could best be addressed with a prospective study using a diverse sample that was large enough to account for selection factors and other important covariates.

Early reports from the SECCYD focused on three aspects of care during the first 3 years of life—namely, quality, quantity, and type of care—and their associations with child well-being. A key question focused on mother-child attachment because this was the theoretical basis for much of the concern about infant care. Results showed clearly that children in child care were just as likely to be securely attached to their mothers at 15 months of age, and this was true regardless of the number of hours of care children received, the type or quality of care, or the age at which they began care (NICHD ECCRN, 1997). Further analyses of SECCYD data examining other aspects of child well-being indicated that children who received higher quality care throughout their infant, toddler, and preschool years, particularly center-based care, showed gains in cognitive and preacademic skills that were evident as early as age 3 and continued to school entry (NICHD ECCRN, 2002b, 2003, 2005). Those children who experienced higher hours of nonmaternal care, however, were reported to be more aggressive and less cooperative (NICHD ECCRN, 1998, 2002b, 2003); in later analyses, this association was found to be lower for children in high-quality care (McCartney et al., 2010). Along with the SECCYD results, findings from other large-scale studies support the academic benefits of high-quality care (Broberg, Wessels, Lamb, & Hwang, 1997; Peisner-Feinberg & Burchinal, 1997). Yet reports of children's social development showed mixed results (e.g., Belsky, 2001; Howes, Phillips, & Whitebook, 1992), leaving open the question of the links between child care experience and child social behavior.

Although infant child care was a primary concern driving research during the 1990s, issues regarding child care and early education for children in the 3- to 5-year age range have become more prominent, especially because of the increased academic demands placed on children during the early years of school. In their preschool years, most U.S. children attend center-based programs, either part- or full-day. The quality of this care, in terms of adult involvement with children, the presence of a positive emotional climate, and the availability of appropriately challenging preacademic activities, is important to children's well-being and their success in the transition to school (e.g., Mashburn et al., 2008). Increasingly, states are recognizing the importance of quality care and early education for preschoolers. To date, more than 25 states have adopted quality rating and improvement systems (QRIS), intended to provide parents with information about program quality as well as to establish program standards that rise above basic health and safety criteria. In addition, in recognition that quality preschool programs contribute to children's later school success, states are increasingly providing funding specifically for pre-kindergarten programs as part of the public education system, often for children who are perceived to be at risk for school difficulties. Research consistently shows that high-quality child care during the preschool years is linked to positive outcomes for children in terms of language and academic skills (e.g., Peisner-Feinberg et al., 2001).

SUMMARY

Despite decades of concern about mothers' employment and nonmaternal child care, the weight of evidence does not support negative effects on children or families. In fact, when young children receive high-quality care, there appear to be significant benefits. These consistent findings of the importance of child care quality suggest an increased emphasis on research to identify the specific aspects of child care and early education settings that contribute to positive outcomes for children.

Prospects for Future Research: Examining Quality in Child Care

Within the child care literature, quality has been defined in two general ways: by *structural* characteristics including adult-child ratio, group size, teacher training, and other regulable factors; and by *process* characteristics that describe aspects of the experience of children in the setting. Structural quality indices include caregiver training, staff-child ratios, group size, and space available; because these characteristics are straightforward and readily measurable, they are the focus of most licensing and regulation policies. In one study examining change in structural regulations, it was found that process quality was enhanced when licensing standards were raised (Howes, Smith, & Galinsky, 1995). Moreover, analyses from the SECCYD showed structural quality to be related to child outcomes indirectly through its association with process quality (NICHD ECCRN, 2002a). At the same time, meeting state licensing requirements does not guarantee quality care, and licensing generally does not extend to home-based child care settings, where many U.S. children, especially infants and toddlers, receive care.

To index process quality in child care, researchers usually focus on caregiver behavior, particularly such aspects of behavior as the sensitivity of care providers to children, the extent to which they maintain positive affect, their involvement in children's activities, and the amount, level, and quality of language they use with children. Process quality is generally found to be related to child social-emotional and cognitive functioning both concurrently and prospectively, but these relations are often relatively weak (e.g., Peisner-Feinberg et al., 2001; Vandell, Belsky, Burchinal, Steinberg, & Vandergrift, 2010). We still do not know what specific aspects of caregiver-child interactions or other factors present in the child care environment are linked to positive outcomes and do not understand the mechanisms by which child care experiences contribute to concurrent or long-term child behavior and learning. In the following sections, we address some questions about quality in child care that are emerging in current research.

IS GLOBAL QUALITY SUFFICIENT TO CAPTURE CHILDREN'S EXPERIENCE?

Most investigators examining child care quality have used relatively broad indices, with the idea that they capture the overall climate of the care setting and the usual experiences of children in that setting. Several investigators have called for a closer look at quality and the disaggregation of components of quality (Dowsett, Huston, Imes, & Gennetian, 2008; Kontos, Burchinal, Howes, Wisseh, & Galinsky, 2002; Zaslow, Martinez-Beck, Tout, & Halle, 2011). In support of this idea, recent theoretical work and empirical studies of parents suggest that interaction quality is domain specific (Davidov & Grusec, 2006; Grusec & Davidov, 2010; Leerkes, Blankson, & O'Brien, 2009); that is, individual caregivers may vary widely in their sensitivity across different situations, and this variability is important to children's experience. For example, caregivers may be sensitive when children are happily involved in play but insensitive or dismissive when children are upset or distressed. It is likely that sensitivity to child distress is particularly important to children's regulatory and emotional development because it meets a child's need for protection (Grusec & Davidov, 2010). In studies of mothers, sensitivity to infant distress has been found to be related to later social development, whereas globally rated measures of sensitivity were not (Leerkes et al., 2009), and sensitive responses to 6- and 8-year-old children's distress were associated with better regulation of negative emotions, whereas overall parental warmth was not (Davidov & Grusec, 2006). Times when children are distressed, particularly in child care where parents are not present, may be particularly salient episodes, and caregivers' responses in these situations are likely to make a big difference in the level of comfort a child feels in the child care environment. To date, no research has been done in child care settings to distinguish between caregiver responses to children in distressing versus nondistressing situations.

Similarly, a focus on global sensitivity is unlikely to provide a picture of caregivers' skill at supporting children's cognitive development by providing stimulation and instruction that is appropriate to the child's age and developmental level. Grusec and Davidov (2010) label this domain "guided learning." In a child care setting, guided learning includes the overall structure that supports teaching and learning, the selection of materials that are appropriately challenging, the caregiver's level of involvement with children as they explore and use materials, the quality and amount of language directed toward children, and the extent of informative feedback provided to children as they work on problem solving or complex tasks. Recent research suggests that even sensitive caregiving that includes attention to cognitive development may not be as effective in promoting positive outcomes as the implementation of a focused curriculum that embeds sensitive caregiver interactions within a developmental learning framework (e.g., Justice & Ezell, 2002; Wasik & Hindman, 2011). Effective curricula provide a structure within which caregivers are able to ensure that children master one set of skills and then move to more challenging tasks at the next level (Gettinger & Stoiber, 2012). Successful implementation of such curricula requires extensive in-service training and professional development for caregivers, who must be able to follow recommended practices but also respond flexibly and individually to children in order to take advantage of learning opportunities (Pianta, Barnett, Burchinal, & Thornburg, 2009). With a growing emphasis placed on academic preparation for kindergarten, the structure and support for learning provided to children prior to school entry has increased in importance.

To date, the most frequently used index of quality in child care has been the Early Childhood Environment Rating Scale (ECERS; Harms & Clifford, 1980). Several national and widely cited studies, including Cost, Quality, and Child Outcomes (Helburn et al., 1995) and the National Child Care Staffing Study (Whitebook, Howes, & Phillips, 1990), have used this measure. Furthermore, many of the states implementing quality rating and improvement systems rely on the ECERS as a measure of program quality. Because the ECERS aims to capture a general picture of quality across a wide range of domains, including both structural and process indicators, it is not likely to provide enough specificity to link program quality to child outcomes (La Paro, Thomason, Lower, Kintner-Duffy, & Cassidy, 2012). If we are to move forward in defining the specific aspects of quality that make a difference to children, some additional measures of child care environments are needed.

Based broadly on the Observational Rating of the Child-care Environment (ORCE) and the Classroom Observation System (COS) developed for the NICHD SECCYD, the Classroom Assessment Scoring System (CLASS; Pianta,

La Paro, & Hamre, 2008) represents an attempt to pull apart specific dimensions of quality. For example, the pre-k and early elementary versions of the CLASS include indices of instructional quality separate from emotional support. These two dimensions have been found in several studies to be related to different aspects of children's school readiness: instructional quality is generally associated with academic and language performance and emotional support with social skills (Burchinal, Vandergrift, Pianta, & Mashburn, 2010; Mashburn et al., 2008). Caregivers in infant, toddler, and preschool-aged child care settings often tend to emphasize emotional quality over instructional quality (LoCasale-Crouch et al., 2007) and may not take full advantage of opportunities to enhance child learning. Use of more structured curricula, especially those that include a social-emotional as well as an academic focus, has the potential to help caregivers provide a better balance between instructional and emotional quality (Bodrova & Leong, 2009; Raver et al., 2011).

CAN WE CAPTURE INDIVIDUAL CHILDREN'S EXPERIENCE OF QUALITY?

Most research into child care has been conducted as if all children in a care setting have the same experiences. Current approaches to developmental science emphasize child-by-environment interactions, highlighting the importance of examining individual variation in the effects of experience (Coll, Bearer, & Lerner, 2004; Gottlieb, 1996; Keating, 2011). Some investigators have applied these ideas to the study of child care, proposing the examination of niches within child care settings and the possibility that the same classroom may have different effects on different children, depending on children's individual characteristics (Jeon et al., 2010; Pluess & Belsky, 2009; Watamura, Phillips, Morrisey, McCartney, & Bub, 2011).

To date, the individual child characteristics most frequently examined in research have been aspects of temperament. Several researchers have examined the question of whether children who are inhibited or anxious have difficulty adapting to child care environments and coping with peer interactions, which may be difficult and stressful. In one study, home-based child care appeared to be beneficial for anxious children, reducing their anxiety over time, whereas either center-based care or mother-at-home care did not (Coplan, Findlay, & Schneider, 2010). It may be that the exposure to peers in a small group setting allows anxious children to learn peer interaction skills without becoming overwhelmed. Tarullo, Milner, and Gunnar (2011) examined the social experiences of preschool-aged children reported by caregivers to be "inhibited" and "exuberant." The inhibited children were less well integrated socially into the classroom whereas the exuberant children were dominant in their peer groups but also showed more anger in peer interactions and tended to have more conflictual friendships. It is likely that these individual differences in children interact with aspects of the child care setting to result in different outcomes. However, researchers examining the question of whether children with "difficult" temperaments benefit more from high-quality child care than do other children have found no child-by-environment effects but only positive outcomes related to high-quality care for all children (Crockenberg & Leerkes, 2005; Wachs, Gurkas, & Kontos, 2004).

Although research into child-by-environment effects to date has focused on social experiences and social-emotional outcomes, opportunities for cognitive development are also experienced differently by different children in a classroom. Children are active participants in creating and learning from their environments. Once they can move about independently, children have many opportunities to choose what they will do and with whom they will do it, choices that affect what they will learn. Children who are curious, persistent, and alert to their surroundings need less support from caregivers and an organized, structured environment than do children with lower executive function and cognitive skills. Shy children, who may be reluctant to become involved in group activities or initiate interactions with caregivers, may be particularly at risk in unstructured and less well organized child care environments (Blankson, O'Brien, Leerkes, Marcovitch, & Calkins, 2011; Dominguez, Vitiello, Maier, & Greenfield, 2010). Unfortunately, it is likely to be those children least able to elicit and structure their own learning opportunities who are overlooked or not challenged by caregivers. Further research is needed to identify and implement teaching strategies that engage all children in learning, encourage their curiosity, challenge their thinking, and increase their understanding.

HOW DO VARIATIONS IN CHILD CARE QUALITY AFFECT CHILDREN'S BEHAVIOR AND DEVELOPMENT?

Stress is one proximal factor that is frequently suggested as the mechanism by which low-quality child care or many hours of child care may have negative effects on children. Children who find their day-to-day environments stressful are called on to exert substantial behavioral control, thereby challenging their still immature regulatory systems. Stress in child care has been a topic of considerable interest in recent years, and a growing body of research using cortisol as an index of stress has developed. In general, child care appears to be a relatively stressful environment for children, as indicated by the fact that children's cortisol levels tend to rise during the day in child care but decrease across the day when children are at home (Vermeer & van IJzendoorn, 2006). Heightened cortisol levels in child care are most pronounced when care is considered low in quality and/or when children are rated by teachers as having low social skills (Dettling, Parker, Lane, Sebanc, & Gunnar, 2000). Thus, stress is most likely to be experienced by a child who is involved in negative interactions with other children or adults or who spends many hours in a disorganized environment not knowing what will happen next.

Child-by-environment interactions are relevant in the study of stress in child care, and some recent work has shown intriguing findings about individual differences in children's behavioral responses when their physiological state indicates stress. For example, in one study of children in home-based care, it was found that girls responded to high cortisol levels with anxiety whereas boys whose cortisol levels were high tended to show anger and aggression (Gunnar, Kryzer, Van Ryzin, & Phillips, 2010). These patterns suggest sex differences in stress responses beginning at an early age, with girls tending to overregulate and boys to underregulate their emotional states. Watamura, Kryzer, and Robertson (2009) found variation in cortisol levels among children in high-quality child care programs and suggested that some children had more positive experiences than others even within the same classroom. Tarullo and colleagues (2011) found that highly inhibited preschool children maintained or increased their high cortisol levels across a school year, whereas other children showed a decrease as time went on, indicating that they adapted to the child care environment and found it less stressful over time. Furthermore, the level of children's social integration and dominance had different effects on cortisol reactivity in inhibited versus exuberant children. For inhibited children, an outwardly successful social experience appeared to be inwardly stressful, as indexed by high cortisol levels, whereas exuberant children were stressed by the lack of social success.

Although studies of stress in child care are only beginning and to date have been largely descriptive, these early findings suggest that examining individual children's experiences in child care is an important goal. There are many potential sources of stress in a child care environment. Separation from parents, conflictual interactions with caregivers and other children, a disorganized and chaotic environment that leaves children confused about expectations, inadequate resources, harsh or insensitive demands for behavioral control—all of these factors may create stress that, when experienced on a daily basis, can lead to long-term changes in physiology, behavior, and health (Caserta et al., 2008; Johnston-Brooks, Lewis, Evans, & Whalen, 1998). In fact, Watamura, Coe, Laudenslager, and Robertson (2010) report high cortisol levels in child care to be related, concurrently, to low antibody levels and more child illnesses reported by parents. To date, studies have not addressed the specific aspects of child care environments that create stress for children who come to those environments with specific characteristics of their own, and this is a key component of the future research agenda in child care.

HOW DO PEERS CONTRIBUTE TO CHILDREN'S EXPERIENCES IN CHILD CARE?

A major distinction between mother-at-home care and nonmaternal child care is the presence of other children, sometimes a large number of other children, often of the same age. Recently, several authors have suggested that peer influences are likely to be highly salient to children, especially those in center-based child care settings (Fabes, Hanish, & Martin, 2003; Kontos et al., 2002) but to some extent in home-based care as well (Kryzer, Kovan, Phillips, Dornagall, & Gunnar, 2007).

In classroom observations, Kontos and colleagues (2002) found that caregivers tended to intervene in children's peer interactions when problems arose but otherwise kept their distance. These findings suggest that the functioning of peer groups in child care settings is largely independent of adult involvement.

Few research studies have examined how children's time in child care is spent. Data from the NICHD SECCYD on how children spent their time while in child care at 36 and 54 months show that children at 36 months interacted with caregivers only 10% of the time; they played alone or were unoccupied 28% of the time and were interacting with peers approximately 30% of the time (times when children had no choice of activity, as during meals, were not included in these totals). At 54 months, children were observed to spend more time in interaction with caregivers, approximately 18% of their time, but played alone almost 25% of the time and spent approximately 40% of their time playing with or near other children. These data lend support to the idea that peer interactions are an important and overlooked aspect of children's experiences in care.

What is it that children may be learning from one another? Presumably, children gain social and cognitive skills from observing other children and participating in shared activities, but little research has examined naturally occurring peer-to-peer learning in child care settings. Mashburn, Justice, Downer, and Pianta (2009) reported that preschool-aged children experienced greater gains in language skills when they attended a child care classroom with children who had higher language skills at the beginning of the year. These findings suggest that high-level language-based interactions with other children may help to promote language learning. Longitudinal data from the SECCYD has shown that children who experience high rates of positive peer interactions in child care are more socially competent at third grade than are other children, whereas those who experience more negative peer interactions tend to be more aggressive and have lower social skills (NICHD ECCRN, 2008). Further research that looks more closely at the nature and quality of peer interactions in child care settings and examines both social-emotional and academic outcomes for children based on these experiences would help to identify key ingredients of the peer culture and climate that contribute positively to children's development.

One aspect of young children's peer groups that may contribute to different patterns of development is that they are usually segregated by sex. Maccoby (1998) described sex-segregated peer groups as essentially separate cultures guiding what boys and girls learn (see also Liben, Bigler, & Hilliard, Chapter 1). According to Maccoby (1998), girls' groups tend to emphasize cooperation and to involve more verbal, rather than physical, interaction; girls usually are more behaviorally regulated than boys as well, and therefore their peer play tends to be calmer and less challenging to a child with limited social skills. The smaller groups that girls form are less stable in their dominance hierarchies than are those of boys. Thus, girls may have more opportunities to be dominant in some groups at some times, whereas the relative social positions of boys are likely to remain constant over time.

Boys' groups are larger, less likely to be influenced by adults, and therefore less rule-bound and more likely to involve physical contact and dysregulated behavior (Carpenter, Huston, & Holt, 1986). These different peer experiences of boys and girls have the potential to be reflected in both social-emotional and cognitive development. Fabes and colleagues (2003) report data showing that preschool-aged boys in child care classrooms spend dramatically more time than girls in activities that explicitly involve science and math, whereas girls are more involved in activities involving language; the authors suggest that these patterns are fostering different skills for boys and girls (see also Eccles, Chapter 2).

Other researchers have also found sex differences in boys' and girls' experiences in preschool settings. Within publicly funded preschool classrooms, Early et al. (2010) observed girls to spend more time in language/literacy, art, and fine motor activities than did boys, who spent more time in science and social studies activities and gross motor play. Kontos and colleagues (2002) observed preschool-aged girls to be involved in more complex interactions with peers than are boys, and this was especially true when girls were interacting *without* teacher involvement. When children spend much of their time in one type of activity, they are likely to gain specific skills and knowledge related to that activity as well as a repertoire of behavior appropriate to the other children who participate in that activity. If preschool-aged boys and girls select different activities, it would be expected they would start school with different sets of skills and behaviors, some of which will be more adaptive and successful than others. Thus, the contention of Fabes et al. (2003), that child care centers are promoting sex-differentiated learning, is one that calls for additional research.

SUMMARY

An underlying assumption in much of the current literature on child care is that quality is largely defined by the presence of caregivers who are sensitive and engaged with children. Although having such caregivers may be necessary to high quality, this aspect of care is not sufficient to ensure that all children will receive quality care in all situations. Future research is needed to identify specific components of caregiver sensitivity that contribute to positive social-emotional development and specific approaches to involvement in children's play and learning activities that contribute to cognitive development. In addition, we need to know more about the extent to which children's individual characteristics make them more or less able to benefit from specific aspects of child care environments and more or less vulnerable to particular environmental arrangements. Finally, there has been a long-standing belief that sensitive caregiving promotes positive peer interactions and complex peer play, but the processes by which adult-child interaction is transferred to child-child interaction in child care settings have not been described. In sum, a priority for future research is to take a closer look at children's experiences in child care in order to identify the characteristics of care environments that promote positive social, emotional, and cognitive outcomes for all children.

Conclusion: Translating Child Care Research into Practice and Policy

For research on child care to make a difference in the quality of care children receive, the results of basic research into children's experiences in child care settings need to become the foundation for caregiver and early childhood teacher training programs at universities, community colleges, and community-based in-service programs. Framing research findings in ways that can be used as concrete training components could have a direct effect on quality across a wide range of child care settings. Several successful in-service professional development programs have shown the promise of research-based approaches to caregiver training. For example, the Chicago School Readiness Project provides in-classroom consultation for Head Start staff to assist them in dealing with child behavior problems (Raver et al., 2008), the Exceptional Coaching for Early Language and Literacy program uses intensive caregiver training in book reading and conversation to promote literacy (Wasik & Hindman, 2011), and the My Teaching Partner program uses web-based technology to provide preschool caregivers with individual consultation (Downer, Kraft-Sayre, & Pianta, 2009; Pianta, Mashburn, Downer, Hamre, & Justice, 2008).

The issues discussed in this chapter have profound implications for public policy surrounding child care. These implications are the focus of Chapter 4 by Zaslow, Crosby, and Smith and are therefore not discussed in detail here. It is clear that an expanded focus on policy-relevant research in child care is needed because child care is an issue that affects all U.S. children and families and our educational system (Palley, 2010). Only by expanding the access of all families to quality early care and education can we be assured that U.S. children are given maximum opportunity for success.

References

Bodrova, E., & Leong, D. J. (2009). Tools of the Mind: A Vygotskian-based early childhood curriculum. *Early Childhood Services: An Interdisciplinary Journal of Effectiveness, 3*, 245–262.

Belsky, J. (2001). Developmental risks (still) associated with early child care. *Journal of Child Psychology and Psychiatry, 42*, 845–859.

Bianchi, S. M., Robinson, J. P., & Milkie, M. A. (2006). *Changing rhythms of American family life.* New York: Russell Sage.

Blankson, A. N., O'Brien, M., Leerkes, E. M, Marcovitch, S., & Calkins, S. D. (2011). Shyness and vocabulary: The role of executive functioning and home environmental stimulation. *Merrill-Palmer Quarterly, 57*, 105–128.

Booth, C. L., Clarke-Stewart, K. A, Vandell, D. L., McCartney, K., & Owen, M. T. (2002). Child-care usage and mother-infant "quality time." *Journal of Marriage and Family, 64*, 16–26.

Bowlby, J. (1958). The nature of the child's tie to his mother. *International Journal of Psychoanalysis, 39*, 350–371.

Bowlby, J. (1969). *Attachment and loss* Vol. 1: *Attachment*. London, UK: Hogarth.

Broberg, A. G., Wessels, H., Lamb, M. E., & Hwang, C. P. (1997). Effects of day care on the development of cognitive abilities in 8-year-olds: A longitudinal study. *Developmental Psychology, 33*, 62–69.

Brooks-Gunn, J., Han, W., & Waldfogel, J. (2010). First-year maternal employment and child development in the first 7 years. *Monographs of the Society for Research in Child Development, 296, 75(2)*.

Buehler, C., & O'Brien, M. (2011). Mothers' part-time employment: Associations with mother and family well-being. *Journal of Family Psychology, 25*, 895–906.

Buehler, C., O'Brien, M., & Walls, J. K. (2011). Mothers' part-time employment: Child, parent, and family outcomes. *Journal of Family Theory and Review, 3*, 256–272.

Burchinal, M., Vandergrift, N., Pianta, R., & Mashburn, A. (2010). Threshold analysis of association between child care quality and child outcomes for low-income children in pre-kindergarten programs. *Early Childhood Research Quarterly, 25*, 166–176.

Carpenter, C. J., Huston, A. C., & Holt, W. (1986). Modification of preschool sex-typed behaviors by participation in adult-structured activities. *Sex Roles, 14*, 603–615.

Caserta, M. T., O'Connor, T. G., Wyman, P. A., Wang, H., Maynihan, J., Cross, W., et al. (2008). The associations between psychosocial stress and the frequency of illness, and innate and adaptive immune function in children. *Brain, Behavior, and Immunity, 22(6)*, 933–940.

Clarke-Stewart, A., & Allhusen, V. D. (2005). *What we know about childcare*. Cambridge, MA: Harvard University Press.

Coleman, J. S. (1988). Social capital in the creation of human capital. *American Journal of Sociology, 94*, 95–120.

Coley, R. L., Lohman, B., Votruba-Drzal, E., Pittman, L. D., & Chase-Lansdale, P. L. (2007). Maternal functioning, time, and money: The world of work and welfare. *Children and Youth Services Review, 29*, 721–741.

Coll, C. G., Bearer, E. L., & Lerner, R. M. (2004). *Nature and nurture: The complex interplay of genetic and environmental influences on human behavior and development*. Mahwah, NJ: Lawrence Erlbaum Associates.

Coplan, R., Findlay, L. C., & Schneider, B. H. (2010). Where do anxious children "fit" best? Childcare and the emergence of anxiety in early childhood. *Canadian Journal of Behavioral Science, 42(3)*, 185–193.

Crockenberg, S. C., & Leerkes, E. M. (2005). Infant temperament moderates associations between childcare type and quantity and externalizing and internalizing behaviors at 2½ years. *Infant Behavior & Development, 28*, 20–35.

Davidov, M., & Grusec, J. E. (2006). Untangling the links of parental responsiveness to distress and warmth to child outcomes. *Child Development, 77*, 44–58.

Dettling, A. C., Parker, S. W., Lane, S., Sebanc, A., & Gunnar, M. R. (2000). Quality of care and temperament determine changes in cortisol concentrations over the day for young children in childcare. *Psychoneuroendocrinology, 25*, 819–836.

Dominguez, X., Vitiello, V. E., Maier, M. F., & Greenfield, D. B. (2010). A longitudinal examination of young children's learning behavior: Child-level and classroom-level predictors of change throughout the preschool year. *School Psychology Review, 39,* 29–47.

Downer, J. T., Kraft-Sayre, M., & Pianta, R. C. (2009). On-going, web-mediated professional development focused on teacher-child interactions: Feasibility of use with early childhood educators. *Early Education & Development, 20,* 321–345.

Dowsett, C. J., Huston, A. C., Imes, A. E., & Gennetian, L. (2008). Structural and process features in three types of child care for children from high and low income families. *Early Childhood Research Quarterly, 23,* 69–93.

Doyle, A. B. (1975). Infant development in daycare. *Developmental Psychology, 11,* 655–656.

Early, D. M., Iheoma, U. I., Ritchie, S., Barbarin, O. A., Winn, D.-M., Crawford, G. M., et al. (2010). How do pre-kindergarteners spend their time? Gender, ethnicity, and income as predictors of experiences in pre-kindergarten classrooms. *Early Childhood Research Quarterly, 25,* 177–193.

Fabes, R. A., Hanish, L. D., Martin, C. L. (2003). Children at play: The role of peers in understanding the effects of childcare. *Child Development, 74,* 1039–1043.

Gettinger, M., & Stoiber, K. C. (2012). Curriculum-based early literacy assessment and differentiated instruction with high-risk preschoolers. *Reading Psychology, 33,* 11–46.

Goldberg, W. A., Prause, J. A., Lucas-Thompson, R., & Himsel, A. (2008). Maternal employment and children's achievement in context: A meta-analysis of four decades of research. *Psychological Bulletin, 134,* 77–108.

Gottlieb, G. (1996). Developmental psychobiological theory. In R. B. Cairns, G. H. Edler, & S. J. Costello (Eds.), *Developmental science* (pp. 63–77). New York: Cambridge University Press.

Grusec, J. E., & Davidov, M. (2010). Integrating different perspectives on socialization theory and research: A domain-specific approach. *Child Development, 81,* 687–709.

Gunnar, M. R., Kryzer, E., Van Ryzin, M. J., & Phillips, D. A. (2010). The rise in cortisol in family day care: Associations with aspects of care quality, child behavior, and child sex. *Child Development, 81,* 851–869.

Harms, T., & Clifford, R. M. (1980). *Early Childhood Environment Rating Scale* New York: Teachers College Press.

Helburn, S., Culkin, M. I., Morris, J., Mocan, N., Howes, C., Phillipsen, L., et al. (1995). *Cost, quality, and child outcomes in child care centers, public report* (2nd ed.). Denver, CO: Economics Department, University of Colorado at Denver.

Howes, C., Phillips, D. A., & Whitebook, M. (1992). Thresholds of quality: Implications for the social development of children in center-based child care. *Child Development, 63,* 449–460.

Howes, C., Smith, E., & Galinsky, E. (1995). *The Florida child care quality improvement study.* New York: Families and Work Institute.

Huston, A. C., & Aronson, S. R. (2005). Mothers' time with infants and time in employment as predictors of mother-child relationships and children's early development. *Child Development, 76,* 467–482.

Jeon, H. J., Langill, C. C., Peterson, C. A., Luze, G. J., Carta, J. J., & Atwater, J. B. (2010). Children's individual experiences in early care and education: Relations with overall classroom quality and children's school readiness. *Early Education and Development, 21,* 912–939.

Johnston-Brooks, C. H., Lewis, M. A., Evans, G. W., & Whalen, C. K. (1998). Chronic stress and illness in children: The role of allostatic load. *Psychosomatic Medicine, 60,* 597–603.

Justice, L. M., & Ezell, H. K. (2002). Use of storybook reading to increase print awareness in at-risk children. *American Journal of Speech-Language Pathology, 85,* 388–396.

Keating, D. P. (Ed.). (2011). *Nature and nurture in early child development.* New York: Cambridge University Press.

Kontos, S., Burchinal, M., Howes, C., Wisseh, S., & Galinsky, E. (2002). An eco-behaviorial approach to examining the contextual effects of early childhood classrooms. *Early Childhood Research Quarterly, 17,* 239–258.

Kryzer, E. M., Kovan, N., Phillips, D. A., Domagall, L. A., & Gunnar, M. R. (2007). Toddlers' and preschoolers' experience in family day care: Age differences and behavioral correlates. *Early Childhood Research Quarterly, 22,* 451–466.

La Paro, K. M., Thomason, A. C., Lower, J. K., Kintner-Duffy, V. L., & Cassidy, D. J. (2012). *Examining the definition and measurement of quality in early childhood education: A review of the use of the ECERS-R from 2003 to 2010. Early Childhood Research and Practice, 14.* Retrieved from http://ecrp.uiuc.edu/v14n1/laparo.html

Leerkes, E. M., Blankson, A. N., & O'Brien, M. (2009). Differential effects of sensitivity to infant distress and non-distress on social-emotional functioning. *Child Development, 80,* 762–775.

LoCasale-Crouch, J., Konold, T., Pianta, R., Howes, C., Burchinal, M., Bryant, D., et al. (2007). Observed classroom quality profiles in state-funded pre-kindergarten programs and associations with teacher, program, and classroom characteristics. *Early Childhood Research Quarterly, 22,* 3–17.

Lucas-Thompson, R., Goldberg, W. A., & Prause, J. A. (2010). Maternal work early in the lives of children and its distal associations with achievement and behavior problems: A meta-analysis. *Psychological Bulletin, 136,* 915–942.

Maccoby, E. E. (1998). *The two sexes: Growing up apart, coming together.* Cambridge, UK: Harvard University Press.

Mashburn, A. J., Justice, L. J., Downer, J. T., & Pianta, R. C. (2009). Peer effects on children's language achievement during pre-kindergarten. *Child Development 80,* 686–702.

Mashburn, A. J., Pianta, R. C., Hamre, B. K., Downer, J. T., Barbarin, O. A. Bryant, D., et al. (2008). Measures of classroom quality in prekindergarten and children's development of academic, language, and social skills. *Child Development, 79,* 732–749.

McCartney, K., Burchinal, M., Clarke-Stewart, A., Bub, K. L., Owen, M. T., & Belsky, J. (2010). Testing a series of causal propositions relating time in child care to children's externalizing behavior. *Developmental Psychology, 46,* 1–17.

Moyles, E. W., & Wolins, M. (1971). Group care and intellectual development. *Developmental Psychology, 4,* 370–380.

NICHD Early Child Care Research Network. (1997). The effects of infant child care on infant-mother attachment security: Results of the NICHD Study of Early Child Care. *Child Development, 68,* 860–879.

NICHD Early Child Care Research Network (1998). Early child care and self-control, compliance, and problem behavior at twenty-four and thirty-six months. *Child Development, 69,* 1145–1170.

NICHD Early Child Care Research Network. (2001). Nonmaternal child care and family factors in early development: An overview of the NICHD Study of Early Child Care. *Journal of Applied Developmental Psychology, 22,* 457–492.

NICHD Early Child Care Research Network. (2002a). Child-care structure- process-outcome: Direct and indirect effects of child-care quality on young children's development. *Psychological Science, 13,* 199–202.

NICHD Early Child Care Research Network (2002b). Early child care and children's development prior to school entry: Results from the NICHD Study of Early Child Care. *American Educational Research Journal, 39,* 133–164.

NICHD Early Child Care Research Network. (2003). Does quality of child care affect child outcomes at age 4 ½? *Developmental Psychology, 39,* 451–469.

NICHD Early Child Care Research Network. (2005). Early child care and children's development in the primary grades follow-up results from the NICHD Study of Early Child Care. *American Educational Research Journal, 42,* 537–570.

NICHD Early Child Care Research Network. (2008). Social competence with peers in third grade: Associations with earlier peer experiences in childcare. *Social Development, 17,* 419–453.

Palley, E. (2010). Who cares for children? Why are we where we are with American child care policy? *Children and Youth Services Review, 32,* 155–163.

Peisner-Feinberg, E., & Burchinal, M. (1997). Concurrent relations between child care quality and child outcomes: The study of cost, quality and outcomes in child care centers. *Merrill Palmer Quarterly, 43,* 451–477.

Peisner-Feinberg, E., Burchinal, M., Clifford, R., Culkin, M., Howes, C., Kagan, S. L., & Yazejian, N. (2001). The relation of preschool child-care quality to children's cognitive and social developmental trajectories through second grade. *Child Development, 72,* 1534–1553.

Pianta, R. C., Barnett, W. S., Burchinal, M., & Thornburg, K. R. (2009). The effects of preschool education: What we know, how public policy is or is not aligned with the evidence base, and what we need to know. *Psychological Science in the Public Interest, 10,* 49–88.

Pianta, R., La Paro, K., & Hamre, B. K. (2008). *Classroom Assessment Scoring System* Baltimore, MA: Paul H. Brookes.

Pianta, R., Mashburn, A., Downer, J., Hamre, B., & Justice L. (2008). Effects of web-mediated professional development resources on teacher-child interactions in pre-kindergarten classes. *Early Childhood Research Quarterly, 23,* 431–451.

Pluess, M., & Belsky, J. (2009). Differential susceptibility to rearing experience: The case of childcare. *Journal of Child Psychology and Psychiatry, 50,* 396–404.

Raver, C. C., Jones, S. M., Li-Grining, C. P., Metzger, M., Champion, K. M., Sardin, L. (2008). Improving preschool classroom processes: Preliminary findings form a randomized trial implemented in Head Start settings. *Early Childhood Research Quarterly, 23,* 10–26.

Raver, C. C., Jones, S. M., Li-Grining, C., Zhai, F., Bub, K., & Pressler, E. (2011). CSRP's impact on low-income preschoolers' preacademic skills: Self-regulation as a mediating mechanism. *Child Development, 82,* 362–378.

Robinson, H. B., & Robinson, N. M. (1971). Longitudinal development of very young children in a comprehensive day care program: The first two years. *Child Development, 42,* 1673–1683.

Tarullo, A. R., Milner, S., & Gunnar, M. R. (2011). Inhibition and exuberance in preschool classrooms: Associations with peer social experiences and changes in cortisol across the preschool year. *Developmental Psychology, 47*, 1374–1388.

U.S. Department of Labor, Bureau of Labor Statistics. (2012). Employment characteristics of families—2011. Retrieved from http://www.bls.gov/news.release/famee.nro.htm

Vandell, D. L., Belsky, J., Burchinal, M., Steinberg, L., & Vandergrift, N. (2010). Do effects of early child care extend to age 15 years? Results from the NICHD study of early child care and youth development. *Child Development, 81*, 737–756.

Vermeer, H. J., & Van IJzendoorn, M. H. (2006). Children's elevated cortisol levels at day-care: A review and meta-analysis. *Early Childhood Research Quarterly, 21*, 390–401.

Wachs, T. D., Gurkas, P., & Kontos, S. (2004). Predictors of preschool children's compliance behavior in early childhood classroom settings. *Journal of Applied Developmental Psychology, 25*, 439–457.

Wasik, B. A., & Hindman, A. H. (2011). Improving vocabulary and pre-literacy skills of at-risk preschoolers through teacher professional development. *Journal of Educational Psychology, 103*, 455–469.

Watamura, S. E., Coe, C. L., Laudenslager, M. L., & Robertson, S. S. (2010). Child care setting affects salivary cortisol and antibody secretion in young children. *Psychoneuroendocrinology, 35*, 1156–1166.

Watamura, S. E., Kryzer, E. M., & Robertson, S. S. (2009). Cortisol patterns at home and child care: Afternoon differences and evening recovery in children attending very high quality full-day center-based child care. *Journal of Applied Developmental Psychology, 30*, 475–485.

Watamura, S. E., Phillips, D. A., Morrissey, T. W., McCartney, K., & Bub, K. (2011). Double jeopardy: Poorer social-emotional outcomes for children in the NICHD SECCYD experiencing home and child-care environments that confer risk. *Child Development, 82*, 48–65.

Whitebook, M., Howes, C., & Phillips, D. (1990). *Who cares? Child care teachers and the quality of care in America. Final report: National Child Care Staffing Study.* Oakland, CA: Child Care Employee Project.

Yarrow, L. J. (1961). Maternal deprivation: Toward an empirical and conceptual re-evaluation. *Psychological Bulletin, 58*, 459–490.

Zaslow, M., Martinez-Beck, I., Tout, K., & Halle, T. (Eds.). (2011). *Quality measurement in early childhood settings.* Baltimore, MD: Paul H Brookes.

4

Issues of Quality and Access Emerging from the Changing Early Childhood Policy Context

TOWARD THE NEXT GENERATION OF RESEARCH

Martha Zaslow, Danielle A. Crosby, and Nina Smith

Over the past 50 years, early care and education (ECE) settings have increasingly come to be recognized as a key developmental context, in part because of a dramatic increase in their use, but also because of scientific advancements in understanding the impact of early learning experiences. As described by O'Brien and colleagues (Chapter 3), families' reliance on child care has grown substantially since the 1970s as women have increased their employment in response to changing social norms, labor market trends (e.g., declining wages), and policy initiatives encouraging or requiring employment for low-income parents. Also during this period, as research has provided a better understanding of early brain development and the factors that promote optimal development, families have increasingly sought out organized educational experiences for their young children. Together, these societal trends mean that a majority of children in the United States now spend significant amounts of time in ECE settings prior to school entry, and government spending on early childhood has expanded to unprecedented levels.

Although the ECE field is gradually moving toward a more unified identity, historically, its two major components—child care as a work support and early education as developmental enrichment—have occupied rather distinct and often disconnected tracks within the realms of policy and research (Huston, 2004, 2008). Although policy initiatives around the former have focused primarily on increasing access, policies related to the latter have emphasized quality. In parallel, separate bodies of research have made substantial strides in understanding the impact of each set of policies. The purpose of this chapter is to summarize key issues related to quality and access emerging from these bodies of research. There is growing recognition in the field that framing these as separate or competing goals is counterproductive, given that most families desire both (Huston, 2008; Pianta, Barnett, Burchinal, & Thornburg, 2009). In describing the existing evidence, we are constrained to summarize the work in distinct sections; however, we conclude the chapter by describing some hopeful signs of convergence between policy efforts focused on quality and access. Before summarizing each area of research, we begin by providing a brief overview of the current ECE policy landscape.

Public Investments Related to Early Care and Education Access and Quality

Children in low-income families have long been the primary target of public investments in ECE, given the policy goals of promoting employment among disadvantaged parents (with an emphasis on access to ECE) and reducing socioeconomic-based disparities in child achievement (with an emphasis on quality). Yet, as noted, the funding streams and program structures related to these two goals have remained largely separate (Huston, 2008). Tax credits and child care subsidies serve as the primary policy mechanisms for supporting low-income parents' employment by reducing families' out-of-pocket child care expenses. Funding for subsidies through the Child Care Development Block Grant (CCDBG) has more than doubled since 1996, when welfare reform created new incentives and pressures for low-income mothers (of even very young children) to work. In addition, states have been allowed to direct a portion of their Temporary Assistance to Needy Families (TANF) funds toward facilitating child care access for low-wage workers. In 2010, CCDBG and TANF provided more than $8 billion for subsidies, serving approximately 2.6 million children per month (Schulman & Blank, 2012).

In terms of developmental enrichment, the oldest and largest form of federal investment is the Head Start program, which provides education, health, nutrition, and family support services to more than 1 million preschool-aged children each year; an additional 100,000 infants and toddlers receive a similar suite of services through Early Head Start (Office of Head Start, 2011). Most states have likewise invested heavily in early childhood over the past two decades. Motivated by concerns about skill gaps evident at school entry and mounting evidence on the benefits of early childhood education, a majority of states (39 in 2011) now provide some form of publicly funded pre-kindergarten program, with a total enrollment of more than 1.3 million children (Barnett, Carolan, Fitzgerald, & Squires, 2011).

The shifting ECE policy landscape creates both new opportunities and new challenges. Never before has there been such widespread interest in and support for the care and education of young children, and this interest is shared not only by parents and developmental scientists, but by scholars from a range of disciplines, as well as by business and community leaders, policy makers, and, increasingly, the public at large. As such, the early childhood field has become an exemplar of meaningful connections between scientific theory, empirical research, policy, and practice (Pianta et al., 2009).

This broad (and growing) base of support may be one reason that ECE initiatives on the whole have fared relatively well during the Great Recession. To date, the major ECE funding streams just mentioned have been generally protected in the federal budget. Moreover, the American Recovery and Reinvestment Act of 2009 (ARRA, H. Res 1, 2009) provided short-term supplemental funds for a wide spectrum of ECE services in an effort to compensate for shrinking state budgets (National Association for the Education of Young Children [NAEYC], 2009). In addition, such recent policy initiatives as the establishment of the Maternal, Infant and Early Childhood Home Visiting Program as part of the Affordable Care Act and the Race to the Top-Early Learning Challenge grants from the U.S. Department of Education, working in collaboration with the U.S. Department of Health and Human Services, signal a significant commitment to public investments in early childhood. While ECE programs have been buffered by ARRA funding, and even expanded through specific initiatives, the phasing out of ARRA funds is beginning to alter this picture. For example, constrained state budgets have meant that pre-K funding has declined in the past 2 years (Barnett et al., 2011).

Despite important strides forward, however, the full promise of ECE remains unfulfilled, given that many children do not yet have access to the types of high-quality early educational experiences known to promote development and learning. Many existing ECE settings are rated as being of mediocre to low quality, especially those serving infants and toddlers, and significant numbers of children do not regularly participate in any type of ECE services (Adams, Tout, & Zaslow, 2007). As Pianta and colleagues (2009) note, "even in a policy and program development environment in which early education is valued and prominent...the realities point to a fragile and vulnerable nonsystem through which many of our most fragile and vulnerable citizens pass" (p. 49). It will be important, then, for the next generation of early childhood policies to focus both on improving quality and expanding access, and research has a vital role to play in these efforts. Next, we highlight key research issues related to quality and access, summarizing the current state of the literature on each and identifying new areas for scientific inquiry.

Emerging Policy Research Issues Related to Early Care and Education Quality

LINKAGES BETWEEN QUALITY AND CHILD OUTCOMES

Growing recognition of the importance of ECE to young children's development and readiness for school has meant a greater focus on the quality of early childhood settings. We define quality here as stimulating and supportive interactions that foster young children's development across domains, as well as structural features of quality (such as group size and ratio) that make such interactions more likely. There are concerns about wide variation in quality both within and across types of early childhood settings and a lack of common requirements or standards regarding quality not only across settings but across states as well.

Important developments at both the state and national levels have focused on measuring quality in a way that provides a common platform for different types of ECE settings. As of 2010 (Tout et al., 2010), 26 states and localities had quality rating and improvement systems (QRIS) that differentiate among levels of quality in a way that applies across different types of ECE programs. Ratings of quality within QRIS have important implications in that parents may be more or less likely to select a setting because of the QRIS rating it receives, state or local funding for quality improvement efforts may be contingent on the rating a setting receives, and there may be incentives, such as payment of a higher level of child care subsidies, for children attending a center with a higher rating (Tout & Zaslow, 2003; Tout, Zaslow, Halle, & Forry, 2009). Along with the growing weight placed on quality ratings for early childhood settings has come greater scrutiny of the measures and methods used to assess quality for research and policy purposes (Martinez-Beck, 2011).

One issue being reviewed in this context is the widely held assumption that the relationship between quality and child outcomes is linear: that each increment in quality, at any place along the continuum, is associated with a similar gain in child outcomes (Burchinal, Kainz, & Cai, 2011; Martinez-Beck 2011; Zaslow, Anderson et al., 2010). A careful examination of the relationship between quality and child outcomes has sparked reconsideration of this assumption. In a secondary analysis of data from the NICHD Study of Early Care and Education, the National Center for Early Learning and Development Study, and the FACES 1997 studies, Burchinal and colleagues (Burchinal, Kainz et al., 2011) found some indications that associations between quality and child outcomes are stronger at higher levels of quality. Stronger associations between quality and children's development were also evident when the measure of quality was more specific and the outcome being assessed was more closely aligned (e.g., a measure of language and literacy stimulation considered in relation to language outcomes). A subsequent study, using data from eight large early childhood datasets to test for slope differences in the association between quality and child outcomes in lower and higher quality settings, revealed a similar set of results (Burchinal, Xue, Tien, Auger, & Mashburn, 2011; Martinez-Beck, 2011). It will be important for future work to follow up on these analyses using measures of quality that focus on stimulation in specific domains of development (e.g., early literacy and early math). It will also be important to consider the specificity of quality measures included in state QRIS and how distinctions among levels of quality are set (Zaslow, Martinez-Beck, Tout, & Halle, 2011).

THE NEED FOR A STRONG FOCUS ON THE EARLY CHILDHOOD WORKFORCE

With the proliferation of early childhood programs and an intensified focus on quality, there is growing recognition of the central role of the ECE workforce in children's development. At the same time, concerns have been expressed repeatedly about the extent to which there is indeed a single workforce with a unified set of expectations and criteria of professionalism (Rhodes & Huston, 2012). With different funding streams, histories, and priorities, the three major types of publicly supported ECE programs (Head Start, pre-kindergarten, and child care) also vary widely in their requirements and expectations for personnel. These discrepancies pose a challenge to viewing the early childhood workforce as a single, defined profession and holding it accountable for the quality of education and care provided (Rhodes & Huston, 2012).

A recent national workshop convened on this topic identified several issues critical for improving ECE quality at the system level (Institute of Medicine & National Research Council, 2012). First, a more reliable and comprehensive picture of the ECE workforce is needed, one that can be updated on a regular basis to guide planning and investments in staffing and professional development (Rhodes & Huston, 2012). Definitional issues (e.g., distinctions between such occupations as "pre-kindergarten teacher" and "child care worker") and incomplete information about home-based providers make it difficult to assess the size and characteristics of the workforce. A new National Survey of Early Care and Education will begin to address existing gaps by providing in-depth, nationally representative data about both center- and home-based settings (Goerge, Witte, Gennetian, & Brandon, 2010). However, work is also needed toward a unified set of definitions for recurrent national surveys.

There have also been repeated calls in the field for a more integrated ECE system (across funding streams and program types), within which members of the workforce can receive both professional development and institutional supports on a systematic basis (Pianta et al., 2009; Rhodes & Huston, 2012). In addition, given evidence that quality, although important to all children, is especially so for children in low-income families, it has been suggested that efforts to strengthen the ECE workforce should have a broad reach, intentionally including personnel from the full variety of settings serving children at-risk (Rhodes & Huston, 2012).

EXTENDING THE RESEARCH ON EARLY CHILDHOOD PROFESSIONAL DEVELOPMENT

At the intersection of issues regarding the workforce and high-quality ECE environments are discussions of early childhood professional development. Here, too, we are seeing careful review and reassessment of earlier conceptualizations based on new research (see Zaslow, Tout, Halle, & Starr, 2010). In particular, an early assumption held that professional development aimed at increasing the knowledge of early educators (e.g., completion of a bachelor's degree with a major in early childhood) would result in changes in practice. Recently, however, rigorous tests of the association between higher education degrees, observed quality, and children's development have called into question whether knowledge-focused professional development of this kind leads to higher quality or improved child outcomes (Early et al., 2006, 2007).

Instead, an emerging body of evidence suggests that efforts to enhance the quality of services provided by ECE professionals should have a direct focus on practice. One approach that shows promise is individualized professional development involving coaches who observe and provide feedback on interactions with children and model positive interactions, all within the everyday workplace (Zaslow, Tout, Halle, Whittaker, & Lavelle, 2010). A recent review of evaluation research on coaching finds that many, but not all, studies report improvements in observed quality or child outcomes (Tout, Isner, & Zaslow, 2011). Simply including coaching in professional development efforts, however, does not ensure their effectiveness. Yet the literature to date provides few details about the specific features of coaching that make a difference. A recently launched project will describe how specific components (for example, specific processes undertaken during coaching sessions; staffing patterns) vary across coaching models and will lay the groundwork for a study assessing the role of specific components (see the Head Start Coaching Study: Design Phase 2012–2013, available at www.acf.hhs.gov/programs/opre/research).

Various coaching and mentoring models have been widely implemented within QRIS (Smith, Schneider, & Kreader, 2010; Tout et al., 2010; Zaslow, Tout & Halle, 2012) and have been a special priority within Head Start. As these professional development approaches go to scale, however, gaps in the research are becoming apparent. One identified gap is that the research on coaching focuses primarily at the level of the classroom or group. Research extending beyond this level to take into account center- and system-level issues is very limited (Tout et al., 2011). To illustrate, a recent study of four local QRIS notes that little is known about the extent to which center directors are included in and regularly consulted about coaching models being implemented within their setting (Isner et al., 2011). Directors' understanding of and support for a coaching model may be critical to its full implementation and essential for prioritizing which classrooms receive coaching support, as well as for avoiding multiple contradictory or poorly coordinated curricular approaches being implemented at the same time.

At a broader systems level, the selection, training, and supervision of coaches is emerging as a key issue. The Quality Interventions for Early Care and Education (QUINCE) Evaluation (Bryant et al., 2009) found wide variation in the caseloads and supervision of those providing on-site, practice-focused professional development through existing agencies implementing quality improvement initiatives. This study found wide variation in the fidelity of implementation of the quality improvement approach. It also found high rates of turnover among staff in agencies implementing on-site quality improvement approaches. The researchers call for a greatly increased focus in research on the systems-level supports needed for preparation of coaches and their faithful implementation of coaching approaches.

As attention to the early childhood workforce intensifies, a critical question exists regarding pre-service preparation. Educational attainment requirements have been important markers of professionalization in other fields. However, if a bachelor's degree is not systematically related to either observed quality or children's development, what should be required of those working in this field, given the need for clear professional standards and requirements? The finding that completion of a bachelor's degree is not clearly associated with quality and child outcomes may mean that we need a careful review of the focus and requirements of existing higher education programs. Wide variability in course requirements has been documented (Hyson, Horm, & Winton, 2012). Furthermore, the National Council for Accreditation of Teacher Education (NCATE) has called for a review of the extent to which teacher preparation programs include a focus on developmental science and coordinate high-quality placement experiences with coursework in child development (National Council for Accreditation or Teacher Education Expert Panel [NCATE], 2010; Pianta, Hitz, & West, 2010). There is no reason that college coursework should not include practice-focused professional development, and there are presently efforts undertaken to do so. Future research should examine the effects of such approaches.

Emerging Policy Research Issues Related to Early Care and Education Access

Large federal and state investments in ECE over the past two decades (primarily through Child Care and Development Fund [CCDF] subsidies, Head Start/ Early Head Start, and public pre-kindergarten initiatives) have greatly expanded low-income families' access to ECE. National data link recent increases in public funding for ECE to higher enrollment among children in low-income families, particularly in formal center-based settings (Magnuson, Meyers, & Waldfogel, 2007). Yet, despite these expansions, many of the children eligible to participate in publicly supported ECE programs do not do so. This "underenrollment" may reflect limited availability, barriers to access, parental preferences, or some combination of these factors. Most state child care subsidy programs have waiting lists, and Head Start and state pre-kindergarten programs currently serve only a fraction of the children who are eligible to participate (Matthews & Ewen, 2010).

Of particular concern are children and families who may be "slipping through the cracks" in the current landscape—populations for whom there may be meaningful benefits of participation, but who are not well-served by existing policies, programs, and systems. In this section, we spotlight three such groups to illustrate some of the current gaps in research and policy: children of parents with nonstandard or unpredictable employment, children in immigrant families, and children in families dealing with significant health issues. Each of these populations has grown substantially over the past decade, underscoring the need to better understand their experiences in the emerging ECE landscape. Each group is also quite heterogeneous and by no means distinct from the others; indeed, many children and families find themselves at the intersection of multiple "gaps," a point we return to below. Before highlighting some of the key access issues facing these populations, we first briefly consider what is known about parents' decision-making processes regarding care and education for young children.

UNDERSTANDING HOW FAMILIES NAVIGATE THE EARLY CARE AND EDUCATION LANDSCAPE

The process of selecting, securing, and maintaining ECE arrangements for young children typically requires parents to negotiate a complex set of goals and demands related to the needs of individual family members and the family unit as a whole. These considerations may include parents' employment desires and requirements, as well as their beliefs and preferences regarding beneficial experiences for their children. Decisions about how best to meet family needs and preferences take place within the context of certain opportunities and constraints that exist at multiple levels, ranging from the individual to the systems or structures in which families are located (Chaudry et al., 2011). Among other things, families' options are shaped by the types of programs available in their community, their level of financial resources and/or access to public resources, the time they have available to devote to the search process, and the quantity and quality of information they have regarding various ECE alternatives.

Adding to the complexity of this process is the fact that ECE decisions are almost never made in isolation but happen in conjunction with other decisions about employment, housing, transportation, and family budgets (Meyers & Jordan, 2006; Weber, 2011). And, at the same time, this process is dynamic, as circumstances, priorities, preferences, opportunities, and constraints change over time. Given the complex, multifaceted, and dynamic nature of this process, Meyers and Jordan (2006) have described parents' care decisions as "accommodations" to the realities of work, family, and community life, rather than "choices," which implies a more straightforward process of maximizing preferences among a clear set of options.

The opportunities and constraints shaping parents' ECE decisions are not distributed equally across families. In general, higher levels of income increase the quantity and quality of families' options and make it easier to sustain a set of arrangements (Meyers & Jordan, 2006). Public investments in ECE are intended in large part to address these inequities; however, to achieve these aims, ECE policies and programs must "fit" into families' lives (Chaudry et al., 2011; Lowe & Weisner, 2004). To the extent that they do this, policies can either facilitate access or create barriers. Significant mismatches between policy or program parameters and family needs are likely to hinder participation. We turn now to a discussion of three broad groups of families who are at risk for experiencing this type of mismatch in the current ECE policy landscape.

CHILDREN OF PARENTS WITH NONSTANDARD OR
UNPREDICTABLE EMPLOYMENT

Over the past few decades, the emergence of a 24/7 economy and a proliferation of service sector jobs have substantially altered the parameters of parents' work. As a result, there has been a significant increase in the number of jobs requiring night, evening, weekend, and/or rotating hours. Approximately one-fifth of U.S. workers are subject to a nonstandard schedule, and more than 40% of mothers report working nonstandard hours at some point during the first 3 years of their child's life (Presser, 2003). Single parents, ethnic minority parents, those with low levels of education, and those transitioning from welfare to work—indeed, many of the same families targeted by ECE policies—are overrepresented in the types of jobs that require nonstandard schedules (Presser, 2003).

Although some parents may choose to work nonstandard hours in order to obtain preferred ECE arrangements for their children, most have such schedules because it is required by their job (Presser, 2003). Parents in the low-wage workforce are very likely to work nonstandard hours out of necessity, and they tend to have little control, input, or advance notice regarding their schedules (Henly, Shaefer, & Waxman, 2006; Yoshikawa, Weisner, & Lowe, 2006). This instability and unpredictability, coupled with the fact that fewer care options exist in the evening, at night, or on weekends, mean that parents working nonstandard hours face significant barriers to accessing high-quality ECE programs for their children (Le Bihan & Martin, 2004).

Qualitative studies focused on low-income mothers in the post-welfare reform era reveal significant complexities in coordinating work schedules and care for children. Nonstandard and irregular work hours often require "patchworks" of care arrangements flexible enough to meet schedule demands (Scott, London, & Hurst, 2005) and are associated with greater use of informal care by relatives, friends, or neighbors (Henly & Lyons, 2000). Single mothers who work nonstandard shifts are almost twice as likely to rely on relatives to care for their preschoolers as are single mothers who work standard shifts (88% vs. 45%, respectively) (Presser, 2003). The handful of quantitative studies to examine child care use among mothers working nonstandard schedules generally concur with those in the qualitative literature, showing that nonstandard work is associated with less use of center-based care and greater use of informal arrangements (Kimmel & Powell, 2006). These findings are consistent with the suggestion by Emlen and Weit (1999) that the flexibility and predictability of work and care arrangements are often inversely related.

Several potential areas of "mismatch" exist in the current ECE policy landscape for parents with nonstandard or inconsistent employment. First, the part-day, part-year operating schedule of most public pre-kindergarten and some Head Start programs can make these impractical options for working parents, and perhaps specifically for parents with unpredictable employment schedules. In addition, fluctuating work hours or intermittent employment can make it difficult for families to participate in programs where eligibility is tied closely to parental employment (e.g., child care subsidies) (Chaudry et al. 2011).

CHILDREN IN IMMIGRANT FAMILIES

As noted elsewhere in this volume (see Chapter 5 by Marks, Godoy, & García Coll and Chapter 6 by Nieto & Yoshikawa), the demographic transformation of the United States over the past 50 years has been dramatic. Approximately 25% of young children (birth to age 8) are first- or second-generation immigrants, having at least one parent who was born outside the United States (Hernandez, Denton, & Macartney, 2008). More than half of these children live in low-income families, despite high rates of parental employment and two-parent households (Capps, Fix, Ost, Reardon-Anderson, & Passel, 2005). Given disproportionately higher levels of exposure to poverty and lower levels of exposure to English, young children of immigrants have been identified as an important target for ECE services. Evidence suggests that high-quality programs can promote school readiness skills and English-language learning within this population (Magnuson, Lahaie, & Waldfogel, 2006). Early childhood programs also have the potential to support families' integration into communities and their efforts to build the human, social, and cultural capital needed to help their children navigate the U.S. education system (Vesely, Ewaida, & Kearney, 2012).

Despite potential benefits to participation, data from several sources show that immigrant parents are less likely than U.S.-born parents to access formal ECE programs (Matthews & Jang, 2007). National survey estimates reveal this participation gap for infants, toddlers, and preschoolers, and for every type of care arrangement (Karoly & Gonzalez, 2011). Although roughly 55% of children younger than age 3 in native households are in nonparental care, this is true for only 38% of children in immigrant households; the native-immigrant gap is 71% versus 61% for 3-year-olds and 84% versus 72% for 4-year-olds. Enrollment disparities are not likely to be the result of differences in eligibility; most young children in low-income immigrant families are eligible for publicly supported ECE programs based on their own citizenship status or the fact that some programs (e.g., Head Start) do not collect information about legal status.

Nativity-based disparities in ECE participation have been attributed in part to cultural differences in preferences for maternal employment and care for children; however, recent work suggests this may be a less salient or deterministic factor than previously thought. As Hernandez and colleagues point out (2008), many parents emigrate from countries with universal access to early education. For example, in Mexico, where preschool is free (and compulsory since 2009), 99% of 4-year-olds participate (OECD, 2012). A recent survey of Latino parents in the United States finds that more than 90% believe that preschool is important for their children (Garcia & Garcia, 2012), and relatively high rates of Head Start participation among dual-language learners provide evidence of immigrant families' willingness to engage in ECE programs. Between 2000 and 2009, the percentage of children in Head Start with a non-English home language rose from 18% to 26% (Hulsey et al., 2011).

This is not to say that newcomer families place their young children in non-parental care without reservation or concern. Like all parents, immigrant parents most likely seek arrangements that provide safety, stimulation, and nurturance for children while also fitting family needs in terms of affordability, reliability, and convenience. Yet, accessing such arrangements within a less familiar culture and education system involves a unique set of challenges, which may be compounded if parents also have limited English skills. Nearly 15% of young immigrant children have a parent who is not English proficient, and more than 25% speak a home language other than English (Capps et al., 2005).

Several recent reports on ECE participation for children of immigrants identify a range of access barriers (informational, structural, and bureaucratic) in the current policy environment (e.g., Karoly & Gonzalez, 2011; Matthews & Ewen, 2010). As noted earlier, most children of immigrants are eligible to receive publicly supported ECE services: Head Start and Early Head Start have no citizenship requirements and families can prove income eligibility in a number of ways, and eligibility for federal child care subsidies is based on child rather than parent immigration status. There is evidence, however, that many families are unaware of or misinformed about these policies (Perreira et al., 2012). Moreover, studies reveal fairly high levels of fear and apprehension among immigrant parents (particularly those who are undocumented) about participating in government-subsidized programs because of worries about deportation or potential consequences for efforts to obtain citizenship (Adams & McDaniel, 2009; Perreira et al., 2012). The amount and accuracy of information that parents have about local ECE opportunities depends on a variety of factors at the individual and community level, including language issues and program outreach efforts (Chaudry et al., 2011). Even when immigrant families are aware of and interested in publicly supported ECE services, studies suggest that they may encounter multiple barriers (see reviews by Karoly & Gonzalez, 2011; Matthews & Ewen, 2010). For example, enrollment processes are often complicated, may involve completing forms in English, and may require various forms of documentation (e.g., employment, children's vaccinations). In addition, the transportation issues experienced by many low-income families may be heightened for immigrant families, some of whom are not eligible for a driver's license.

A recent review of state plans for CCDBG funds suggests that most states are investing, at least at some level, in strategies to increase immigrant families' access to ECE programs (Firgens & Matthews, 2012). Such efforts include providing information and application materials in a variety of languages, increasing the number of bilingual staff in state and local agencies, and providing resources to increase the linguistic and cultural competencies of the ECE workforce. For example, 13 states report providing direct subsidy contracts to providers who speak languages other than English. At the same time, only 11 states reported engaging in 10 or more of the activities asked about in the 2012–2013 CCDBG plans related to children and families learning English. As Firgens and Matthews (2012) suggest, a much more detailed evaluation of state policy options and choices is needed.

CHILDREN WITH DISABILITIES OR CHRONIC HEALTH ISSUES

Over the past decade, unprecedented numbers of children have been identified as having special needs because of physical, behavioral, and neurodevelopmental disabilities or chronic health issues. Although prevalence estimates vary based on how the population is defined, rates have nearly doubled since the 1980s (Currie & Kahn, 2012). According to the 2008–09 National Health Interview Survey (NHIS), 4.6% of children aged 5 or younger and 9.5% of children aged 6–11 exhibit the criteria for disability because they are limited from engaging in developmentally appropriate activities because of a chronic medical, behavioral, emotional, or developmental issue (Halfon, Houtrow, Larson, & Newacheck, 2012). The leading causes of limitation reported in the NHIS are speech problems, learning disability, attention deficit-hyperactivity disorder, general emotional or behavioral problems, developmental delay, and asthma; this represents a shift from the 1980s, when physical health conditions were more predominant (Halfon et al., 2012).

The already complex process of making ECE "accommodations" may be even more so for parents of young children with special needs, who can face additional constraints related to the more complex caregiving needs of their children and more limited caregiving options in their community. Although mothers of children with disabilities are slightly less likely than other mothers to be employed, when they are, they tend to work slightly more hours (Ward, Morris, Oldham, Atkins, & Herrick, 2006). At the same time, many families dealing with these issues have limited resources; rates of childhood disability and compromised health are disproportionately higher in socioeconomically disadvantaged families (Halfon et al., 2012; Ward et al., 2006).

One key policy mechanism for facilitating ECE access for children with disabilities is the Individuals with Disabilities Education Act (IDEA), which maintains that all children are entitled to "a free, appropriate, public education in the least restrictive environment." Although the original legislation was enacted in 1975, its attention to and support for early childhood services began a decade later, in 1986, when Part B for school-aged children was extended to 3- to 5-year-olds and Part C was added to address the needs of infants and toddlers. Under these sections of the law, federal grants are made to states to help fund early intervention and educational services for children with developmental delays or disabilities. Indeed, the number of children with special needs being served in inclusive ECE settings has increased substantially over the last decade. Annually, more than 407,000 3- and 4-year-olds participate in public preschool programs with the support of IDEA funds (Barnett, Epstein, Friedman, Hustedt, & Sansanelli, 2008), and nearly

300,000 infants and toddlers receive services under Part C (Blackorby et al., 2010). In addition, up to 10% of the slots in Head Start and Early Head Start are reserved for children with special needs.

Beyond these Figures, however, it is unclear what proportion of children with special needs is being served adequately within these systems. National surveys have not collected consistent information about the full range of child disabilities and health limitations or how these impact families' participation in ECE (Halfon et al., 2012). Nonetheless, several pieces of evidence point to significant gaps for this population. First, according to both parents and providers, there is insufficient capacity in community-based ECE settings to serve children with significant special needs; many providers report lacking the necessary training or resources (Ohlson, 1998; Ward et al., 2006). Parents of children with behavioral problems may experience particular challenges finding and maintaining stable ECE arrangements. One survey of both parents and providers found that more than 25% of young children with a behavioral problem had been expelled from a child care program (Ward et al., 2006). Providers' reluctance to accept children with disabilities or intensive health needs may also partly reflect subsidy rates that do not cover the higher costs of specialized care (Ward et al., 2006).

The difficulties that parents of children with special needs face in accessing appropriately licensed ECE programs are cited as one reason for their greater reliance on informal care and the strategy of piecing together multiple arrangements (Rosman, Yoshikawa, & Knitzer, 2002; Ward et al., 2006). The strain of managing these arrangements may be felt more acutely by parents of children with disabilities, who report more frequent disruptions in child care and employment than do parents of children who are typically developing (Ward et al., 2006). An additional level of coordination is required of families if children are receiving intervention services, which may or may not dovetail with other ECE programs. IDEA requires that Part C services for infants and toddlers be delivered in children's "natural environments" (typically interpreted as the home) and Part B services for preschoolers in the "least restrictive environment"; in reality, delivery modes and settings vary widely across communities (Aron & Loprest, 2012). Specialists report that despite the goal of working with children in their homes and ECE settings, reimbursement rates, program rules, and logistics often make this difficult (Ward et al., 2006). Repeated calls have been made for a more integrated system of services for young children with special needs that effectively blends funding streams and ensures that policies intended to support this population are not working at cross purposes (Aron & Loprest, 2012).

Conclusion

To move closer to realizing the full potential of early childhood education, the next phase of policy making will need to attend both to issues of quality and access. As we have noted, these have often, in the past, been framed as competing goals

(Huston, 2004, 2008). Yet there are several important recent policy developments suggesting greater simultaneous focus on quality and access. These come both from the policies that have traditionally aimed primarily at fostering access and from those that have traditionally focused primarily on fostering school readiness.

From the first perspective, one important example is the new set of reporting requirements for state administrators of child care subsidies for low-income families (see http://www.acf.hhs.gov/programs/occ/ resource/program-instruction-ccdf-acf-pi-2012-02). Although the primary goal of child care subsidies is to improve access for low-income families, a percentage of the funding provided through the CCDF also goes toward improving quality. The new reporting requirements focus on specific indicators of quality and reflect a growing emphasis on the joint importance of quality and access. As an example from the second perspective, whereas many Head Start programs have operated on a part-day and part-week basis, recent analyses indicate that, by 2010, more than half of Head Start programs were operating on a full-day and full-week basis (Schmit & Ewen, 2012). Further policy innovations focus on fostering greater collaboration and coordination across the types of ECE that have their roots in funding streams oriented primarily to supporting parental employment or to supporting children's progress toward school readiness. We have already noted the system-building goals of QRIS. In addition, the 2007 reauthorization of Head Start called for the establishment of State Advisory Councils for Early Care and Education, with one stated goal being to increase collaboration among Head Start, child care, and pre-kindergarten.

The research summarized in this chapter has focused in separate sections on quality and access. We conclude with the hope that the promising policy developments just noted are harbingers of a time when there will be a strong and consistent joint focus on these. We hope that our chapter will need to be updated at some point in the near future to summarize a growing literature focusing on outcomes for children as well as parents, once policy levers are widely utilized that foster both quality and access simultaneously.

References

Adams, G., & McDaniel, M. (2009). *Fulfilling the promise of preschool for all: Insights into issues affecting access for selected immigrant groups in Chicago*. Washington, DC: The Urban Institute.

Adams, G., Tout, K., & Zaslow, M. (2007). *Early care and education for children in low-income families: Patterns of use, quality, and potential policy implications*. Washington, DC: The Urban Institute.

Aron, L., & Loprest, P. (2012). Disability and the education system. *Future of Children, 22*, 97–122.

ARRA, H. Res. 1—111th Congress: American Recovery and Reinvestment Act of 2009. (2009). In www.GovTrack.us. Retrieved from http://www.govtrack.us/congress/bills/111/hr1

Barnett, W. S., Carolan, M. E., Fitzgerald, J., & Squires, J. (2011). *The state of preschool* 2011. Rutgers, NJ: The National Institute for Early Education Research.

Barnett, W. S., Epstein, D. J., Friedman, A. H., Hustedt, J. T., & Sansanelli, R. A. (2008). *The state of preschool 2008.* New Brunswick, NJ: National Institute for Early Education Research. Retrieved from http://nieer.org/yearbook/pdf/yearbook.pdf

Blackorby, J., Schiller, E., Mallik, S., Hebbeler, K., Huang, T., Javitz, H., et al. (2010). *Patterns in the identification and outcomes for children and youth with disabilities (NCEE 2010-4005).* Washington, DC: National Center for Education Evaluation and Regional Assistance, Institute of Education Sciences, U.S. Department of Education.

Bryant, D. M., Wesley, P. W., Burchinal, M., Sideris, J., Taylor, K., Fenson, C., & Iruka, I. U. (2009). *The QUINCE-PFI study: An evaluation of a promising model for child care provider training: Final report.* Chapel Hill: University of North Carolina, FPG Child Development Institute.

Burchinal, M., Kainz, K., & Cai, Y. (2011). How well do our measures of quality predict child outcomes? A meta-analysis and coordinated analysis of data from large-scale studies of early childhood settings. In M. Zaslow, I. Martinez-Beck, K. Tout & T. Halle (Eds.), *Quality measurement in early childhood settings* (pp. 11–32). Baltimore, MA: Paul H. Brookes Publishing.

Burchinal, M., Xue, Y., Tien, H., Auger, A., & Mashburn, A. (April, 2011). Testing for threshold in the association between child care quality and child outcomes. In I. M. Martinez-Beck (Chair), *Child care dosage, thresholds, features and child outcomes: New analyses of data from national studies.* Symposium conducted at the meeting of the Society for Research in Child Development, Montreal, Canada.

Capps, R., Fix, M., Ost, J., Reardon-Anderson, J., & Passel, J. (2005). *The health and well-being of young children of immigrants.* Washington, DC: The Urban Institute.

Chaudry, A., Pedroza, J., Sandstrom, H., Danziger, A., Grosz, M., Scott, M., & Ting, S. (2011). *Child care choices of low-income working families.* Washington, DC: The Urban Institute.

Currie, J., & Kahn, R. (2012). Children with disabilities: Introducing the issue. *Future of Children, 22,* 3–12.

Early, D. M., Bryant, D. M., Pianta, R. C., Clifford, R. M., Burchinal, M. R., Ritchie, S., et al. (2006). Are teachers' education, major, and credentials related to classroom quality and children's academic gains in pre-kindergarten? *Early Childhood Research Quarterly, 21*(2), 174–195.

Early, D. M., Maxwell, K., Burchinal, M., Alva, S., Bender, R., Bryant, D., et al. (2007). Teachers' education, classroom quality, and young children's academic skills: Results from seven studies of preschool program. *Child Development, 78,* 558–580.

Emlen, A. C., & Weit, K. (1999). Quality of care for a child with a disability. In K. J. Exo, L. J. Gordon, P. Jivanjee, & K. Blankenship (Eds.), *Building on family strengths: Research and services in support of children and their families: 1997 conference proceedings* (pp. 84–87). Portland, OR: Portland State University.

Firgens, E., & Matthews, H. (2012). *State child care policies for limited English proficient families.* Washington, DC: Center for Law and Social Policy.

Garcia, E. E., & Garcia, H. E. (2012). *Understanding the language development and early education of Hispanic children.* New York: Teachers College Press.

Goerge, R., Witte, A. D., Gennetian, L. A., & Brandon, R. N. (2010). *National survey of early care and education.* Office of Planning, Research and Evaluation, Administration for Children and Families, U.S. Department of Health and Human Services.

Halfon, N., Houtrow, A., Larson, K., Newacheck, P. W. (2012). The changing landscape of disability in childhood. *Future of Children*, 22, 13–42.

Henly, J. R., & Lyons, S. (2000). The negotiation of child care and employment demands among low-income parents. *Journal of Social Issues*, 56, 683–706.

Henly, J. R., Shaefer, L., & Waxman, E. (2006). Nonstandard work schedules: Employer- and employee-driven flexibility in retail jobs. *Social Service Review*, 80, 609–634.

Hernandez, D. J., Denton, N. A., & Macartney, S. E. (2008). Children in immigrant families: Looking to America's future. *Social Policy Report*, 22(3), 3–22.

Hulsey, L. K., Aikens, N., Kopack, A., West, J., Moiduddin, E., & Tarullo, L. (2011). *Head Start children, families, and programs: Present and past data from FACES*. OPRE Report 2011-33a. Washington, DC: Office of Planning, Research and Evaluation.

Huston, A. C. (2004). Child care for low income families: Problems and promise. In A. C. Crouter & A. Booth (Eds.). *Work-family challenges for low-income parents and their children* (pp. 139–164). New York: Erlbaum

Huston, A. C. (2008). How can public policy improve quality of early care and education? *International Journal of Child Care and Education Policy*, 2(1), 1–14.

Hyson, M., Horm, D. M., & Winton, P. J. (2012). Higher education for early childhood educators and outcomes for young children. In R. C. Pianta (Ed.), *Handbook of early childhood education* (pp. 553–583). New York: Guildford Press.

Institute of Medicine and National Research Council. (2012). *The early childhood care and education workforce: Challenges and opportunities: A workshop report*. Washington, DC: National Academies Press.

Isner, T., Tout, K., Zaslow, M., Soli, M., Quinn, K., Rothenberg, L., & Burkhauser, M. (2011). *Coaching in early care and education programs and quality rating and improvement systems (QRIS): Identifying promising features*. Washington, DC: Child Trends.

Karoly, L. A., & Gonzalez, G. (2011). Early learning environments: Child care and preschool arrangements for children in immigrant families. *Future of Children*, 211, 71–101.

Kimmel, J., & Powell, L. M. (2006). Nonstandard work and child care choices of married mothers. *Eastern Economic Journal*, 32, 397–419.

Le Bihan, B., & Martin, C. (2004). Atypical working hours: Consequences for child-care arrangements. *Social Policy and Administration*, 38, 565–590.

Lowe, T., & Weisner, T. S. (2004). "You have to push it—who's gonna raise your kids?": Situating child care in the daily routines of low- income families. *Children and Youth Services Review*, 26, 143–171.

Magnuson, K., Lahaie, C., & Waldfogel, J. (2006). Preschool and school readiness of children of immigrants. *Social Science Quarterly*, 87, 1241–1262.

Magnuson, K. A., Meyers, M. K., & Waldfogel, J. (2007). Public funding and enrollment in formal child care in the 1990s. *Social Service Review*, 81(1), 47–83.

Martinez-Beck, I. (2011). Why strengthening the measurement of quality in early childhood settings has taken on new importance. In M. Zaslow, I. Martinez-Beck, K. Tout & T. Halle (Eds.), *Quality measurement in early childhood settings* (pp. xvii–xxiv). Baltimore: Paul H. Brookes Publishing.

Matthews, H., & Ewen, D. (2010). *Early education programs and children of immigrants: Learning each other's language*. Washington, DC: The Urban Institute.

Matthews, H., & Jang, D. (2007). *The challenges of change: Learning from the child care and early education experiences of immigrant families*. Washington, DC: Center for Law and Social Policy. Retrieved from: http://clasp.org/publications/challenges_change.htm

Meyers, M. K., & Jordan, L. P. (2006). Choice and accommodation in parental child care decisions. *Community Development*, 37(2), 53–70.

National Association for the Education of Young Children (2009). *Using the American recovery and reinvestment act to advance high quality professional development for early childhood educators.* Retrieved from: http://oldweb.naeyc.org/policy/arra/pdf/PDARRA.pdf

National Council for Accreditation or Teacher Education Expert Panel (2010). *The road less traveled: How the developmental sciences can prepare educators to improve student achievement.* Retrieved from: www.ncate.org

OECD. (2012). *Education at a glance 2012: Highlights.* OECD Publishing. Retrieved from: http://dx.doi.org/10.1787/eag_highlights-2012-en

Office of Head Start, Administration for Children and Families Early Childhood Learning & Knowledge Center. (2011). *Head Start program facts fiscal year 2011.* Retrieved from http://eclkc.ohs.acf.hhs.gov/hslc/mr/factsheets/docs/hs-program-fact-sheet-2011-final.pdf

Ohlson, C. (1998). Welfare reform: Implications for young children with disabilities, their families, and service providers. Journal of Early Intervention, 21, 191–206.

Perreira, K. M., Crosnoe, R., Fortuny, K., Pedroza, J., Ulvestad, C., Weiland, C., et al. (2012). *Barriers to immigrants' access to health and human services programs.* Washington, DC: The Urban Institute.

Pianta, R. C., Barnett, W. S., Burchinal, M., & Thornburg, K. R. (2009). The effects of preschool education: What we know, how public policy is or is not aligned with the evidence base, and what we need to know. *Psychological Science in the Public Interest, 10,* 49–88.

Pianta, R., Hitz, R., & West, B. (2010). *Increasing the application of developmental sciences knowledge in educator preparation: Policy issues and recommendations.* National Council for Accreditation of Teacher Education. Retrieved from:

Presser, H. B. (2003). *Working in a 24/7 economy: Challenges for American families.* New York: Russell Sage Foundation.

Rhodes, H., & Huston, A. (2012). Building the workforce our youngest children deserve. *Social Policy Report, 26* (1), 1–32.

Rosman, E. A., Yoshikawa, H., & Knitzer, J. (2002). Towards and understanding of the impact of welfare reform on children with disabilities and their families: Setting a research policy agenda. *Social Policy Reports of the Society for Research in Child Development, 16*(4), 1–16.

Schmit, S., & Ewen, D. (2012). *Putting children and families first: Head Start programs in 2010.* Brief No. 10. Washington, DC: Center for Law and Social Policy, Inc. (CLASP).

Schulman, K., & Blank, H. (2012), *Downward slide: State child care assistance policies 2012.* Washington, DC: National Women's Law Center.

Scott, E. K., London, A. S., & Hurst, A. (2005). Instability in patchworks of child care when moving from welfare to work. *Journal of Marriage and Family, 67*(2), 370–386.

Smith, S., Schneider, W., & Kreader, J. L. (2010). *Features of professional development and on-site assistance in child care quality rating improvement systems: A survey of state-wide systems.* National Center for Children in Poverty Retrieved from: http://www.nccp.org/

Tout, K., Isner, T., & Zaslow, M. (2011). *Coaching for quality improvement: Lessons learned from Quality Rating and Improvement Systems.* Washington, DC: Child Trends. http://www.childtrends.org/Files/Child_Trends-2011_04_27_FR_CoachingQuality.pdf

Tout, K., Starr, R., Soli, M., Moodie, S., Kirby, G., & Boller, K. (2010). *Compendium on quality rating systems and evaluations.* Washington, DC: U.S. Department of Health and Human Services, Administration for Children and Families, Office of Planning, Research and Evaluation.

Tout, K., & Zaslow, M. (2003). *Tiered reimbursement in Minnesota child care settings: A report of the Minnesota Child Care Policy Research Partnership.* St. Paul: Minnesota Department of Children, Families, and Learning.

Tout, K., Zaslow, M., Halle, T., & Forry, N. (2009). *Issues for the next decade of quality rating and improvement systems.* OPRE Issue Brief #3. Washington, DC: Child Trends. Retrieved from http://www.acf.hhs.gov/programs/opre/resource/issues-for-the-next-decade-of-quality-rating-and-improvement-systems

Vesely, C., Ewaida, M., & Kearney, K. (2012). *Capitalizing on early childhood education: Low-income immigrant mothers' use of ECE to build human, social, and navigational capital.* Retrieved from: http://www.researchconnections.org/childcare/resources/23761/pdf

Ward, H., Morris, L., Oldham, E., Atkins, J., & Herrick, A. (2006). *Child care and children with special needs: Challenges for low income families.* Portland, ME: Edmund S. Muskie School of Public Service.

Weber. R. (2011). *Understanding parents' child care decision-making: A foundation for policy making,* OPRE Research-to-Policy, Research-to-Practice Brief OPRE 2011-12. Washington, DC: Office of Planning, Research and Evaluation.

Yoshikawa, H., Weisner, T. S., & Lowe, E. (Eds.) (2006). *Making it work: Low-wage employment, family life, and child development.* New York: Russell Sage Foundation.

Zaslow, M., Anderson, R., Redd, Z. Wessel, J., Tarullo, L., & Burchinal, M. (2010). *Quality dosage, thresholds, and features in early childhood settings: A review of the literature,* OPRE 2011-5. Washington, DC: Office of Planning, Research and Evaluation, Administration for Children and Families, U.S. Department of Health and Human Services. Retrieved from: http://www.acf.hhs.gov/sites/default/files/opre/quality_review_0.pdf

Zaslow, M. Martinez-Beck, I., Tout, K., & Halle, T. (Eds.). (2011). *Quality measurement in early childhood settings.* Baltimore, MD: Paul H. Brookes Publishing.

Zaslow, M., Tout, K., & Halle, T. (2012). *On-site approaches to quality improvement in Quality Rating and Improvement Systems: Building on the research on coaching.* Research-to-Policy, Research-to-Practice Brief OPRE 2012-40. Washington, DC: Office of Planning, Research and Evaluation, Administration for Children and Families, U.S. Department of Health and Human Services.

Zaslow, M., Tout, K., Halle, T., & Starr, R. (2010). Professional development for early educators: Reviewing and revising conceptualizations. In S. Neuman & D. Dickinson (Eds.), *Handbook of early literacy research, vol. 3* (pp. 425–434) New York: Guilford Publications.

Zaslow, M., Tout, K., Halle, T., Whittaker, J. V., & Lavelle, B. (2010). *Towards the identification of features of effective professional development for early childhood educators.* Prepared for Policy and Program Studies Service, Office of Planning, Evaluation and Policy Development, U.S. Department of Education.

Cultural Contexts and Immigrant Families

5

An Ecological Approach to Understanding Immigrant Child and Adolescent Developmental Competencies

Amy K. Marks, Camila Godoy, and Cynthia García Coll

Immigrant youth are the fastest growing population of children in the United States. Currently, 16 million children have at least one immigrant parent, comprising 23% of the population. A full quarter of the U.S. population under the age of 10 is either a first- (foreign-born) or second- (U.S.-born to foreign-born parents) generation immigrant (Hernandez, Denton, & Macartney, 2008). By 2030, this youth population will likely grow to about 35%, the majority of whom are Hispanic or Asian, with many recent refugees from Eastern Europe and Africa as well. Most of these children are U.S. citizens, of which nearly 5 million have at least one undocumented parent. Strikingly, today, approximately 1.7 million children themselves are undocumented yet have lived in this country for most of their lives and do not know another country of origin (C. Suarez-Orozco, 2010). The United States is experiencing unprecedented diversity among its immigrant youth by migration type (e.g., migratory, transnational, multiple resettlements), documentation status (e.g., citizen, undocumented, refugee), ethnicity, and language. The field of developmental psychology is consequently growing in its awareness of the many unique contextual considerations regarding the healthy development of immigrant youth.

This chapter reviews several key aspects of immigrant youth development within an ecological framework. In contrast to risk/deficit models of minority development, we draw from perspectives emphasizing resiliency and highlight research on developmental competencies among immigrant youth (García Coll et al., 1996). Although growing rapidly in numbers, immigrant youth continue to be an understudied and underserved child population in the United States. With an absence of political representation, unclear legal statuses or gateways to citizenship, and lacking access to social, educational, and medical services, many immigrant families and children face unique challenges to a healthy everyday life in the United States (C. Suarez-Orozco, 2010). These challenges include racism and discrimination, which can negatively impact the development of any child (and, in particular, children of color in the United States) regardless of their culture of origin or family socioeconomic status (García Coll et al., 1996). Nevertheless, many immigrant children and adolescents thrive developmentally in spite of these social and economic barriers, and researchers are documenting these noteworthy pathways of success. In particular, there is increasing discussion around the "immigrant paradox," a phenomenon in which the most recently immigrated youth (who are also most likely to reside in poverty, have parents with low-wage work, and experience barriers to social services) exhibit superior educational and behavioral outcomes when compared to more highly acculturated same-ethnicity peers (García Coll & Marks, 2011). Given these recent trends emphasizing the developmental promise of immigrant youth, this chapter reviews recent research on several developmental *competencies* particularly salient for immigrant children. These include the developmental tasks of becoming bicultural in social and family relationships, developing healthy multiethnic identities, and building cognitive and social skills that yield facility in multiple languages (i.e., bilingualism). We contend that developing these competencies is of singular importance for supporting the overall healthy growth and development of youth in immigrant families, and supporting them should be a focus of research and intervention efforts moving forward.

To situate these developmental competencies in context, ecological perspectives explicating child-environment interactions within social settings also frame this review (Bronfenbrenner & Morris, 2006). We focus on research capturing *microsystems,* the everyday social settings including home, school, peer, and neighborhoods, that shape the above-mentioned developmental competencies (see Chapter 9 by Gershoff & Benner). We focus on microsystems primarily because a relatively large proportion of context-related immigrant youth development research resides at the microsystem level (compared to direct measurement and consideration of macrosystem or exosystem research). We also attend to research of the *mesosystem* when possible, capturing transactions involving immigrant youth across multiple microsystem settings. Strong alliances across social settings allow immigrant children to access and coordinate their varied sources of developmental support and promote their own and their family's well-being (García Coll & Marks, 2009). Parent-school involvement interactions, for example, are commonly studied mesosystem processes that are known to widely support children's and adolescents' academic successes (Cheung & Sin-Sze, 2012). By emphasizing interactions among social settings, in this chapter we hope to highlight opportunities for public policies and interventions that might support developmental competencies among immigrant children and their families (see Chapter 6 by Nieto & Yoshikawa). By situating our review of the bicultural, ethnic identity, and bilingual developmental competencies so vital to the health and development of immigrant youth in these ecological settings, we hope to stimulate ideas for future research that may expand our appreciation for and understanding of immigrant youth-context interactions.

Becoming Bicultural Across Immigrant Youth's Everyday Settings

Immigrant children in the United States are tasked not only with learning to read, write, and build healthy self-care skills and relationships, they also must grow and develop while acculturating. Psychological acculturation has been conceptualized in varying ways but is most typically considered a slowly occurring process of cultural exchange occurring on immersion in a new country or culture (Berry, 1997). This exchange involves the active and passive adoption of new cultural skills (e.g., languages), customs, values, beliefs, and identities, the characteristics of which are highly context dependent. Importantly, the age at which an individual arrives in the United States influences how quickly he or she is likely to acculturate; the types of ethnic self-labels adopted, the behavioral and academic child outcomes, and the parenting practices within families are all influenced by an individual's age at entry to the United States (Portes & Rumbaut, 2001). Individuals who arrive during early or middle childhood are more likely to adopt behaviors, language preferences, and ethnic labels that are more congruent with the native U.S. population. In contrast, immigrants who arrive during adolescence or adulthood are more likely to retain preferences and behaviors from their native countries. In particular, for first- and second-generation immigrant youth, acculturation to school and peer groups outside their families' ethnic enclaves will likely be faster and qualitatively different from their parents' experiences living in the United States (C. Suarez-Orozco & Suarez-Orozco, 2001).

At the heart of these acculturation complexities is the notion of being bicultural. Scholars have described immigrant biculturalism as maintaining a balance between the old (i.e., the parent or child's culture of origin) and new (i.e., the U.S.) ways of life (Berry, Phinney, Sam, & Vedder, 2006). Generally speaking, biculturalism is the effective social integration of an immigrant child into U.S. contexts (including schools) while maintaining and developing the cultural skills to be well-integrated within the home context as well (Coatsworth, Maldonado-Molina, Pantin, & Szapocznik, 2005). Biculturalism is a particularly salient area of developmental competency for immigrant youth who can claim membership in multiple ethnic groups either through residency (i.e., as first-generation immigrants themselves, living in multiple countries) or family heritage (i.e., as second-generation youth practicing their parents' culture of origin while being born in the United States; see Padilla, 2006). From an ecological perspective, biculturalism may be understood as a quintessential mesosystem-level developmental competency. Most immigrant children must learn to speak to and interpersonally connect with English-speaking teachers and build bonds and friendships with U.S.-born peers, all while further developing and maintaining family values, languages, and customs in daily life (García Coll & Marks, 2009). Such coordination of social transactions across multiple settings (i.e., school, community, and home) exemplifies a mesosystem approach to conceptualizing biculturalism. Importantly, the general benefits of biculturalism for immigrant youth have been shown for a variety of developmental outcomes, including greater academic competencies, greater social-emotional health, and fewer problem behaviors when compared to more assimilated peers (i.e., peers who have highly adopted U.S. culture without maintaining or building home cultural practices; Cassels, Chan, Chung, & Birch, 2010; Coatsworth et al., 2005).

Becoming and being bicultural across multiple social contexts, however, can be a challenging process. Within the family microsystem, parents and children alike learn their new host language(s), practice new social customs, and adopt new values (Portes & Rumbaut, 2001). And yet the ways and paces with which parents and their children acculturate often vary widely from one another. For example, parents are much less likely to spend time in the U.S. education system than are their children. Parents and their children are exposed to different peer groups, attend different community activities, and prefer to engage in different leisure activities, with children engaging in more "American" activities and parents maintaining ethnic traditions (C. Suarez-Orozco & Suarez-Orozco, 2001). Within-family acculturation asynchronies can present challenges and may increase inter-personal conflict in parent-child dyadic relationships (Marks, Patton, & Coyne, 2011), as well as increase risk for adolescent substance misuse (Unger, Ritt-Olson, Soto, & Baezconde-Garbanati, 2009).

Conversely, many youth and families can and do practice successful bicultural-ism across children's everyday social settings, with positive impacts on immigrant youth development. In a study of Chinese immigrant families, for example, bicul-tural synchrony between parents and adolescents was linked with fewer adoles-cent depressive symptoms when compared to parent-adolescent dyads exhibiting differing acculturation styles (Weaver & Kim, 2008). Importantly, parents and families utilize a variety of approaches to promote biculturalism among their chil-dren and adolescents. One line of contemporary research attempts to explain how immigrant parents actively build their children's bicultural competencies through cultural socialization or the "practices that teach children about their racial or ethnic heritage and history; that promote cultural customs and traditions; and that promote children's cultural, racial, and ethnic pride either deliberately or implic-itly" (Hughes et al., 2006, p. 749). Cultural socialization within families includes parents' intentional and unintentional exposure of their children to customs, their use of native language, and their education of their children about the family's country of origin. For instance, many immigrant families continue to practice their previously upheld cultural traditions and to maintain their original cultural values, including those emphasizing family obligations and filial respect. Such traditional values can offer children a strong basis for academic motivation and healthy psychological adjustment in school (Fuligni, Alvarez, Bachman, & Ruble, 2005). Many voluntary migrant families also remain strongly connected through travel and filial relationships to their country of origin, thus providing children with enriching cross-cultural social experiences that enhance social skills in peer and friendship contexts (García Coll & Marks, 2009).

In addition to parents' culture-of-origin socialization practices at home, immigrant parents directly and indirectly support their children's integration into U.S. social settings in a variety of ways. One recent qualitative study of Taiwanese-American mothers documented the practice of purposefully enrolling young children in English-speaking child care settings in order to build and promote bicultural and bilingual competencies. Parents were confident that enrollment in English-speaking early education environments would, alongside their efforts to engage their children in Taiwanese cultural experiences at home and in the community, promote their children's bicultural competencies and social skills (Uttal & Han, 2011). Active parent involvement in their children's English-based school-related activities with the goal of promoting biculturalism also has been documented in Chinese-American families (Lu, 2001). Moreover, parents' own bicultural orientation has been linked with more adaptive child behavioral and social outcomes in preschool (Calzada, Brotman, Huang, Bat-Chava, & Kingston, 2009). At the level of the school context, educational programming supporting bilingualism also provides support for bicultural identities and skills. Curricula embracing narratives and poetry, as well as mathematical instruction, in both English and native languages have been shown to both improve children's literacy and quantitative skills and promote bicultural social skills and identities (Kenner, Gregory, Ruby, & Al-Azami, 2008).

Although there appear to be numerous associations among child developmental competencies and parent and child biculturalism across family and school contexts, little research has attended to bicultural processes at the mesosystem level. In other words, future studies aimed at understanding *how* the coordination of home-school bicultural practices promotes developmental competencies in immigrant youth is warranted. Greater attention should also be paid to the ways in which diversity in socioeconomic status (e.g., parent education) and migration history (e.g., voluntary vs. refugee) impact immigrant youth's mesosystems. Such research might employ mixed-methods and longitudinal designs to better examine the mesosystem-level transactions (e.g., parent-child cultural socialization as it relates to parent-teacher communications) that support biculturalism in immigrant youth and how these transactions subsequently shape developmental outcomes. Also relatively absent from the extant research has been attention to bicultural competencies within the contexts of peer and friendship networks. Scholars have recently argued for the use of egocentric measurement of friendship and peer networks that may situate child and adolescent acculturation processes within broader social ecological contexts beyond the individual level (Tseng & Yoshikawa, 2008). As these authors noted, acculturation research, including research on biculturalism, typically theorizes about acculturation as a highly context-dependent psychological process but most commonly measures acculturation solely at the level of the individual. Future studies of biculturalism should take into account not only the broad-level cultural values and practices at the individual level that typically are used to measure biculturalism but also should explore and measure these values and practices alongside the acculturation-related character-istics of the micro- and mesosystem contexts they are enacted in.

Developing Healthy Ethnic Identities in Youth's Everyday Settings

A primary and critical psychological component of development among immi-grant youth is the establishment and maintenance of healthy ethnic identities. Although some early perspectives in acculturation research used the concepts of acculturation and ethnic identity interchangeably or to define one another (i.e., achieving an "American identity" meant being highly acculturated or assimilated, whereas having a strong ethnic identity was an indication of low levels of accul-turation), the psychological processes of acculturation and ethnic identification are quite distinct. Beginning in early childhood and extending actively through adolescence and adulthood, ethnic identities are formed as part of the indi-vidual's sense of self with respect to ethnic, racial, and cultural groups to which he or she may belong. This sense of self may include feelings of pride in his or her family's country-of-origin culture and the U.S. culture, as well as awareness of personal and social challenges stemming from group membership with mar-ginalized or stigmatized groups. Ethnic identity development plays an important role in supporting overall personal identity development in early adulthood and in supporting healthy psychosocial functioning overall (Schwartz, Zamboanga, Weisskirch, & Wang, 2010). Furthermore, among ethnic minority group mem-bers, having a strong, positive ethnic identity is related to more positive academic outcomes, fewer behavioral and mental health issues, and protection from risky behaviors such as substance use, drug use, and smoking (e.g., Phinney, Horenczyk, Liebkind, & Vedder, 2001; Schwartz, Zamboanga, Ham et al., 2010). Researchers are just beginning to tease apart the mechanisms linking ethnic identity with posi-tive immigrant youth development, with some studies supporting ethnic iden-tity's role as a largely indirect path through self-esteem (Schwartz, Zamboanga, & Jarvis, 2007). Studies are needed to further these lines of research, attending to these ethnic identity-self esteem-adjustment mechanisms early in the lifespan and examining how characteristics of ecological settings relate to and support these mechanisms.

Starting in early childhood, it appears that immigrant children with strong ethnic identities also exhibit more positive peer social preferences, an important microsystem-level developmental competency. For example, in a study of second-generation immigrant children of Dominican or Cambodian heritage, children who endorsed higher levels of ethnic pride in their family's culture of origin also were more likely to report wanting to play with children from both their own and other ethnic backgrounds as well (Marks, Szalacha, Lamarre, Boyd, & García Coll, 2007). Other research, however, has shown that, as children age, greater levels of ethnic identity can correlate with *both* positive and negative social biases regarding ethnic outgroup members (Pfeifer et al., 2007). Taken together, these complexities may reflect that the development of early ethnic identities in childhood plays an important role in developing immigrant children's overall awareness, exploration, and understanding of interethnic group social differences. In adolescence, research suggests that Asian-American adolescents with predominantly same-ethnic and mixed-ethnic friendships have higher levels of ethnic identity exploration than do adolescents with predominantly other-ethnic friendships (Kiang, Peterson, & Thompson, 2011). Importantly, immigrant adolescents with greater levels of ethnic identity were also more likely to report higher perceived discrimination than were adolescents with lower levels of ethnic identity.

It may be that these relationships between self-esteem-building ethnic identification processes and awareness of interethnic group biases may be adaptive for immigrant children who will need to navigate community stereotypes and prejudice as ethnic/racial minorities or immigrants as they age. For example, in adolescence and adulthood, positive ethnic identities can mediate the negative impacts of ethnic and racial discrimination (Lee, 2005). Research has documented that immigrant youth with healthy ethnic identities often cope with and adapt better to "negative social mirroring," an interpersonal process by which children and adolescents receive negative messages about immigrants or ethnic groups, and suffer problems of self-worth and identity because of these messages (M. Suarez-Orozco & Suarez-Orozco, 2000). Such negative social-contextual cues and messages, which can emanate from many settings at macro- and microsystem ecological levels, have been documented by children and adolescents in schools and their communities, for example:

"Most Americans think that we are lazy, gangsters, drug addicts that only come to take their jobs away." (14-year-old Mexican boy)
"Most Americans think that we are bad like all Latinos." (12-year-old Central American boy)
"Most Americans think that we don't exist." (12-year-old Mexican boy) (M. Suarez-Orozco & Suarez-Orozco, 2000, p. 27)

Although maintaining positive ethnic identities appears protective against potential detriments to self-worth caused by these negative interpersonal interactions and cues, we still know little about how immigrant children or adolescents navigate negative peer, friendship, school, and community discrimination messages and how the adaptations children and adolescents make to these cues vary across settings. Do some contexts' messages make more potent impacts on children's ethnic identities and feelings of self-worth than others? Can the benefits of positive ethnic identity development in one ecological domain (e.g., home) fully or partially mediate the negative impacts of discrimination received in other contexts? How do mesosystem transactions across contexts impact immigrant children's early ethnic identity development? Research is needed that specifically addresses the characteristics of and interactions among social settings as they relate to the efficacy of positive ethnic identities that serve self-protective functions against discrimination in immigrant youth development.

As is the case with building bicultural skills, parents and the home context play critical roles in facilitating the development of healthy ethnic identities across childhood and adolescence. Bicultural parenting beliefs and practices that reflect both culture of origin *and* traditional U.S. authoritative styles appear to be particularly supportive of healthy adolescent ethnic identity development (Farver, Xu, Bakhtawar, Narang, & Lieber, 2007). Furthermore, research with second-generation youth suggests that fathers' (but not mothers') support of their adolescents' autonomous ethnic identity exploration yields overall positive adolescent ethnic identities, biculturalism, and well-being (Abad & Sheldon, 2008). Parent education level—both a family setting and larger socioeconomic level factor—appears to be related to ethnic identity development in immigrant children as well. In a large, longitudinal study of recent immigrant children and adolescents of Haitian, Mexican, and Chinese origin, higher levels of parent education were associated with children retaining their culture-of-origin identities over time (Song, 2010). The mechanisms behind these socioeconomic-ethnic identity linkages are currently unclear. It may be that the strategies immigrant parents use or have available to them for culturally socializing their children in the United States vary by socioeconomic status (SES). For example, early childhood research with immigrants has revealed important nuances and moderating effects among indicators of SES and immigrant generation such that maternal education may have particularly strong impacts on parent language practices among immigrant families when compared to native families (Mistry, Biesanz, Chien, Howes, & Benner, 2008). Future research in this area is warranted, given the central importance of parents' roles in supporting and maintaining their children's healthy ethnic identities and the critical contributions that socioeconomic factors can make to child and adolescent functioning.

Although numerous studies demonstrate the critical roles that school and classroom characteristics have on immigrant youth academic engagement and achievement outcomes (e.g., Crosnoe, 2005), comparatively less research has focused on examining specifically how school context characteristics shape ethnic identities. In one recent classroom-level study from the Netherlands, 40 hours of seventh- and eighth-grade classroom lesson recordings revealed that the "discursive patterns" characterizing majority-minority ethnic group members' verbal interactions had direct impacts on children's academic and ethnic identities (Haan, Keizer, & Elbers, 2010). These discursive patterns revealed that ethnic majority children often assumed roles of leadership and authority within classroom lessons, with ethnic minority children taking more passive roles in lesson activities. Such power dynamics were observed primarily in academic-related discourse; in more casual, nonacademic discourse, opposite examples of power dynamics were observed, with ethnic minority children asserting knowledge dominance over ethnic majority children, particularly in support of their own cultural practices and ethnic identities. The power of discourse has been noted elsewhere in quantitative research with mixed ethnic and mixed immigrant/nonimmigrant adolescents, with ethnic discrimination from both adults and peers in school being associated with more negative perceptions of one's own ethnic group (Rivas-Drake, Hughes, & Way, 2009). From these studies, it appears that school- and classroom-based microsystem power dynamics and discriminatory messages play key roles in immigrant children's and adolescents' ethnic group affiliations and evaluations. Future studies are needed to focus specifically on how these school and classroom-based socialization characteristics relate to ethnic identity development over time among immigrant youth.

Being Bilingual Across Immigrant Youths' Everyday Settings

As we have detailed so far, creating a sense of biculturalism and building healthy ethnic identities are developmental processes of central importance for immigrant youth. They also inform and support one another. Generally speaking, as children and adolescents build healthy bicultural skills, their ethnic identity exploration increases and develops. Furthermore, as reviewed earlier, various aspects of social settings that promote biculturalism also support immigrant youth in their ethnic identity development. There exists yet another developmental competency that connects with and informs these two psychological processes as well: bilingualism. For the vast majority of U.S. immigrant children, acquiring English-language proficiency and maintaining or learning the language of their family's culture of origin are also primary developmental tasks. Most immigrant families maintain their primary country-of-origin language(s), providing children with multilingual social and cognitive benefits when compared to monolingual children (e.g., Schwartz, Share, Leikin, & Kozminsky, 2008). Furthermore, becoming bilingual-proficient involves developing high-order cognitive skills, such as "frame switching" or moving between two sets of cultural interpretative frames, including the different languages, customs, and values of each, in response to social and environmental cues (Benet-Martinez, Leu, Lee, & Morris, 2002). Bilingualism has been linked to many positive developmental outcomes, including gains in early childhood mathematical skills (Kempert, Saalbach, & Hardy, 2011), greater family cohesion, and higher GPAs, for boys in particular (Lutz & Crist, 2009). Further, "language brokering," a bilingual practice by which children translate for their parents in everyday social settings, has been linked with promoting positive psychosocial adjustment and ethnic identity development into early adulthood (Weisskirch et al., 2011).

Yet, as with developing bicultural skills, becoming bilingual can be a challenging process. In a recent school-setting micro-ethnographic study of three second-grade Hispanic English Language Learners (ELLs) classrooms, teachers' emphases on promoting English proficiency came at the cost of overlooking important aspects of immigrant children's other burgeoning academic and social skills (Iddings & Katz, 2007). Importantly, the focus on ELLs appeared to prevent teachers from fully appreciating the children's characteristic strengths, cultural identities, and home cultural practices. The authors noted the importance of creating space in the classroom for children's cultural activities—in essence, supporting biculturalism—as a key component to promoting the early academic success of young ELLs. In adolescence, learning English can have both positive and negative effects on peer and friendship microsystems. On the one hand, ELLs benefit socially by increasing their positive associations with larger and multiethnic peer networks; however, on the other hand, being labeled a second-language learner can yield distress due to stereotype threats within the peer network (Tsai, 2006).

Among second-generation immigrant youth, learning the heritage or culture-of-origin language (as opposed to English) most frequently becomes the task for establishing bilingualism. Whereas ELL status has demonstrated benefits for first-generation youth, heritage language learning (HLL) status has benefits for second-generation youth. A recent study of Hispanic and Asian second-generation immigrant adolescents demonstrated that proficiency in the home language coincided with more positive parent-adolescent relationships and ethnic identities (Oh & Fuligni, 2008). In another mixed-ethnicity sample of second-generation adolescents, Phinney and colleagues found support for a theorized model wherein parent cultural maintenance predicts adolescents' home-language learning and subsequently supports adolescent ethnic identity development (Phinney, Romero, Nava, & Huang, 2001). Furthermore, in an analysis of a nationally representative sample of Asian and Latino adolescents in the Adolescent Health Study, increased use of home languages among second-generation youth served a protective function against developing a number of delinquency-related behaviors (Marks, Guarini, Patton, & García Coll, in preparation).

Discussion and Future Directions

These three developmental competencies—being bicultural, being bilingual, and developing healthy ethnic identities—are particularly influenced by social settings but often are measured at the level of the individual without direct consideration of the micro- or mesosystem influences that shape them. As seen in the research examples given in this chapter, many (although certainly not all) studies that directly incorporate ecological settings into studies of these immigrant youth developmental competencies are qualitative or preliminary in nature. Moreover, it is still common that studies focusing on "immigrant youth" do not always make clear theoretical or analytical distinctions between the immigrant generations being studied (i.e., first vs. second) or attend to the variability in cultural practices among ethnic groups that make up larger pan-ethnic study populations (i.e., Asian, Hispanic). Taking a carefully measured ecological approach to understanding the developmental competencies of immigrant youth is of central importance in moving the field forward, not only for teasing apart important contextual mechanisms that support healthy identity development and personal adjustment, but for designing and implementing effective interventions (see Nieto & Yoshikawa, Chapter 6).

We focused our review primarily on studies undertaken in the past decade, and we note that the majority of studies that attempt to capture a contextual view of biculturalism, bilingualism, or ethnic identity development focus on the family context. This has been noted in a recent review of the literature on contexts and ethnic group differences in child and adolescent development (Chao & Otsuki-Clutter, 2011). Studies have also examined the roles of teachers, peers, and schools, particularly as they relate to biculturalism and bilingualism. Notably absent from the literature have been studies that link other ecological characteristics (e.g., the exosystem, or relationships between adults in children's lives that may impact their well-being; the macrosystem, including public policies) to these immigrant youth developmental competencies. Nevertheless, at the level of the community context, many examples of macro- and microsystems forces can be conceptualized as influencing ethnic identity development, as well as biculturalism and bilingualism. Families' perceptions of neighborhood safety, police-community relations, and bilingual community service availability are all examples of community characteristics that may promote positive or negative influences on immigrant families' ethnic identities. Instances of discrimination within communities, neighborhood safety and interethnic group relations also are important to shaping immigrants' acculturation experiences. Few studies have attempted to identify the specific characteristics of community setting mechanisms that directly or indirectly shape immigrant youths' ethnic identities or bicultural/bilingual practices. Instead, communities are used to characterize the receiving context of immigrants and interpret research findings therein. The presence or absence of social mobility ladders, for example, has been theorized as important in shaping the overall adaptation of immigrants in a given community, who may have few (downward assimilation) or plentiful (upward assimilation) education and labor opportunities (Portes & Zhou, 1993). Although this type of framework provides a compelling approach to understanding community-level influences on immigrant youth adjustment, studies that specifically measure and link the qualities and quantities of the presence or absence of mobility ladders are rare (we have not noted any in recent peer-reviewed publications). A new wave of research directly examining community characteristics and their influences on immigrant youth developmental competencies is needed. For instance, a recent qualitative study of Vietnamese immigrant adolescents revealed the nuanced ways in which residing in an ethnic versus a nonethnic enclave can shape ethnic identity development, including the social and cultural influences enacting on ethnic identities, as well as adolescents' emotional responses to ethnic identity exploration (Vo-Jutabha, Dinh, McHale, & Valsiner, 2009). Using purposive sampling techniques at the community level and employing direct observations and measurements of community-level characteristics may enable researchers to test theoretical notions of communities that are thought to support immigrant youth development.

In sum, the qualities of experiences and outcomes immigrant children have in building healthy ethnic identities and becoming bilingual and bicultural are highly influenced by the contexts of their development (e.g., Phelan, Davidson, & Yu, 1998). Children may experience significant facilitation building these developmental skills in some contexts, but experience significant barriers in other contexts. Children also co-construct their cultural developmental competencies within family, school, and neighborhood contexts, shaping, in turn, the characteristics of the families, schools, and neighborhoods they reside in. Just as with any child (immigrant or not), these settings impact a variety of other health and developmental outcomes as well. How do immigrant children build these culture-related developmental competencies within family, school, and neighborhood contexts? How do the qualities of these contexts broadly impact immigrant youth health and development? We look forward to new horizons of research that bring ecological settings and creative approaches to their measurement to the forefront of developmental competency research with immigrant youth.

References

Abad, N. S., & Sheldon, K. M. (2008). Parental autonomy support and ethnic culture identification among second-generation immigrants. *Journal of Family Psychology*, 22(3), 652–657.

Benet-Martinez, V., Leu, J., Lee, F., & Morris, M. W. (2002). Negotiating biculturalism: Cultural frame switching in biculturals with oppositional versus compatible cultural identities. *Journal of Cross-Cultural Psychology*, 33(5), 492–516.

Berry, J. W. (1997). Immigration, acculturation, and adaptation. *Applied Psychology: An International Review*, 46, 5–68.

Berry, J. W., Phinney, J. S., Sam, D. L., & Vedder, P. (2006). Immigrant youth: Acculturation, identity and adaptation. *Applied Psychology: An International Review*, 55(3), 303–332.

Bronfenbrenner, U., & Morris, P. A. (2006). The bioecological model of human development. In R. M. Lerner & W. Damon (Eds.), *Handbook of child psychology* (6 ed., vol. 1, pp. 793–828). Hoboken, NJ: Wiley.

Calzada, E. J., Brotman, L. M., Huang, K., Bat-Chava, Y., & Kingston, S. (2009). Parent cultural adaptation and child functioning in culturally diverse, urban families of preschoolers. *Journal of Applied Developmental Psychology*, 30(4), 515–524.

Cassels, T. G., Chan, S., Chung, W., & Birch, S. A. J. (2010). The role of culture in affective empathy: Cultural and bicultural differences. *Journal of Cognition and Culture*, 10, 309–326.

Chao, R. K., & Otsuki-Clutter, M. (2011). Racial and ethnic differences: Sociocultural and contextual explanations. *Journal of Research on Adolescence*, 21(1), 47–60.

Cheung, C., & Sin-Sze, E. M. (2012). Why does parents' involvement enhance children's achievement? The role of parent-oriented motivation. *Journal of Educational Psychology, 104*(3), 820–832.

Coatsworth, J. D., Maldonado-Molina, M., Pantin, H., & Szapocznik, J. (2005). A person-centered and ecological investigation of acculturation strategies of Hispanic immigrant youth. *Journal of Community Psychology, 33*(2), 157–174.

Crosnoe, R. (2005). Double disadvantage or signs of resilience? The elementary school contexts of children from Mexican immigrant families. *American Educational Research Journal, 42*(2), 269–303.

Farver, J. M., Xu, Y., Bakhtawar, R. B., Narang, S. K., & Lieber, E. (2007). Ethnic identity, acculturation, parenting beliefs, and adolescent adjustment. *Merrill-Palmer Quarterly, 53*(2), 184–215.

Fuligni, A. J., Alvarez, J., Bachman, M., & Ruble, D. N. (2005). Family obligation and the academic motivation of young children from immigrant families. In C. Cooper (Ed.), *Developmental pathways through middle childhood: Rethinking contexts and diversity as resources* (pp. 261–282). Mahwah, NJ: Lawrence Erlbaum Associates.

García Coll, C., Lamberty, G., Jenkins, R., McAdoo, H. P., Crnic, K., Wasik, B. H., & García, H. V. (1996). An integrative model for the study of developmental competencies in minority children. *Child Development, 67*, 1891–1914.

García Coll, C., & Marks, A. K. (2009). *Immigrant stories: Ethnicity and academics in middle childhood.* New York: Oxford University Press.

García Coll, C., & Marks, A. K. (2011). *The immigrant paradox in children and adolescents: Is becoming American a developmental risk?* Washington, DC: American Psychological Association.

Haan, M., Keizer, R., & Elbers, E. (2010). Ethnicity and student identity in schools: An analysis of official and unofficial talk in multiethnic classrooms. *European Journal of Psychology of Education, 25*, 176–191.

Hernandez, D., Denton, N. A., & Macartney, S. E. (2008). Children in immigrant families: Looking to America's future. *Social Policy Report, 22*(3), 3–22.

Hughes, D., Rodriguez, J., Smith, E. P., Johnson, D. J., Stevenson, H. C., & Spicer, P. (2006). Parents' ethnic-racial socialization practices: A review of research and directions for future study. *Developmental Psychology, 42*(5), 747–770.

Iddings, A. C., & Katz, L. (2007). Integrating home and school identities of recent-immigrant Hispanic English language learners through classroom practices. *Journal of Language, Identity, and Education, 6*(4), 299–314.

Kempert, S., Saalbach, H., & Hardy, I. (2011). Cognitive benefits and costs of bilingualism in elementary school students: The case of mathematical word problems. *Journal of Educational Psychology, 103*(3), 547–561.

Kenner, C., Gregory, E., Ruby, M., & Al-Azami, S. (2008). Bilingual learning for second and third generation children. *Language, Culture and Curriculum, 21*(2), 120–137.

Kiang, L., Peterson, J. L., & Thompson, T. L. (2011). Ethnic peer preferences among Asian American adolescents in emerging immigrant communities. *Journal of Research on Adolescence, 21*(4), 754–761.

Lee, R. M. (2005). Resilience against discrimination: Ethnic identity and other-group orientation as protective factors for Korean Americans. *Journal of Counseling Psychology, 52*, 36–44.

Lu, X. (2001). Bicultural identity development and Chinese community formation: An ethnographic study of Chinese schools in Chicago. *The Howard Journal of Communications,*
   12, 203–220.
Lutz, A., & Crist, S. (2009). Why do bilingual boys get better grades in English-only
   America: The impacts of gender, language and family interaction on academic achievement of Latino/a children of immigrants. *Ethnic and Racial Studies, 32*(2), 346–368.
Marks, A. K., Guarini, T. E., Patton, F., & García Coll, C. (In preparation). *Bilingualism as*
   a mediator of the immigrant paradox in adolescent risky behaviors.
Marks, A. K., Patton, F., & Coyne, L. C. (2011). Acculturation-related conflict across
   generations in immigrant families. In R. Moreno & S. S. Chuang (Eds.), *Immigrant*
   Children: Change, adaptation and cultural transformation (pp. 255–270). Lexington,
   MA: Rowman & Littlefield Publishers.
Marks, A. K., Szalacha, L. S., Lamarre, M., Boyd, M. J., & García Coll, C. (2007). Emerging
   ethnic identity and interethnic group social preferences in middle childhood: Findings
   from the Children of Immigrants Development in Context (CIDC) study. *International*
   Journal of Behavioral Development, 31(5), 501–513.
Mistry, R. S., Biesanz, J. C., Chien, N., Howes, C., & Benner, A. D. (2008). Socioeconomic status,
   parental investments, and the cognitive and behavioral outcomes of low-income children
   from immigrant and native households. *Early Childhood Research Quarterly, 23,* 193–212.
Oh, J. S., & Fuligni, A. (2008). The role of heritage language development in the ethnic
   identity and family relationships of adolescents from immigrant backgrounds. *Social*
   Development, 19(1), 202–220.
Padilla, A. M. (2006). Bicultural social development. *Hispanic Journal of Behavioral*
   Sciences, 28(4), 467–497.
Pfeifer, J. H., Ruble, D. N., Bachman, M. A., Alvarez, J. M., Cameron, J. A., & Fuligni, A. J.
   (2007). Social identities and intergroup bias in immigrant and non-immigrant chil-
   dren. *Developmental Psychology, 43*(2), 496–507.
Phelan, P., Davidson, A. L., & Yu, H. C. (1998). *Adolescents' Worlds: Negotiating Family,*
   Peers, and School. New York: Teachers College Press.
Phinney, J. S., Horenczyk, G., Liebkind, K., & Vedder, P. (2001). Ethnic identity, immigra-
   tion, and well-being: An interactional perspective. *Journal of Social Issues, 57*(3), 493–510.
Phinney, J. S., Romero, I., Nava, M., & Huang, D. (2001). The role of language, parents, and
   peers in ethnic identity among adolescents in immigrant families. *Journal of Youth and*
   Adolescence, 30(2), 135–153.
Portes, A., & Rumbaut, R. G. (2001). *Legacies: The story of immigrant second generation.*
   Berkeley: University of California Press.
Portes, A., & Zhou, M. (1993). The new second generation: Segmented assimilation and its
   variants. *Annals of the American Academy of Political and Social Sciences, 530,* 74–96.
Rivas-Drake, D., Hughes, D., & Way, N. (2009). A preliminary analysis of associations
   among ethnic-racial socialization, ethnic discrimination, and ethnic identity among
   urban sixth graders. *Journal of Research on Adolescence, 19*(3), 558–584.
Schwartz, M., Share, D. L., Leikin, M., & Kozminsky, E. (2008). On the benefits of bi-
   literacy: Just a head start in reading or specific orthographic insights? *Reading and*
   Writing, 21(9), 905–927.
Schwartz, S. J., Zamboanga, B. L., Ham, L. S., Park, I. J., Kim, S. Y., Weisskirch, R. S.,
   et al. (2010). Dimensions of acculturation: Associations with health risk behaviors

among college students from immigrant families. *Journal of Counseling Psychology,* 58(1), 27–41.

Schwartz, S. J., Zamboanga, B. L., & Jarvis, L. H. (2007). Ethnic identity and acculturation in Hispanic early adolescents: Mediated relationships to academic grades, prosocial behaviors, and externalizing symptoms. *Cultural Diversity and Ethnic Minority Psychology,* 13(4), 364–373.

Schwartz, S. J., Zamboanga, B. L., Weisskirch, R. S., & Wang, S. C. (2010). The relationships of personal and cultural identity to adaptive and maladaptive psychosocial functioning in emerging adults. *The Journal of Social Psychology,* 150(1), 1–33.

Song, S. (2010). Finding one's place: Shifting ethnic identities of recent immigrant children from China, Haiti and Mexico in the United States. *Ethnic and Racial Studies,* 33(6), 1006–1031.

Suarez-Orozco, C. (2010). In the best interest of our children: Examining our immigration enforcement policy. *Ad-hoc hearing of the United States House of Representatives, July 15.* American Psychological Association.

Suarez-Orozco, C., & Suarez-Orozco, M. M. (2001). *Children of immigration.* Cambridge, MA: Harvard University Press.

Suarez-Orozco, M., & Suarez-Orozco, C. (2000). Some conceptual considerations in the interdisciplinary study of immigrant children. In H. Trueba & L. Bartolome (Eds.), *Immigrant voices: In search of educational equity* (pp. 17–36). Oxford, UK: Rowman & Littlefield.

Tsai, J. (2006). Xenophobia, ethnic community, and immigrant youths' friendship network formation. *Adolescence,* 41(162), 285–298.

Tseng, V., & Yoshikawa, H. (2008). Reconceptualizing acculturation: Ecological processes, historical contexts, and power inequities. *American Journal of Community Psychology,* 42, 355–358.

Unger, J. B., Ritt-Olson, A., Soto, D. W., & Baezconde-Garbanati, L. (2009). Parent-child acculturation discrepancies as a risk factor for substance use among Hispanic adolescents in Southern California. *Journal of Immigrant and Minority Health,* 11(3), 149–157.

Uttal, L., & Han, C. Y. (2011). Taiwanese immigrant mothers' childcare preferences: Socialization for bicultural competency. *Cultural Diversity and Ethnic Minority Psychology,* 17(4), 437–443.

Vo-Jutabha, E. D., Dinh, K. T., McHale, J. P., & Valsiner, J. (2009). A qualitative analysis of Vietnamese adolescent identity exploration within and outside an ethnic enclave. *Journal of Youth and Adolescence,* 38, 672–690.

Weaver, S. R., & Kim, S. Y. (2008). A person-centered approach to studying the linkages among parent-child differences in cultural orientation, supportive parenting, and adolescent depressive symptoms in Chinese American families. *Journal of Youth and Adolescence,* 37, 36–49.

Weisskirch, R. S., Zamboanga, B. L., Bersamin, M., Kim, S. Y., Schwartz, S. J., & Umana-Taylor, A. J. (2011). Cultural influences for college student language brokers. *Cultural Diversity and Ethnic Minority Psychology,* 17(1), 43–51.

{ 6 }

Beyond Families and Schools

FUTURE DIRECTIONS IN PRACTICE AND POLICY FOR CHILDREN IN IMMIGRANT FAMILIES

Ana Maria Nieto and Hirokazu Yoshikawa

Since Bronfenbrenner first introduced the concept of the "ecology of human development" (Bronfenbrenner, 1977), social scientists have been assessing the significance of social contexts in determining children's developmental trajectories. Although the importance of contexts for human development beyond those including children's daily interactions may seem obvious from a theoretical standpoint, this is not necessarily the case in practice and policy. Programs and policies to improve children's developmental outcomes are often limited to targeting *microsystems* for change—that is, the settings that directly include children such as families, schools, and child care programs. Such an approach may disregard the potential for productive targeting of interactions between these proximal settings (the *mesosystem*); the relationships between adults in settings that do not involve the child him- or herself (the *exosystem*); and other *macrosystem* forces, such as policies targeting adults that were not designed with children in mind but that still have substantial impacts on their day-to-day lives.

In particular, interventions aimed at improving children's lives by intervening with families tend to be based on commonly held assumptions that nuclear families work as closed systems and that "parents have nearly full responsibility for determining their children's outcomes" (sometimes termed the "family bubble," Frameworks Institute, 2002, p. 14). We contend that these assumptions are especially problematic in the pursuit of promoting the healthy development of children in immigrant families because they disregard crucial aspects of immigrant parents' experiences outside of the home context that affect their children's development.

In this chapter, we address three examples of common limitations in the literature on programs and policies for children in immigrant families related to this prevailing approach. We present each of the following three limitations alongside solutions: (a) assuming that individual families, and more specifically parenting practices within families, are the primary locus for developmental intervention; (b) assuming that, as a society, we can enhance the well-being of children in immigrant families without addressing the political incorporation of their parents; and (c) assuming that policy and program innovations to benefit these children should be researcher-driven. We argue that dealing with these assumptions by building on the strengths of immigrant communities will more effectively address the contextual barriers faced by children in immigrant families.

We focus on initiatives from the fields of family and community engagement in education, poverty reduction, and political incorporation to illustrate the mechanisms through which realities faced by immigrant parents at multiple ecological levels may impact their children's development. Our review of promising programs, policies, and civic actions does not aim to be exhaustive but rather aims to identify particularly innovative yet overlooked approaches with the potential to improve the developmental trajectories of children in immigrant families. We underscore the need to consider contextual processes that are unique to immigrant families in program and policy design and of supporting initiatives aimed at shifting political structures that hinder the ideal of equal opportunity for all children.

Expanding the Locus of Change Beyond the Family Context: Strengthening Networks of Immigrant Parents

In this section, we challenge the assumption that programs should focus solely on immigrant parent's interactions with the child by examining two specific pathways through which their experiences outside of the family unit impact their children's development—parent's participation in schools and adult's economic well-being. We urge an expansion of the locus of developmental interventions for children in immigrant families to address these adult experiences outside the home context and present parents' social networks as fruitful intervention targets in program and policy design.

STRENGTHENING PARENT NETWORKS FOR SCHOOL ENGAGEMENT

The relationship between parents and schools is perhaps the most cited example used to illustrate the *mesosystem*—broadly defined as the relationship between the multiple proximal settings in children's lives (Bronfenbrenner, 1977). Decades of research have established that parent involvement in children's education, both in the home and in school contexts, is associated with positive academic outcomes for students, especially those from low-income families (Fan & Chen, 2001). In many immigrant families, children spend significantly more time in the U.S. education system than their parents; such school involvement differences can lead to acculturation asynchronies and concomitant interpersonal conflict in parent-child dyadic relationships (Marks, Godoy, & García Coll, Chapter 5). Increasing immigrant parents' participation in schools is thus an important strategy to support the positive development of children in immigrant families.

Foreign-born parents can face a myriad of difficulties when participating in schools, ranging from common language and cultural home–school divides (e.g., Turney & Kao, 2009) to more specific barriers, such as fears of retaliation from school personnel due to past experiences during times of severe political repression or civil war in home countries (Carlock, 2011). Researchers have urged schools systems to carry on efforts such as hiring bilingual staff, providing high-quality translation and interpretation services, creating family liaison positions, and holding school events at convenient hours that can accommodate immigrant parents' work schedules (e.g., Turney & Kao, 2009). Others have pointed to the potential of teacher home visits to promote bicultural understanding and foster trust between schools and immigrant families (Bowne, 2011; Hong, 2011). Although these types of school-based interventions can play a crucial role in lowering many of the barriers to participation faced by individual immigrant parents, there is also a need to build immigrant parents' strengths to overcome home–school divisions.

Literature on social capital highlights the importance of social networks as determinants of immigrant parents' participation in their children's education. *Social capital* refers to the benefits obtained by individuals through their social connections and the norms of reciprocity and trustworthiness that arise from them (Coleman, 1988; Putnam, 2000). Following this theory, Kao and Rutherford (2007) coined the concept of *school-specific social capital* to refer to the social networks that allow parents to attain information and resources to support their children's education. Louie (2004) found that the success of a group of Chinese-American children was a consequence of the cross-class social relationships within their ethnic enclave and the concomitant flow of knowledge of educational issues. The tight relationships between parents and other community members in ethnic enclaves can also benefit children by reinforcing educational values across multiple contexts and providing parents with information about how to leverage school systems (Coleman, 1988).

Interventions that transcend parent education to target the relationships among immigrant parents have shown positive effects in promoting their participation in children's education, both in school and community contexts. Although immigrant parents may form strong social networks outside of schools, strengthening these networks in the school environment may be a particularly effective approach to improving children's outcomes, particularly for children in immigrant families living in ethnic enclaves with low cross-class ties and little transnational wealth (Louie, 2012). McDonald et al. (2006) found that an intervention held in schools and involving multifamily support groups for low-income Latino families had a positive impact on children's academic performance and classroom behaviors (including aggression and social skills) compared to a more traditional intervention consisting of eight behavioral parenting pamphlets, follow-up phone calls, and a lecture on parenting. Implementing this type of interventions will require district policies that support the recruitment, hiring, and development of personnel who are effective at building authentic relationships with immigrant parents.

Support groups are a vital means through which immigrants seek and share informational resources (Oh & Yoshikawa, 2011). Parent support groups held in community-based organizations can also be effective at shifting immigrant parents' relationships with schools. For example, a case study about community-based parent-to-parent support groups for Spanish-speaking mothers of school-aged children with disabilities found that participating mothers felt "like a family," received emotional support from their fellow group members, and gained information that was not being effectively communicated by the educational, legal, or health systems (Mueller, Milian, & Islas Lopez, 2009). In addition, parent-to-parent support networks may provide more of the opportunities to engage in building parenting skills, rather than simply being exposed to didactic information about parenting. A recent meta-analysis found that early childhood programs that provide such opportunities were more effective in improving preacademic outcomes among children birth to age 5 than those that simply provided didactic parenting education (Grindal et al., 2013).

Adult English classes are another promising environment for building social capital and promoting parent engagement among non–English-speaking parents. English classes can help overcome the widely documented participation barriers that result from a lack of translation and interpretation resources during school communications and events (Turney & Kao, 2009). These educational spaces are also propitious environments to foster support networks and counteract feelings of isolation. More important, through an emphasis on school engagement, adult English classes can be effective at promoting changes in the relationships between immigrant parents and school personnel. School districts such as the Boston Public Schools and community-based organizations like the Welcome Project in Somerville, Massachusetts, provide English classes in which teachers emphasize relationship building among parents and foster discussions about education in schools, thereby allowing parents to become familiar with the expectations for their involvement in the American school system. Such an approach also provides opportunities to overcome fears of retaliation by school staff, develop confidence in approaching school personnel, and question ingrained beliefs about what is deemed appropriate communication between parents and schools. Parent's English classes offered at schools can also help reduce the perceived home–school barrier by increasing parents' perception of openness and of being welcomed, thus increasing trust and improving home–school communication (Hong, 2011).

STRENGTHENING IMMIGRANT PARENT NETWORKS FOR ECONOMIC WELL-BEING

Taken together, research on the effects of antipoverty programs on developmental outcomes (see Chapter 8 by Duncan & Weisner) and an analysis of the unique work experiences of low-income immigrants indicates that programs and policies focused on parental economic well-being are particularly important for children in low-income immigrant families. The innovative approaches presented in this section are aimed at building low-income immigrant parents' social capital as an effective mechanism to improve economic well-being.

Theories aiming to explain income differences between different immigrant groups point to individual differences in *human capital*, the specific sets of skills acquired by individuals through education and job experience required for a job, as well as to social networks and contexts of reception as important determinants of economic well-being (Portes and Rumbaut, 2006). For example, these authors found that human capital factors explained one-fourth of the income differences between immigrant groups. Yet substantial income variation between groups persisted, even after accounting for such characteristics as education level, English knowledge, length of U.S. residency, and gender. These results signal the need to consider both individual characteristics and broader economic and social contexts in antipoverty programs intended to benefit immigrant families.

The *ethnic enclave* literature, which studies concentrations of businesses in physical space that employ a significant proportion of workers from the same minority (Wilson & Portes, 1980), highlights factors beyond intensive human-capital development that can be crucial in supporting immigrant families' movement out of poverty. Ethnic enclaves can support the creation of entire business chains (e.g., shipping of raw products, clothing manufacturing factory owners, wholesale clothing buyers, boutiques and small business clothing stores, and customers) that function with little dependence on mainstream networks (Chin, 2005; Zhou, 1992). Adult relationships within ethnic enclaves may also promote economic mobility for individuals through the development of social capital. Co-ethnic networks provide valuable sources of information about employment inside and outside of the community, as well as sources of credit and support for entrepreneurial activities (Portes & Rumbaut, 2006; Portes & Zhou, 1993). Some argue, however, that such patterns do not always hold and that other factors, such as the average socioeconomic status level of the particular immigrant group and local labor market conditions, serve as important moderators (Damm, 2009). Others have pointed out that interethnic networks between different immigrant groups can also produce a mix of symbiotic and exploitative relationships. For example, restaurants, markets, and other service providers in Koreatowns offer job opportunities for recently arrived Latino immigrants at very low salaries (Min, 2008). Strong partnerships among local government, ethnic community leadership, and advocacy organizations can be determinant in taking advantage of these mechanisms to expand and improve the economic development opportunities for immigrant parents.

Innovative poverty reduction efforts are moving away from individual-level theories of change to strategies that take advantage of existing social networks at the neighborhood level, an approach that is particularly appropriate for immigrant families living in residential ethnic enclaves. The Family Independence Initiative (FII), a privately funded nonprofit organization, focuses on bringing working families out of poverty by giving them the space to support each other in taking control of crafting and following their own pathway to economic independence. By joining FII, members of working poor families, a large proportion of whom are first-generation immigrants, self-organize into peer support groups and commit to meeting once a month for 2 years. They set goals for their households, such as raising children's grades, improving credit scores, addressing health or mental health in the family, or building savings, and they receive cash for reporting their monthly progress through an online reporting system. Participants receive $25–$30 dollars for each action they plan and complete, up to a total of $600 per quarter and $2,400 per year (Stuhldreher & O'Brien, 2011). This total represents more than the amount ($1,500–$2,000 per year) suggested by recent welfare-to-work evaluations as necessary to produce detectable improvements in children's achievement (Duncan, Huston, & Weisner, 2007). All resources and formal supports are provided by other households, rather than by formal service providers. Notably, this emphasis on peer leadership breaks with the tradition of bringing in outside "experts," thus building local capacity while at the same time cutting program costs.

Families participating in the FII have shown important improvements in their economic well-being in a short time frame. After completing the 2-year participation period, families in Oakland and San Francisco had average increases in their incomes of 27% and 20%, respectively (Stuhldreher & O'Brien, 2011). Six months after the beginning of the program, families in Boston showed a 13% increase in their salaries (Family Independence Initiative, 2011). An independent review using a pre-post, within-subject design found that for the core group in San Francisco, total families' liabilities (including automobile loans, bank loans, credit card debt, home loans, personal loans, and other liabilities) had decreased from an average of $6,867 to $2,654 at the 2-year mark and continued to decrease after families were no longer receiving quarterly awards. After 3 years of enrollment in the program, families' average savings increased from $437 to $1,433 (Moore Kubo, McKenna, Baum, & Andrews, 2011).

The FII's neighborhood-based approach builds social capital in immigrant enclave communities. Because of the program's emphasis on within-network resources, rather than drawing in other resources through referrals or formal service systems, it provides an unusually focused emphasis on social capital building that may ultimately be more sustainable than a time-limited program. As such, it is particularly suited to immigrant communities, particularly the facilitation of networks between the most newly arrived and more established immigrants.

Beyond Social Capital: Mobilizing Immigrant Parent Networks Toward Political and Civic Engagement

The initiatives reviewed so far point to the potential of efforts aimed at strengthening the social capital of immigrant parents to overcome barriers for their children's development both at the *mesosystem* (i.e., parent's participation in schools) and *exosystem* (i.e., parent's economic well-being) levels. Nevertheless, additional contextual barriers located at the *macrosystem*, or the political level, warrant approaches that go beyond the strengthening of parents' social networks to effect broader change. In this section, we present pathways through which macrosystem policies targeted at broad populations of immigrant adults nonetheless impact children's day-to-day lives and the ways through which immigrant parents and communities can affect macrosystemic changes to improve their own children's lives. We advocate for the need to promote civic and political incorporation and empowerment of immigrant parents.

For recent waves of low-income immigrants and their children, undocumented status is an important macrosystem-based barrier, driven by legislation and a focus on legal personhood in the polity. As pathways to citizenship have increasingly been shut off since the 1986 Immigration Reform and Control Act (Yoshikawa, 2011), entire generations of immigrant families have been affected by this barrier. Parents' undocumented status influences roughly 4.5 million citizen children in the United States. Undocumented parents cannot fully participate in the labor market because their status prevents them from taking better job offers, asking for wage raises, or receiving employer benefits such as sick days, overtime, and flexibility for parenting needs (Yoshikawa, 2011). Undocumented workers are also much more likely than documented immigrant workers to earn wages below the legal minimum (Bernhardt et al., 2009; Yoshikawa, 2011). Documentation status also impacts children's lives by increasing barriers to services and benefits that positively affect child development. Compared to documented families, mixed-status families—families with members who are citizens/legal residents and members who remain undocumented—benefit at lower rates from services that their citizen children are entitled to, such as child care subsidies (Yoshikawa, 2011), health care (Perreira et al., 2012), and other social welfare benefits like Temporary Assistance for Needy Families (Fomby & Cherlin, 2004).

Immigrant organizations can play a determinant role in devising alternative institutional mechanisms to overcome access barriers related to undocumented status. In New York City, for example, the requirement of a photo ID to enter the school in which one's child is enrolled dissuaded many low-income immigrant parents who did not have drivers' licenses from attending school events (Anderson, 2011). In response, the New York Immigration Coalition pressed for legislation to allow consular identification as an acceptable form of photo ID and worked with the consulates of Mexico and Ecuador to conduct identification drives in neighborhoods with high concentrations of low-income immigrants. These provide access to the *matricula consular*, the identification document that can aid in access to programs and resources in New York City (Anderson, 2011). Alternative forms of identification for undocumented adults, in general, hold promise as an indirect pathway to increase access to resources for children in mixed-status families.

Civic action is a direct approach to overcoming exo- and macrosystem barriers that have an impact on immigrant families' economic well-being and thus on children's development. Labor rights have been an increasingly important site of action and collective mobilization for immigrants (Gleeson, 2008). Community organizations and labor unions have shown important successes in organizing day laborers, garment workers, and undocumented immigrants to demand working rights. Examples of campaigns include the Service Employees International Union's (SEIU) "Justice for janitors" campaign in Los Angeles (Milkman, 2006) and cross-ethnic demonstrations for immigrant rights (Ramakrishnan & Bloemraad, 2008; Wong, 2006). Most recently, years of large-scale organizing by undocumented youth activists for the federal DREAM Act resulted in the Obama Administration's June 2012 executive action, Deferred Action for Childhood Arrivals, to stop deportation proceedings for young undocumented immigrants who came to the United States before age 16 and who are under 31 years of age; who are in school or are high school graduates or military veterans; and who have no criminal records. Work authorizations for up to 2 years are being provided (U.S. Department of Homeland Security, 2012). This organizing effort clearly exemplifies the dynamic way in which actions intended to affect macrosystemic policies can improve the everyday experiences of youth in immigrant families. In addition, the organizing actions generated opportunities for strengthening collective identity and solidarity among parents and children, potentially mitigating some of the negative effects of intergenerational conflict (see Marks, Godoy, & García Coll, Chapter 5).

Community organizing also holds promise in increasing the participation of immigrant adults in local decision-making processes that affect children's education. Community organizing initiatives have been successful at impacting educational policy formation to improve struggling schools (Mediratta, Shah, & McAlister, 2009) and at transforming traditional relations among school staff, families, and communities (Warren & Mapp, 2011). These efforts have also been successful in promoting civic and political engagement in predominately immigrant working-class neighborhoods around community issues that can harm children's development. In Los Angeles, for example, Latino parents from the Fernangeles Elementary School pressured Waste Management, a landfill owner, to drop its bid to raise the height of a nearby dumping site by another 43 feet (Catone, Chung, & Oh, 2011). Throughout the campaign, immigrant parents developed collaborative partnerships with OneLA organizers, school staff, and local churches to address a neighborhood problem that was directly affecting their children's health and thereby negatively affecting school attendance, academic engagement, and achievement (Catone et al., 2011). The close mesosystemic interactions among families, schools, and churches were instrumental in building relational power that promoted exosystemic changes and ultimately enhanced children's microsystemic experiences.

Community organizing efforts have also been successful in mobilizing immigrant communities for electoral purposes. The resulting shift in government representations may lead to the design and funding of programs and policies that consider immigrant families. Mexican Americans in the southwest and Cuban

Americans in Miami are examples of immigrant communities that have ensured political representation by mobilizing around issues of ethnicity (as opposed to social class) as the fundamental determinant for political action (Portes & Rumbaut, 2006). Electoral mobilization of Mexican immigrants in California has been characterized by massive naturalization and electoral registration campaigns, especially in response to anti-immigration initiatives such as proposition 187 and bill HR 4437. On their part, many political organizations in Miami were founded in response to the discrimination toward Cuban immigrants after the massive Mariel immigration in the early part of 1980 and the anti-bilingual referendum in November of that same year (Portes & Rumbaut, 2006).

These successful examples point to the potential of community organizing efforts in promoting political incorporation, increasing electoral representation, and bringing about policy changes that positively impact children's development, such as access to services, labor rights, and education policy. Nevertheless, there are limitations to this approach that must be taken into account. Most community organizing efforts are supported by nonprofit community-based organizations (CBOs), which are currently filling the gap left by traditional parties in politically educating and mobilizing the newer wave of immigrants for electoral and non-electoral political activities (Wong, 2006). The current political landscape poses important barriers to promoting immigrant incorporation into mainstream political processes, especially in areas with low immigrant concentrations. Although CBOs are trusted settings, with the potential to promote political mobilization, their role as sites of political incorporation into mainstream political institutions, and thus their potential to impact policy formation, is less clear than in the case of political parties—for instance, their functions often concentrate on increasing human and social capital, rather than political power. Local unions, which tend to be relatively strong and involved in politics, may be better equipped in issues of advocacy and public policy; however, these organizations may not necessarily take up issues related to immigrant workers, especially since very few immigrants are union members (Ramakrishnan & Bloemraad, 2008). Community-based organizations working with immigrant populations that integrate human and social capital with advocacy, organizing, and political power hold greater promise in achieving the goals of political incorporation and empowerment of immigrant parents and of shifting the policy landscape in ways that will benefit their children (Oh & Yoshikawa, 2011; Yoshikawa et al., 2012).

Assuming that CBOs will remain a critical site for immigrant political incorporation, there is a need to understand ways to promote their effectiveness. Examples of successful community organizing efforts tend to come either from large, well-structured and funded CBOs, from existing unions that have taken on the immigrant cause, or from alliances between these types organizations (Carlock, 2011; Ramakrishnan & Bloemraad, 2008). Supportive government policies can mitigate political stratification and level the playing field between ethnic and nonethnic organizations by boosting resources for those organizations serving marginalized communities (Ramakrishnan & Bloemraad, 2008). Alliances and coalitions constitute another pathway to strengthen CBOs. Advocacy organizations that work with multiple social service-oriented organizations have achieved important cross-organizational change. The New York Immigration Coalition, an umbrella organization with more than 200 organizations as members, many of which focus more on social services, provides training and technical assistance to organizations on issues of advocacy and policy change. The Coalition organized the massive 2006 marches in New York City at the time of congressional and federal debate over comprehensive immigration reform.

In the longer term, political incorporation should be strengthened through structural changes to the political system that shift the current context and promote immigrant representation. Analysts suggest the creation of district, proportional, and cumulative voting systems of representation and other measures that would increase party competition, such as open primaries and balanced electoral districts (Ramakrishnan & Bloemraad, 2008). Local governments can also increase political incorporation by creating posts for immigrants at local boards and fostering stronger communications with non–English speaking groups through special liaisons and commissions (Ramakrishnan & Bloemraad, 2008).

Expanding the Nexus of Research, Practice, and Policy: Valuing Research Approaches That Privilege Action, Empowerment, and Transformation of Reality

Research has greatly advanced the documentation of the various barriers to healthy development faced by immigrant populations and, in some instances, the evaluation of effective interventions designed to address developmental barriers. However, the immigrant youth development literature is dominated by an emphasis on the microsystem, without sufficient consideration of the interactions between social settings (mesosystem); the relationships between adults in children's lives that may impact their well-being (exosystem); and the influence of macrosystem factors, such as public policies (Marks, Godoy, & García Coll, Chapter 5). Studies that have considered immigrant parents' experiences focus on parenting skill or human capital development. In addition, the majority of interventions do not take advantage of the knowledge of practitioners or communities. In other words, program and polices' theories of change continue to be largely designed for—not by—the communities they aim to help (Yoshikawa & Ramos Olazagasti, 2010). In our view, this is a limited approach to encouraging innovation in programs and policies, and to strengthening the links among research, practice, and policy that will bring about deeper change for immigrant children.

The prevention science paradigm, a prominent approach to developing evidence-based programs for children and youth, privileges researcher-driven innovation (National Research Council and Institute of Medicine, 2009). Theories of change based on risk and protective factors are the principal source of innovation in such preventive and promotive interventions. This approach has, in fact, produced many remarkable advances in interventions. However, there are many alternative frameworks—perhaps a universe of alternatives (Sarason, 1982)—that can be equally productive in producing innovations for the next generation of programs and policies targeting children in immigrant families. Bottom-up approaches that see communities as competent, knowledgeable, and capable of informing policy and program design and evaluation hold promise in informing culturally relevant interventions (Yoshikawa & Ramos Olazagasti, 2010).

Several frameworks privilege innovation that is already occurring in communities and bring such innovations to light in order to disseminate and illuminate processes of change. For example, Rappaport (2000) highlights, as an alternative to prevention science, community narratives as sources of innovation and social change because such narratives draw from available knowledge within the community and provide specific knowledge about how to adapt interventions. The narratives that diverse community stakeholders construct as they engage in community change are neglected sources of innovation in programs and policies. The cultural dimensions of such community narratives, in particular, can help address the lack of cultural specificity in traditional policy analysis as well as prevention science (Yoshikawa & Ramos Olazagasti, 2010). For example, Yoshikawa et al (2003) identified the cultural practice of women gatherings at the network level and of youth-organized media interventions at the community level as promising approaches to contextual HIV prevention in Asian and Pacific Islander communities.

Recent studies have taken on the task of documenting the specific processes through which immigrant communities embark on the process of shifting power relations from challenging initial conditions (Carlock, 2011). In-depth ethnographic studies allow following longitudinal changes and uncovering the complex social processes that keep barriers in place, as well as the ways in which communities can begin to shift them. Ethnographic approaches also allow the creation of spaces where people feel enough trust and comfort to uncover and confront the negative feelings, fears of reprisal, and insecure self-conceptions that prevent them from voicing their opinions and fighting for their interests (Lukes, 2005). In this way "the research process may itself serve as a form of empowerment, allowing the expression of interests that previously had been withheld by the participant" (Carlock, 2011, p. 30).

Participatory action research approaches allow diverse stakeholders to come together to create innovative strategies that are grounded on particular contexts and at different ecological levels. The work conducted by Luis Moll and his collaborators (1992) in Tucson highlights the instrumental role of educational researchers in transforming the relationships between schools and immigrant families. In the classic study *Funds of Knowledge for Teaching*, anthropologists developed collaborative partnerships with teachers and working-class Mexican families to devise innovative teaching practices that integrated the knowledge and skills found in local households into the curriculum (Moll, Amanti, Neffi, & Gonzalez, 1992). This approach, which promotes the coordination of home–school bicultural practices, may have positive effects on youth development by reducing the cultural gulf that often exists between home and school for immigrant communities (Marks, Godoy, & García Coll, Chapter 5).

Research projects undertaken by the Kafka Brigade, an independent, not-for-profit action research team in the United Kingdom dedicated to reducing red tape for citizens and businesses (Kafka Brigade, 2012) constitute another effective "bottom-up" approach to policy design. As in traditional research, these research projects allow practitioners and policy makers to develop an understanding of the functioning of access barriers from the perspective of the user. However, this group moves away from the traditional practice of making recommendations based on their findings. Instead, they bring all of the relevant stakeholders around a particular policy problem into a conversational space that fosters the creation of specific commitments and actions that will alter the status quo. This approach is especially promising in overcoming barriers associated with cultural diversity because it gives voice to frontline service providers and the people who are affected by the programs and policies.

Social science has produced remarkable advances in our understanding of human development and potential pathways to effect change (Shonkoff & Phillips, 2000). As we move forward, there is a need to conduct research that will support innovations for the next generation of programs and policies for children in immigrant families. Findings obtained through community narratives, ethnographic approaches, and participatory action research can inform more culturally specific theories of change and strengthen the design of both qualitative and quantitative evaluation studies. The integration of these different research paradigms may also broaden our societal understanding of innovation in efforts to improve developmental outcomes among children in immigrant families (Small, 2011; Yoshikawa, Weisner, Kalil, & Way, 2008). Innovative research approaches go beyond documenting the barriers faced by immigrant families to supporting the processes through which different actors can take actions to transform reality.

Conclusion

Prevention programs and public policies to improve the lives of children in immigrant families are often limited to initiatives targeted at the family and, more specifically, at parenting practices. In this chapter, we have argued that, in order to address the particular contextual barriers faced by children in immigrant families, there is a need to expand the focus of change from parents to target broader populations of immigrant adults and their economic well-being and political incorporation. Approaches aimed at strengthening social networks and political capital in immigrant communities hold promise in shifting developmental barriers at different levels of the ecological system. Research efforts that approach immigrant communities as competent, knowledgeable, and capable of informing policy and program design and evaluation can support the development of more culturally and ecologically grounded theories of change.

We focused on participation in schools, working conditions, and political incorporation as three specific pathways through which immigrant parents' experiences outside of the home context may impact their children. We call on others to conduct similar analyses for other significant pathways, such as family separation and reunification; refugee experiences and trauma; and experiences of violence, repression, or racism in the receiving context. Research efforts to understand these pathways by giving voice and empowering immigrant communities can be an important source of innovation in promoting the healthy development of children in immigrant families in the United States.

References

Anderson, N. (2011, October 13). New initiative draws immigrant parents into schools. *The Brooklyn Ink.* Retrieved from http://thebrooklynink.com/2011/10/13/30582-new-initiative-draws-immigrant-parents-into-schools/

Bernhardt, A., Milkman, R., Theodore, N., Heckathorn, D., Auer, M., DeFilippis, J., et al. (2009). *Broken laws, unprotected workers: Violations of employment and labor laws in America's cities.* New York: National Employment Law Project.

Bowne, J. (2011). *Home visits as a catalyst to effective parent-teacher relationship in pre-kindergarten and kindergarten classrooms: A dyadic qualitative analysis.* Unpublished manuscript, Harvard Graduate School of Education, Cambridge, MA.

Bronfenbrenner, U. (1977). Toward an experimental ecology of human development. *American Psychologist, 32,* 513–531.

Carlock, R. (2011). *"La union hace la fuerza": Community organizing for democratic school governance: An ethnographic study in an immigrant community.* Unpublished manuscript, Harvard Graduate School of Education, Cambridge, MA.

Catone, K., Chung, C., & Oh, S. (2011). "An appetite for change": Building relational cultures for educational reform and civic engagement in Los Angeles. In M. Warren & K. Mapp (Eds.), *A match on dry grass: Community organizing as a catalyst for school reform* (pp. 66–98). Oxford, UK: Oxford University Press.

Chin, M. (2005). *Sewing women: Immigrants and the New York City garment industry.* New York: Columbia University Press.

Coleman, J. (1988). Social capital in the creation of human capital. *American Journal of Sociology, 94*(Supplement), S95–S120.

Damm, A. P. (2009). Ethnic enclaves and immigrant labor-market outcomes: A quasi-experimental study. *Journal of Labor Economics, 27,* 281–314.

Duncan, G. J., Huston, A. C., & Weisner, T. S. (2007). *Higher ground: New Hope for the working poor and their children.* New York: Russell Sage.

Family Independence Initiative. (2011). *FII–Boston families: The first six months.* Retrieved from http://www.fiinet.org/writable/resources/documents/boston_update_april_2011-1.pdf

Fan, X., & Chen, M. (2001). Parental involvement and students' academic achievement: A meta-analysis. *Educational Psychology Review, 13*, 1–22.

Frameworks Institute. (2002). *Promoting school readiness and early child development: Findings from cognitive elicitations.* Retrieved from http://www.frameworksinstitute.org/assets/files/ECD/school_readiness_and_ecd.pdf

Fomby, P., & Cherlin, A. J. (2004). Public assistance use among U.S.-born children of immigrants. *International Migration Review, 38,* 584–610.

Gleeson, S. (2008). Organizing for immigrant labor rights: Latino immigrants in San Jose and Houston. In S. K. Ramakrishnan & I. Bloemraad (Eds.), *Civic hopes and political realities: Immigrants, community organizations, and political engagement* (pp. 107–133). New York: Russell Sage Foundation.

Grindal, T., Bowne, J., Yoshikawa, H., Schindler, H., Duncan, G., & Magnuson, K. (2013). *The added impact of parent-education services in early childhood education programs on child cognitive and pre-academic skills: A meta analysis.* Manuscript under review.

Hong, S. (2011). *A cord of three strands: A new approach to parent engagement in schools.* Cambridge, MA: Harvard Education Press.

Kao, G., & Rutherford, L. (2007). Does social capital still matter? Immigrant minority disadvantage in school-specific social capital and its effects on academic achievement. *Sociological Perspectives, 50,* 27–52.

Kafka Brigade. (2012). *About Us.* Retrieved from http://www.kafkabrigade.org.uk/about/

Louie, V. (2004). *Compelled to excel: Immigration, education, and opportunity among Chinese Americans.* Palo Alto, CA: Stanford University Press.

Louie, V. (2012). *Keeping the immigrant bargain: The costs and rewards of success in America.* New York: Russell Sage Foundation.

Lukes, S. (2005). *Power: A radical view* (2nd ed.). New York: Palgrave McMillan.

McDonald, L., Moberg, P., Brown, R., Rodriguez-Espiricueta, I., Flores, N., Burke, M., & Coover, G. (2006). After-school multifamily groups: A randomized controlled trial involving low-income, urban, Latino children. *Children & Schools, 28,* 25–34.

Mediratta, K., Shah, S., & McAlister, S. (2009). *Community organizing for stronger schools.* Cambridge, MA: Harvard University Press.

Milkman, R. (2006). *L.A. story: Immigrant workers and the future of the U.S. labor movement.* New York: Russell Sage Foundation.

Min, P. G. (2008). *Ethnic solidarity for economic survival: Korean greengrocers in New York City* New York: Russell Sage Foundation.

Moll, L., Amanti, C., Neffi, D., & Gonzalez, N. (1992). Funds of knowledge for teaching: Using a qualitative approach to connect home and classrooms. *Theory Into Practice, 31,* 132–141.

Moore Kubo, M., McKenna, A., Baum, B., & Andrews, A. (2011). *Family independence initiative: Pathways out of poverty for San Francisco families.* Retrieved from http://www.fiinet.org/writable/resources/documents/fii_quantitative_report_sf-2.pdf

Mueller, T. G., Milian, M., & Islas Lopez, M. (2009). Latina mothers' views of a parent-to-parent support group in the special education system. *Research and Practice for Persons with Severe Disabilities (RPSD), 34,* 113–122.

National Research Council and Institute of Medicine. (2009). *Preventing mental, emotional, and behavioral disorders among young people: Progress and possibilities.* Committee on Prevention of Mental Disorders and Substance Abuse among Children, Youth and

Young Adults: Research Advances and Promising Interventions. M. E. O'Connell, T. Boat, & K. E. Warner (Eds.). Washington, DC: National Academies Press.

Oh, S. S., & Yoshikawa, H. (2011). Examining spiritual capital across ecological systems: Developmental implications for children and adolescents in immigrant families. In C. García Coll (Ed.), *The impact of immigration on children's development* (pp. 77–98). Basel, Switzerland: Karger.

Perreira, K. M., Crosnoe, R., Fortuny, K., Pedroza, J. M., Ulvestad, K., Weiland, C., et al. (2012). *Barriers to immigrant families' access to health and human services (ASPE Research Brief)*Washington, DC: DHHS Office of the Assistant Secretary for Planning and Evaluation.

Portes, A., & Rumbaut, R. (2006). *Immigrant America: A portrait*. Berkeley: University of California Press.

Portes, A., & Zhou, M. (1993). The new second generation: Segmented assimilation and its variants. *Annals of the American Academy of Political and Social Science, 530,* 74–96.

Putnam, R. (2000). *Bowling alone: The collapse and revival of American community*. New York: Simon & Schuster Press.

Ramakrishnan, S. K., & Bloemraad, I. (2008). *Civic hopes and political realities: Immigrants, community organizations, and political engagement*. New York: Russell Sage Foundation.

Rappaport, J. (2000). Community narratives: Tales of terror and joy. *American Journal of Community Psychology, 28,* 1–24.

Sarason, S. B. (1982). *The culture of the school and the problem of change* (2nd ed.). Boston, MA: Allyn and Bacon.

Shonkoff, J. P., & Phillips, D. A. (2000). *From neurons to neighborhoods: The science of early childhood development*. Washington, DC: National Academy Press.

Small, M. L. (2011). How to conduct a mixed methods study: Recent trends in a rapidly growing literature. *Annual Review of Sociology, 37,* 57–81.

Stuhldreher, A., & O'Brien, R. (2011). *The family independence initiative: A new approach to help families exit poverty*. Retrieved from http://www.fiinet.org/writable/resources/documents/newamericafiipaper-1.pdf

Turney, K., & Kao, C. (2009). Barriers to school involvement: Are immigrant parents disadvantaged? *Journal of Educational Research, 102,* 257–271.

U.S. Department of Homeland Security. (2012). *Exercising prosecutorial discretion with respect to individuals who came to the United States as children*. Washington, DC: U.S. Department of Homeland Security.

Warren, M., & Mapp, K. (2011). *A match on dry grass: Community organizing as a catalyst for school reform*. Oxford, UK: Oxford University Press.

Wilson, K. L., & Portes, A. (1980). Immigrant enclaves: An analysis of the labor market experiences of Cubans in Miami. *American Journal of Sociology, 86,* 295–319.

Wong, J. (2006). *Democracy's promise: Immigrants & American civic institutions*. Ann Arbor: University of Michigan Press.

Yoshikawa, H. (2011). *Immigrants raising citizens: Undocumented parents and their young children* New York: Russell Sage Foundation.

Yoshikawa, H., & Ramos Olazagasti, M. A. (2010). The neglected role of community narratives in culturally anchored prevention and public policy. In M. S. Aber, K. Maton, & E. Seidman (Eds.), *Empowering settings and voices for social change (pp. 173–192)*. New York: Oxford University Press.

Yoshikawa, H., Weiland, C., Ulvestad, K., Fortuny, K., Perreira, K., & Crosnoe, R. (2012). *Ensuring access of low-income immigrant families to health and human services: The role of community-based organizations* (Policy Brief No. 4, Immigrant Access to Health and Human Services Project). Washington, DC: The Urban Institute and U.S. Department of Health and Human Services, Assistant Secretary for Planning and Evaluation.

Yoshikawa, H., Weisner, T. S., Kalil, A., & Way, N. (2008). Mixing qualitative and quantitative research methods in developmental science: Uses and methodological choices. *Developmental Psychology, 44,* 344–354.

Yoshikawa, H., Wilson, P. A., Hsueh, J., Rosman, E. A., Kim, J., & Chin, J. (2003). What frontline CBO staff can tell us about culturally anchored theories of change in HIV prevention for Asian/Pacific Islanders. *American Journal of Community Psychology, 32,* 143–158.

Zhou, M. (1992). *Chinatown: The socioeconomic potential of an urban enclave.* Philadelphia, PA: Temple University Press.

Child Poverty as a Limiting Context of Development

Poverty and Children's Development

FAMILIAL PROCESSES AS MEDIATING INFLUENCES

Vonnie McLoyd, Rashmita S. Mistry, and Cecily R. Hardaway

Poverty touches the lives of millions of American children and is linked to a range of difficulties in child functioning. In this chapter, we discuss various perspectives that have emerged as explanations of the link between poverty and children's development, review research evidence relevant to these perspectives, and identify important areas for future research. Illuminating the processes that underlie the association between poverty and children's development is important for aiding policy and intervention efforts designed to alleviate the hardships faced by families in poverty and improve the long-term economic, educational, and social prospects of their children. To minimize repetition with several other excellent reviews of this topic (e.g., Conger, Conger, & Martin, 2010; Evans, 2004; Huston & Bentley, 2010; McLoyd, Aikens, & Burton, 2006) and overlap with other chapters in this volume (see O'Brien, Weaver, Burchinal, Clarke-Stewart, & Vandell, Chapter 3; Crosnoe & Leventhal, Chapter 10; Weisner & Duncan, Chapter 8; Gershoff & Benner, Chapter 9; Zaslow & Crosby, Chapter 4), we limit our review to school-aged children and youth and emphasize recent advances in knowledge.

THE DEMOGRAPHICS AND PSYCHOSOCIAL CORRELATES OF CHILDHOOD POVERTY IN THE UNITED STATES

Child poverty rates in the United States have soared in the new millennium and show few signs of improving in the near future. In 2011, 16.1 million children and adolescents—21.9% of all children in the United States—lived in families with incomes below the federal poverty threshold (FPT; $23,021 for a four-person household; DeNavas-Walt, Proctor, & Smith, 2012). Of these, more than 7.3 million (9.8%) lived in extreme poverty, defined as family income 50% below FPT (DeNavas-Walt et al., 2012). A measure of *absolute* poverty, the FPT identifies a basic standard of living below which families are deemed officially poor or disadvantaged by societal standards. It is widely used to determine eligibility for a host of social services aimed at reducing material hardships among poor families (e.g., housing subsidies, food stamps, utility assistance) and increasing family income (e.g., Earned Income Tax Credits). There is broad agreement, however, that families with incomes between 100% and 200% of the FPT (i.e., between $23,021 and approximately $46,000 for a family of four), often called *working poor, near poor,* or *low income,* also face significant challenges to making ends meet (Huston & Bentley, 2010). Estimates that combine the number of children living in poor families and working poor families are even more dire; 44% of all American children (32.6 million) live in families with incomes below 200% FPT (DeNavas-Walt et al., 2012).

As staggering as these statistics are, it is important to remember that income poverty is often just one of a myriad of risk factors confronting children who are poor, particularly those dealing with chronic as compared with transitory poverty (Huston & Bentley, 2010). Other prominent status risk factors include single-parent family structure, low parent education, and minority ethnic group membership. For example, ethnic minority children are disproportionately more likely to experience poverty as compared with non-Hispanic White children; in 2011, 37% of African-American, 34% of Hispanic, and 13% of Asian children lived in poverty, as compared with 12.5% of non-Hispanic White children (DeNavas-Walt et al., 2012). Rates of childhood poverty are also substantially higher among female-headed households (DeNavas-Walt et al., 2012) and immigrant families (Borjas, 2011). Although space limitations prohibit an in-depth discussion of how children's experiences of poverty vary across other markers of social status, it is important to keep this within-group variability in mind when evaluating the impact of socioeconomic disadvantage on the quality of children's lives and chances for success. Additional factors that account for variation in children's adjustment and well-being include the child's age at the time family poverty is experienced, the duration and depth of poverty, and the frequency of poverty entries and exits (Huston & Bentley, 2010).

There is robust evidence linking family income and poverty to virtually all domains of child and adolescent development (see reviews by McLoyd, 1998; McLoyd et al., 2006). Results from both correlational and experimental studies demonstrate that, whereas higher levels and increases in family income are associated with better child outcomes, children's experiences of poverty, low income, and income loss correlate with lower levels of academic achievement and educational attainment, higher levels of mental health problems and disorders, drug use and delinquency, and more physical health problems (e.g., obesity) (e.g., Duncan, Huston, & Weisner, 2007; Gershoff, Aber, Raver, & Lennon, 2007; Goodman, 1999; Guo, 1998; Jarjoura, Triplett, & Brinker, 2002; Reardon, 2011; Votruba-Drzal, 2006; Wadsworth, Raviv, Compas, & Connor-Smith, 2005). During adolescence, low-income children's educational aspirations decrease, levels of perceived barriers to educational and occupational achievement increase, and achievement values become tied to perceived barriers (Kao & Tienda, 1998; Taylor & Graham, 2007). Youth from lower socioeconomic status (SES) backgrounds report lower overall levels of educational expectations than do youth from higher SES backgrounds (Diemer & Li, 2012) and are less likely to attend or graduate from college or pursue advanced degrees than nonpoor adolescents (Adelman, 2004). Income-related educational disparities of this nature are particularly unsettling, given overwhelming evidence of the positive payoff to both individuals and society of postsecondary education (Haskins, Holzer, & Lerman, 2009).

Accounting for Linkages Between Poverty and Children's Development: Contrasting Perspectives

As this brief overview indicates, childhood poverty is linked to many difficulties for children and youth, both concurrently and in the long term. Over the course of the past two decades, three perspectives have emerged as explanations for these links. A *social causation* perspective espouses the view that poverty and the conditions strongly linked to poverty lead to variations in children's growth and development (Conger et al., 2010). A great deal of the research guided by a social causation perspective emphasizes familial processes, although it has also informed the study of such extrafamilial contexts as schools and neighborhoods (see Chapter 9 by Gershoff & Benner for a discussion of the latter). Social causation models also undergird experimental studies testing the efficacy of interventions that aim to raise family income and reduce poverty—such as the New Hope intervention discussed in Chapter 8, Weisner and Duncan's complementary chapter. A *social selection* perspective maintains that the traits and dispositions of future parents lead to variation in economic well-being, variation in parents' relationships with their children, and, ultimately, variation in children's development through the endowments and dispositions that parents pass on to their children (Conger et al., 2010). Finally, an *interactionist* perspective contends that the relation between SES/poverty and development involves both social selection and social causation processes. In the sections that follow, we review research evidence relevant to each of these perspectives.

SOCIAL CAUSATION PERSPECTIVE

A growing body of literature identifies two family-based pathways through which SES broadly and poverty more specifically affect child functioning—*parental investments* and *family stress* (see reviews by Conger et al., 2010; Huston & Bentley, 2010). Extant scholarship provides strong support for both perspectives, across families diverse with respect to race/ethnicity, family structure, and nativity status. Further, there is some evidence that parental investment pathways are better able to account for variations in children's cognitive and academically oriented outcomes, whereas family stress pathways appear to matter more for children's socioemotional outcomes.

Parental Investments

The *parental investment model* (PIM) has its roots in economic and sociological perspectives and emphasizes purchasing power. PIM posits that the link-
age between SES and children's outcomes is through parents' procurement of
goods and services that enhance children's economic and educational prospects. Higher-SES parents have both the means and opportunities to provide
their children with the material goods and experiences associated with social
mobility (Lareau, 2003). This includes the provision of learning materials in the
home (e.g., books, educational materials) and parents' direct (e.g., reading with
child) and indirect (e.g., visits to museums and libraries, tutoring, extracurricular activities) support of learning. For example, studies have consistently shown
that lower SES mothers talk less frequently to and engage less often in literacy
activities (e.g., reading and owning books, listening to music) with their young
children as compared with higher SES mothers (Hart & Risley, 1995; Lareau,
2003). These differences, in turn, have been linked to substantial differences
in children's vocabulary growth and language development and overall school
adjustment and attainment (e.g., Hoff, 2003; Snow, 2006). Recent studies demonstrate that educationally enriching activities and experiences mediate the
effects of family income and poverty on school-aged children's cognitive, academic, and behavioral outcomes (see Gershoff et al., 2007) and, furthermore,
that increases in family income are intertwined with improvements in the quality of the home learning environment and children's cognitive and academic
outcomes in both observational and welfare-to-work experimental studies
(Huston & Bentley, 2010).

A second PIM pathway is through parents' attitudes, values, and beliefs, as
well as more targeted efforts designed to ensure their child's success at school
(Magnuson, 2007). A voluminous research literature points to parental attitudes as
antecedents of academic outcomes among low-income adolescents and as mediators of the link between family income and academic outcomes among adolescents (e.g., Benner & Mistry, 2007; Hango, 2007; Hill et al., 2004; Schoon, Parsons,
& Sacker, 2004). For example, levels of academic achievement are higher among
low-income adolescents whose parents have higher educational expectations for
them (Schoon et al., 2004; Wood, Kaplan, & McLoyd, 2007). Higher educational
expectations among low-income parents are also associated with better adjustment to secondary school, which, in turn, fosters higher educational attainment
(Schoon et al., 2004).

Lareau (2003), based on ethnographic findings, contends that SES disparities
in children's developmental trajectories are largely driven by social class-based
child-rearing practices that reflect parents' beliefs about their role in children's
development. As evidence, she finds that middle-class parents, as compared with
working-class/poor parents, more consistently and intensely engage in a parenting
style she terms *concerted cultivation* (CC), whereby they actively foster their child's
cognitive, academic, and social skills through communicative and discipline

strategies that rely heavily on reasoning, directives, and negotiation, and through enrolling their children in multiple leisure and extracurricular activities. In contrast, low-income parents espouse lower levels of involvement in their children's activities and are likely to rely on *the accomplishment of natural growth* as a primary child-rearing strategy.

More recently, Cheadle (2008; Cheadle & Amato, 2011) operationalized Lareau's notion of CC using nationally representative survey data and found support for a three-dimensional classification of parental investments: an index of children's participation in extracurricular activities, parents' use of educational materials in the home, and parents' level of school involvement, such as interactions with school officials and participation in school functions. Cheadle (2008) reported strong evidence of the association between families' use of CC strategies and higher levels of academic achievement at school entry, as well as growth in children's math and reading scores through third grade. Concerted cultivation also mediated, albeit partially, SES-related disparities in children's initial achievement levels and, less consistently, growth in achievement across the first 3 years of schools, indicating that it accounts for some, but not all, of the observed association between SES and children's developmental outcomes.

Family Stress

A second set of family-based processes through which SES and poverty are proposed to matter for children's well-being is posited by a *family stress model* (FSM). The model derives from Glen Elder's seminal study of the effects of parental job and income loss on family functioning and child development during the Great Depression (Elder, 1974), Conger and colleagues' (Conger & Elder, 1994) study of family changes brought about by the U.S. farming crisis of the 1980s, and McLoyd's (1990) extension of the model to African-American families living in poverty. Empirical tests of FSM yield robust confirmatory evidence of the pathways by which economic stress affects children's socioemotional well-being among diverse families, including rural and urban families and families across multiple cultural communities within and outside of the United States (e.g., Benner & Kim, 2010; Mistry, Vandewater, Huston, & McLoyd, 2002; Parke et al., 2004; Solantaus, Leinonen, & Punamaki, 2004).

FSM states that economic hardship (i.e., income declines or living in poverty) induces economic strain and felt pressure in parents. The strain associated with the daily hassles of making ends meet in turn takes a toll on parents' mental health, increases interparental conflict and discord, and ultimately interferes with high-quality parenting. Surprisingly, few studies of economic hardship model family income and material deprivation separately in their analyses (Huston & Bentley, 2010). A recent study by Gershoff and colleagues (Gershoff et al., 2007) provides strong empirical support for modeling *indirect* effects of family income—through material hardship and parent stress—on children's cognitive and social-emotional competence. Specifically, they reported that when *both* income and material hardship were included in a model estimating child outcomes, the influence of income on parental stress was due almost entirely to a reduction in material hardship. Parent stress in turn influenced both parental investments and positive parenting behavior, each of which significantly predicted increases in cognitive skills and social-emotional competence, respectively. These associations were generally consistent for families from diverse socioeconomic and race/ethnic backgrounds (Raver, Gershoff, & Aber, 2007).

Another central premise of FSM, but one that has been less well tested empirically, is that more than absolute levels of income and economic resources, it is parents' perceived financial inadequacy that significantly affects children's well-being. Some of Mistry and colleagues' recent work found that parents felt pressure to meet not only their family's material needs (e.g., rent, food, utility bills) but also to provide more discretionary, modest "extras" (e.g., birthday presents and Christmas gifts for their children), which had important downstream consequences for their own mental health and parenting behaviors (Mistry & Lowe, 2006; Mistry, Lowe, Benner, & Chien, 2008). Keeping abreast of monthly bills was associated with feeling "okay," but affording some, even very modest, extras were associated with feelings of accomplishment and of being a successful provider and parent and, in turn, was a stronger predictor of children's social-emotional adjustment than was meeting basic needs. The findings highlight that inclusion of both dimensions of economic pressure are essential for advancing the understanding of why economic hardship matters for child well-being.

Of all the constructs in the FSM framework, parenting problems are posited as the most proximal link to children's compromised development resulting from economic hardship (Elder, 1974; McLoyd, 1990). Economic stress reduces parents' ability to interact with children in a nurturing, supportive, and responsive manner; decreases their level of involvement and attentiveness toward their children; and increases reliance on more coercive, inconsistent, and harsher parenting practices (Conger, Ge, Elder, Lorenz, & Simons, 1994; Elder, Nguyen, & Caspi, 1985; McLoyd, Jayaratne, Ceballo, & Borquez, 1994). FSM contends that economic strain, depression, and marital conflict make it difficult for poor parents to engage in positive, child-centered parenting, even if they possess strong parenting skills. Low-SES parents do not necessarily lack good parenting skills but may simply be too compromised by the effects of poverty-related stress to engage in it. Importantly, a new family strengthening intervention developed by Wadsworth and colleagues (Wadsworth et al., 2011) to address the key parts of FSM—strengthening the interparental relationship, improving coping and reducing stress, and teaching child-centered parenting—resulted in improvements in parenting, parental coping, and depression, which in turn predicted fewer child internalizing and externalizing symptoms. Translation of FSM from theory to practice is an exciting future direction for work in this area.

Critiques of the Focus on Family Processes as Mediators of Poverty Effects

In recent years, scholars who themselves espouse a social causation perspective have criticized the literature's predominant focus on family processes for explaining poverty's impact on child and adolescent development. Evans (2004) faults research of this ilk largely on the grounds that it lacks an ecological perspective, a core tenet of which is that development is the result of multiple underlying agents and processes of varying proximity to the child. Evans argues that psychologists have largely attended to parenting and home environmental factors while ignoring the physical settings that poor children inhabit and their cumulative exposure to a daunting array of suboptimal psychosocial and physical environmental risk factors known to impact human development (e.g., proximity to toxic waste dumps, elevated levels of exposure to lead and pesticides, ambient air pollution). In their study of rural, White 8- to 10-year-olds, Evans and English (2002) found that those who were poor were more likely than their middle-class counterparts to experience not only psychosocial stressors (e.g., family turmoil, community violence) but physical stressors (e.g., substandard housing, high levels of noise, crowding) as well. Cumulative exposure to these stressors partially mediated the link between poverty and children's psychosocial adjustment (i.e., anxiety, depression, behavioral conduct problems, low self-worth). Moreover, cumulative stressor exposure was a much more powerful mediator of the link between poverty and children's adjustment than were the individual physical and psychosocial stressors.

Of course, scholars who have tested the FSM, PIM, and variants of these models are not unaware of the multiple disadvantages that accompany poverty and low income. More than two decades ago, McLoyd (1990) underscored the complex, multifaceted nature of poverty. Drawing on a rich body of literature, she pointed out that chronic poverty is distinguished by a high contagion of negative life *events* occurring in the context of adverse *conditions* such as inadequate housing, residence in low-resource and sometimes dangerous neighborhoods, and exposure to aversive physical conditions. For this reason, McLoyd and Wilson (1990) cautioned against viewing negative parental behavior as the primary pathway through which poverty undermines children's socioemotional functioning, noting that "the multifaceted nature of poverty, especially if it is chronic, appears to require more complex models of causality" (p. 52). McLoyd (1990) also presumed that chronic poverty has direct effects on the child because it is "longstanding and defines the child's immediate environment, almost in its entirety" (p. 314).

Nonetheless, Evans' (2004) criticism is valid because mediational models centered around family processes scarcely reflect the multiple disadvantages that poor children experience in extrafamilial contexts and the physical environment. That scholars (mostly psychologists) who have directed focal attention to parenting and home environmental factors as mediators of poverty have not made significant forays into extrafamilial processes that may mediate poverty effects (e.g., schools) can be credited, in part, to limited training and expertise in these extrafamilial domains and the challenges of establishing interdisciplinary collaborations.

Conversely, their strong focus on parenting and psychosocial characteristics within the family reflects two key contextual influences: (a) a large contingent of these scholars works in the area of family studies, and (b) the conceptual under-pinnings of FSM rest, to a major extent, on Elder's research on economic loss, in which parenting and family processes are central mediating pathways.

The fact that poor children experience multiple stressors and cumulative disad-vantages has also prompted reservations about the value of research that privileges poverty over other stressors associated with poverty. Sameroff, Gutman, and Peck (2003) assert that focusing on a single risk factor such as poverty or negative par-enting does not address the reality of most children's lives because children often experience multiple adverse conditions and recurring stressors. In their view, "multiple settings and multiple systems must be examined simultaneously because risk factors tend to cluster in the same individuals" (p. 367).

The standard way of capturing such co-occurrences is to create a multiple or cumulative risk score by totaling the number of risk factors for each family or child (with poverty counted as one risk factor). Sameroff and his colleagues (Sameroff, Bartko, Baldwin, Baldwin, & Seifer, 1998) found no differences in child compe-tence by income level when groups of children with the same number of risk factors were compared. They concluded that income seems to make a major dif-ference in child development not because it is an overarching variable in itself, but because it is strongly associated with a combination of other familial and extrafa-milial risk factors. For example, in their study of adolescents in almost 500 families in Philadelphia who varied widely in SES and racial composition, 39% of poor children lived in high-risk families with more than seven risk factors, whereas only 7% of affluent children did. The cumulative risk measure has been employed in numerous studies with economically diverse samples of children and adoles-cents. In general, these studies report that as the number of risk factors increases, the number or severity of behavioral and psychological problems increases and the level of cognitive functioning decreases (e.g., Ackerman, Brown, & Izard, 2004; Mistry, Benner, Biesanz, Clark, & Howes, 2010).

Scholars who study childhood poverty as a focal or overarching variable do so partly because income poverty both precipitates and thwarts efforts to miti-gate adverse conditions and recurring stressors and stands as a distinctly common correlate of these conditions and stressors. Undoubtedly, evidence that chronic poverty is more detrimental to children's development than transitory poverty (Duncan & Brooks-Gunn, 1997) is rooted partly in the fact that chronic poverty, compared to transitory poverty, is more strongly linked to a range of adverse con-ditions, recurring stressors, and risk factors. Another key impetus for the focus on income poverty is that it is generally easier to design and implement programs that alter family income (e.g., increasing welfare benefits, tax credits, and mini-mum wage) than programs that modify the many family- and context-related risk factors with which it is correlated (e.g., low parental education, neighborhood poverty) (Duncan, Yeung, Brooks-Gunn, & Smith, 1998). Family income below a certain threshold is a common criterion for participation in many child- and adolescent-focused programs and interventions that aim to prevent or ameliorate some of the behavioral, cognitive, and attitudinal correlates of poverty and life circumstances linked to poverty.

SOCIAL SELECTION PERSPECTIVE

Proponents of social selection perspectives argue that individual-level personality and cognitive traits are major contributors to poverty and that failure to take these individual characteristics into account results in an overestimation of the environmental effects of poverty (Mayer, 1997; Rowe & Rodgers, 1997). Detailed in her book, *What Money Can't Buy*, Mayer used five analytic strategies for estimating what she termed the *true* effect of income on children's development—that is, the effect of income after controlling all parental characteristics, both observed and unobserved, that might influence parents' income and children's outcomes. One strategy, for example, involved comparing various sources of parental income in relation to child outcomes on the grounds that some sources of income (e.g., interest or child support payments) are less strongly related to parental traits than are other sources (e.g., earnings); the extent to which income from the former sources correlate with child outcomes is therefore considered a better estimate of income's *true* effect. Another strategy involved comparing the apparent effect of parental income measured before an outcome, such as an adolescent dropping out of school, with the apparent effect of parental income after the outcome occurs. If later income predicts an earlier outcome, argues Mayer, it is in a sense a proxy for parental characteristics that existed before the outcome. Mayer points out that parental characteristics that affect children's outcomes "may be partly innate, but even then their expression depends on parents' own childhood experiences and their adult attitudes, values, goals, and predispositions, which are in turn influenced by social structure and institutions" (p. 152).

Based on findings from research using the five analytic strategies, Mayer concluded that (a) "conventional" models of the relationship between parental income and children's outcomes (such as those used in the studies reviewed in the previous section) overstate the importance of income to children's outcomes, and (b) the effect of income per se on most child outcomes is fairly small and considerably smaller than many researchers have thought, probably because, as Mayer contends, "most children in America, have had their basic material needs met" and that "once children's basic material needs are met, characteristics of their parents become more important to how they turn out than anything additional money can buy" (p. 12).

Mayer's conclusions warrant caution because her analytic strategies, although clever, have significant limitations. As Duncan and Brooks-Gunn (2000) point out, despite evidence that poverty and low income status during early and middle childhood have much stronger links to cognitive ability and school achievement than poverty and low-income status during adolescence (Duncan & Brooks-Gunn,

1997), Mayer's strategies do not estimate differential effects of income for different stages of childhood. They also are not well-suited for estimating the effects of income from different sources at the bottom of the income scale. The analysis comparing various sources of parental income in relation to child outcomes is problematic because income from sources that Mayer argues are less strongly related to parental traits (e.g., interest or child support payments) tends to be miniscule (Duncan & Brooks-Gunn, 2000).

Like Mayer (1997), Rowe and Rodgers (1997) contend that conventional analytic strategies overstate the magnitude of poverty effects on children's development, but their arguments center on the role of genetic endowment. They are critical of investigations conducted within biologically related individuals (as discussed in the previous section) on the grounds that they (a) confound genetic and environmental effects and (b) ignore the possibility that poverty itself, the environments provided by parents, and children's developmental outcomes are influenced by genetic factors. They argue that research should be directed to poverty as the dependent variable rather than the independent variable, with a focus placed on heritable individual differences in abilities and personality characteristics that determine poverty. Behavioral genetic studies are deemed essential to provide strong tests of environmental influences.

These points were core elements of Rowe and Rodgers' (1997) critique of the *Child Development* special issue on Children in Poverty edited by Huston, García Coll, and McLoyd (1994). In their response, Huston, McLoyd, and García Coll (1997) argued that parents' poverty or affluence is partly a function of societal values, public policy, economic and social structural conditions, and opportunity structures available to them as a consequence of their race, ethnicity, gender, and other individual characteristics. They acknowledged that parents' poverty or affluence is likely due in part to individual abilities and personality characteristics and that it is unlikely that relations among family environments and child outcomes are exclusively the result of environmental influences. However, they were critical of Rowe and Rodgers' proposal to rely exclusively on behavioral genetics methods on the grounds that these methods do not measure environment directly and do not include the contributions of any environmental factors other than the parents' level of the characteristic being measured.

Despite advances in research design and methodology in the study of childhood poverty, 15 years after Rowe and Rodgers levied their critique, there is still considerable distance to travel toward truly integrative research that incorporates strong assessment of genetic and biological constructs with a sophisticated view and appraisal of the environment at both the individual and social structural levels.

INTERACTIONIST PERSPECTIVE

One step in this direction is a conceptual model proposed by Conger et al. (2010) that incorporates both social selection and social causation processes. A recent study using a three-generational dataset involving 271 European-American rural families found empirical support for this model (Schofield et al., 2011). Consistent with the social selection perspective, *alpha* personality characteristics (i.e., high levels of agreeableness and conscientiousness, low levels of neuroticism) of future parents (second-generation) measured in adolescence (ninth and tenth graders) predicted their adulthood SES (indexed by per capita income and educational attainment), level of family stress (e.g., economic pressure, parental psychological distress, marital conflict), and emotional investments in their children (e.g., parental warmth, monitoring, consistent discipline). These relations held even when controlling for the SES and emotional investments of their own (first-generation) parents. The personality characteristics of future parents in adolescence directly predicted their children's (third-generation) secure attachment and indirectly predicted children's academic competence and prosocial behavior via emotional investments, family stress, SES, and material investments. These findings lend support to the social selection hypothesis that earlier personal characteristics predict later social circumstances and behaviors. However, except for secure attachment, children's adaptive functioning was not directly predicted by their parents' personality measured in adolescence; rather, the linkages were more indirect. Consistent with the social causation perspective, after controlling for parents' personality during adolescence, (a) parents' SES significantly predicted their material (but not emotional) investments in the child, and (b) family stress and parental investments directly predicted children's adaptive functioning. Although parents' personality predicted family stress and emotional investments, it did not account for the association between parental investments and child functioning. Replications of multigenerational studies of the kind Schofield et al. (2011) conducted, but with samples drawn from different racial and ethnic groups, have the potential to yield important insights about the role of psychological characteristics and familial processes as contributors and mediators of poverty and whether and how these processes interact with race and ethnicity.

Conclusion

At a time when economic prospects remain grim, the social safety net is weakened, and more and more American families face unemployment and struggle to makes ends meet, research on poverty and children's development has never been more relevant or timely. To this end, we suggest that, in order to advance current knowledge about for whom and under what conditions poverty matters, researchers need to pay greater attention to the broader societal contexts in which children live and the more nuanced approaches to understanding how poverty compromises development. The recent Great Recession, for example, has pushed many families into homelessness for the first time, yet homeless children are underrepresented in child poverty research. Estimates indicate that almost 1 million children were identified as homeless during the 2009–2010 school year, a 42% increase since 2007 (National Center on Family Homelessness, 2010). The unique constellation of risk factors faced by homeless children, as compared with housed poor children, necessitates greater attention to the social and economic conditions that make families vulnerable to experiencing bouts of homelessness and dampen children's life chances (Buckner, Bassuk, Weinreb, & Brooks, 1999).

Another important but currently underdeveloped area of exploration is how parents' investment choices, decisions, and socialization processes are conditioned by more macrolevel economic and societal factors. Findings from some recent work (Chien & Mistry, 2013) highlight the impact of one such macrolevel condition—cost-of-living differences across the United States—on family functioning and children's development. Specifically, differences in children's academic achievement outcomes were partially explained by variations in their experiences at home and school: living in a higher cost-of-living area placed greater constraints on poor (as compared with nonpoor) parents' ability to enroll their children in extracurricular activities and participate in their child's school and increased the likelihood that their child attended less well-resourced schools. As discussed in the complementary chapter by Weisner and Duncan (Chapter 8), enhanced understanding of how and why poverty matters can and should help to inform strategies for intervening in the lives of arguably some of America's most vulnerable citizens.

ONE FINAL CONCLUDING POINT

Empirical documentation of the pathways through which poverty influences child and adolescent development has far outpaced the study of resiliency processes among poor children and adolescents. Many healthy and productive adults grew up in poverty, but we have neither a coherent nor well-developed body of knowledge about the factors and processes that underlie positive developmental trajectories in the face of poverty. More work has focused on resilience in the face of specific stressors (e.g., parental alcoholism, child maltreatment) than resilience in the context of poverty.

Although poverty and low-income status are strongly associated with a highly diverse combination of other risk factors, this reality does not preclude examination of protective processes that mitigate the effects of poverty and the cumulative risks associated with it. Because the research literature on children and adolescents living under conditions of socioeconomic hardship has given so little attention to positive adaptation or competence in general, it is unclear which protective factors are overwhelmed under certain circumstances and which positive outcomes are more common than others. Vigorous and systematic study of these issues is important to inform efforts to mitigate the negative impacts of poverty and enhance positive development in poor children.

References

Ackerman, B., Brown, E., & Izard, C. (2004). The relations between persistent poverty and contextual risk and children's behavior in elementary school. *Developmental Psychology, 40* (3), 367–377.

Adelman, C. (2004). *Principal indicators of student academic histories in postsecondary education, 1972–2000.* Washington, DC: U.S. Department of Education, Institute of Education Sciences.

Benner, A. D., & Kim, S. Y. (2010). Understanding Asian American adolescents' developmental outcomes: Insights from the family stress model. *Journal of Research on Adolescence, 20,* 1–12.

Benner, A. D., & Mistry, R. S. (2007). Congruence of mother and teacher educational expectations and low-income youth's academic competence. *Journal of Educational Psychology, 99,* 140–153.

Borjas, G. (2011). Poverty and program participation among immigrant children. *Future of Children, 21*(1), 247–266.

Buckner, J. C., Bassuk, E. L., Weinreb, L. F., & Brooks, M. G. (1999). Homelessness and its relation to the mental health and behavior of low-income school-age children. *Developmental Psychology, 35,* 246–257.

Cheadle, J. E. (2008). Educational investment, family context, and children's math and reading growth from kindergarten through third grade. *Sociology of Education, 81,* 1–31.

Cheadle, J. E., & Amato, P. R. (2011). A quantitative assessment of Lareau's qualitative conclusions about class, race, and parenting. *Journal of Family Issues, 32,* 679–706.

Chien, N. C., & Mistry, R. S. (2013). Geographic variations in cost of living: Associations with family and child well-being. *Child Development, 84* (1), 209–225.

Conger, R. D., Conger, K. J., & Martin, M. (2010). Socioeconomic status, family processes, and individual development. *Journal of Marriage and Family, 72,* 686–705.

Conger R. D., & Elder, G. H., Jr. (1994). *Families in troubled times: Adapting to change in rural America.* New York: Aldine de Gruyter.

Conger, R. D., Ge, X., Elder, G. H., Jr., Lorenz, F. O., & Simons, R. L. (1994). Economic stress, coercive family process and developmental problems of adolescents [Special issue on children and poverty]. *Child Development, 65,* 541–561.

DeNavas-Walt, C., Proctor, B. D., &. Smith, J. C. (2012). U.S. Census Bureau. *Income, poverty, and health insurance coverage in the United States: 2011 (Current Population Reports, P60-243).* Washington, DC: U.S. Government Printing Office.

Diemer, M. A., & Li, C.-H. (2012). Longitudinal roles of pre-college contexts in low-income youths' postsecondary persistence. *Developmental Psychology, 48,* 1686–1693.

Duncan, G., & Brooks-Gunn, J. (Eds.). (1997). *Consequences of growing up poor.* New York: Russell Sage Foundation.

Duncan, G., & Brooks-Gunn, J. (2000). Family poverty, welfare reform, and child development. *Child Development, 71,* 188–196.

Duncan, G., Huston, A. C., & Weisner, T. S. (2007). *Higher ground: New Hope for the working poor and their children.* New York: Russell Sage.

Duncan, G. J., Yeung, W. J., Brooks-Gunn, J., & Smith, J. R. (1998). How much does childhood poverty affect the life chances of children? *American Sociological Review, 63,* 406–423.

Elder, G. H., Jr. (1974). *Children of the Great Depression: Social change in life experience.*
Chicago, IL: University of Chicago Press.

Elder, G. H., Jr., Nguyen, T., & Caspi, A. (1985). Linking family hardship to children's lives.
Child Development, 56, 361–375.

Evans, G. W. (2004). The environment of childhood poverty. *American Psychologist,*
59, 77–92.

Evans, G. W., & English, K. (2002). The environment of poverty: Multiple stressor exposure, psychophysiological stress, and socioemotional adjustment. *Child Development,*
73, 1238–1248.

Gershoff, E. T., Aber, J. L., Raver, C. C., & Lennon, M. C. (2007). Income is not
enough: Incorporating material hardship into models of income associations with parenting and child development. *Child Development, 78,* 70–95.

Goodman, E. (1999). The role of socioeconomic status gradients in explaining differences
in U.S. adolescents' health. *American Journal of Public Health, 89,* 1522–1528.

Guo, G. (1998). The timing of the influences of cumulative poverty on children's cognitive
ability and achievement. *Social Forces, 77,* 257–288.

Hango, D. (2007). Parental investment in childhood and educational qualifications: Can
greater parental involvement mediate the effects of socioeconomic disadvantage? *Social
Science Research, 36,* 1371–1390.

Hart, B., & Risley, T. R. (1995). *Meaningful differences in the everyday experience of young
American children.* Baltimore, MD: Paul H. Brookes Publishing Co.

Haskins, R., Holzer, H., & Lerman, R. (2009). *Promoting economic mobility by increasing postsecondary education.* Washington, DC: Economic Mobility Project, Pew
Charitable Trust.

Hill, N., Castellino, D. R., Lansford, J. E., Nowlin, P., Dodge, K. A., Bates, J. E., & Pettit, G. S.
(2004). Parent academic involvement as related to school behavior, achievement,
and aspirations: Demographic variations across adolescence. *Child Development, 75,*
1491–1509.

Hoff, E. (2003). The specificity of environmental influence: Socioeconomic status affects
early vocabulary development via maternal speech. *Child Development, 74,* 1368–1378.

Huston, A. C., & Bentley, A. C. (2010). Human development in societal context. *Annual
Review of Psychology, 61,* 411–437.

Huston, A. C., García Coll, C., & McLoyd, V. C. (1994). Special issue on children and poverty. *Child Development, 65* (2)

Huston, A. C., McLoyd, V. C., & García Coll, C. (1997). Poverty and behavior: The case for
multiple methods and levels of analysis. *Developmental Review, 17,* 376–393.

Jarjoura, G. R., Triplett, R. A., & Brinker, G. P. (2002). Growing up poor: Examining the
link between persistent childhood poverty and delinquency. *Journal of Quantitative
Criminology, 18,* 159–187.

Kao, G., & Tienda, M. (1998). Educational aspirations of minority youth. *American Journal
of Education, 106,* 349–384.

Lareau, A. (2003). *Unequal childhoods: Race, class, and family life.* Berkeley: University of
California Press.

Magnuson, K. A. (2007). Maternal education and children's academic achievement during
middle childhood. *Developmental Psychology, 43,* 1497–512.

Mayer, S. (1997). *What money can't buy.* Cambridge, MA: Harvard University Press.

McLoyd, V. C. (1990). The impact of economic hardship on Black families and children: Psychological distress, parenting, and socioemotional development. *Child Development, 61*, 311–346.

McLoyd, V. C. (1998). Socioeconomic disadvantage and child development. *American Psychologist, 53*, 185–204.

McLoyd, V., Aikens, N., & Burton, L. (2006). Childhood poverty, policy, and practice. In W. Damon, R. Lerner, K. A. Renninger, & I. Sigel (Eds.), *Handbook of child psychology: Child psychology in practice* (pp. 700–775). Thousand Oaks, CA: Sage.

McLoyd, V. C., Jayaratne, T., Ceballo, R., & Borquez, J. (1994). Unemployment and work interruption among African American single mothers: Effects on parenting and adolescent socioemotional functioning. *Child Development, 65*, 562–589.

McLoyd, V. C., & Wilson, L. (1990). Maternal behavior, social support, and economic conditions as predictors of distress in children. In V. C. McLoyd & C. Flanagan (Eds.), *New directions for child development: Vol. 46. Economic stress: Effects on family life and child development* (pp. 49–69). San Francisco, CA: Jossey-Bass.

Mistry, R. S., Benner, A. D., Biesanz, J. C., Clark, S. L., & Howes, C. (2010). Family and social risk, and parental investments during the early childhood years as predictors of low-income children's school readiness outcomes. *Early Childhood Research Quarterly, 25*, 432–449.

Mistry, R. S., & Lowe, E. (2006). What earnings and income buy: The "basics", plus "a little extra": Implications for family and child well-being. In H. Yoshikawa, T. S. Weisner, & E. D. Lowe (Eds.), *Making it work: Low-wage employment, family life, and child development* (pp. 173–205). New York: Russell Sage Foundation.

Mistry, R. S., Lowe, E., Benner, A. D., & Chien, N. (2008). Expanding the family economic stress model: Insights from a mixed methods approach. *Journal of Marriage and Family, 70*, 196–209.

Mistry, R. S., Vandewater, E. A., Huston, A. C., & McLoyd, V. C. (2002). Economic well-being and children's social adjustment: The role of family process in an ethnically diverse low-income sample. *Child Development, 73*, 935–951.

National Center on Family Homelessness. (2010). *What is family homelessness? (The problem)*. Retrieved from http://www.familyhomelessness.org/facts.php?p=sm

Parke, R., Coltrane, S., Duffy, S., Buriel, R., Powers, J. French, S., & Widaman, K. F. (2004). Economic stress, parenting and child adjustment in Mexican American and European American families. *Child Development, 75*, 1–25.

Raver, C. C., Gershoff, E. T., & Aber, J. L. (2007). Testing equivalence of mediating models of income, parenting, and school readiness for White, Black, and Hispanic children in a national sample. *Child Development, 78*, 96–115.

Reardon, S. F. (2011). The widening academic achievement gap between the rich and the poor: New evidence and possible explanations. In G. J. Duncan & R. J. Murname (Eds.), *Whither opportunity? Rising inequality, schools, and children's life chances* (pp. 91–115). New York: Russell Sage Foundation.

Rowe, D., & Rodgers, J. (1997). Poverty and behavior: Are environmental measures nature and nurture? *Developmental Review, 17*, 358–375.

Sameroff, A., Bartko, W., Baldwin, A., Baldwin, C., & Seifer, R. (1998). Family and social influences on the development of child competence. In M. Lewis & C. Feiring (Eds.), *Familes, risk, and competence* (pp. 177–192). Mahwah, NJ: Erlbaum.

Sameroff, A., Gutman, L. M., & Peck, S. C. (2003). Adaptation among youth facing multiple risks: Prospective research findings. In S. S. Luthar (Ed.), *Resilience and vulnerability: Adaptation in the context of childhood adversities* (pp. 364–391). New York: Cambridge University Press.

Schofield, T. J., Martin, M., Conger, K., Neppl, T., Donnellan, M., & Conger, R. (2011). Intergenerational transmission of adaptive functioning: A test of the interactionist model of SES and human development. *Child Development, 82*, 33–47.

Schoon, I., Parsons, S., & Sacker, A. (2004). Socioeconomic adversity, educational resilience, and subsequent level of adult adaptation. *Journal of Adolescent Research, 19*, 383–404.

Snow, C. E. (2006). What counts as literacy in early childhood? In K. McCartney & D. Phillips (Eds.), *Handbook of Early Childhood Development* (pp. 274–294). Malden, MA: Blackwell.

Solantaus, T., Leinonen, J. A., & Punamäki, R. L. (2004). Children's mental health in times of economic recession: Replication and extensions of the family economic stress model in Finland. *Developmental Psychology, 40*, 412–429.

Taylor, A. Z., & Graham, S. (2007). An examination of the relationship between achievement values and perceptions of barriers among low-SES African American and Latino students. *Journal of Educational Psychology, 99*, 52–64.

Votruba-Drzal, E. (2006). Economic disparities in middle childhood development: Does income matter? *Developmental Psychology, 42*, 1154–1167.

Wadsworth, M. E., Raviv, T., Compas, B. E., & Connor-Smith, J. K. (2005). Parent and adolescent responses to poverty-related stress: Tests of mediated and moderated coping models. *Journal of Child and Family Studies, 14*, 283–298.

Wadsworth, M. E., Santiago, C. D., Einhorn, L., Etter, E., Rienks, S., & Markman, H. J. (2011). Preliminary efficacy of an intervention to reduce psychosocial stress and improve coping in low-income families. *American Journal of Community Psychology, 48*, 257–271.

Wood, D., Kaplan, R., & McLoyd, V. C. (2007). Gender differences in the educational expectations of urban, low-income African American youth: The role of parents and the school. *Journal of Youth and Adolescence, 36*, 417–427.

{ 8 }

The World Isn't Linear or Additive or Decontextualized

PLURALISM AND MIXED METHODS IN UNDERSTANDING THE EFFECTS OF ANTIPOVERTY PROGRAMS ON CHILDREN AND PARENTING

Thomas S. Weisner and Greg J. Duncan

Understanding how work-based support policies might improve the lives of parents and their children is fundamental for informed social policy. We use the example of the New Hope antipoverty intervention to illustrate the plural pathways and diverse responses of working poor parents and families to a well-designed and well-implemented support program. As members of the MacArthur Foundation's Network on Successful Pathways through Middle Childhood directed by Jacque Eccles, the authors, Aletha Huston, and Vonnie McLoyd were part of the program's evaluation team. Robert Granger, then at MDRC, was also a member and provided us with opportunities to add family- and child-based content to the evaluation. Key program publications include Bos, Duncan, Gennetian, and Hill (2007); Duncan, Huston, and Weisner (2007); and Weisner (2011a).

New Hope was a policy experiment that operated for three years in Milwaukee, Wisconsin. It was created by a coalition of community activists and business leaders who believed that work was the best route out of poverty. New Hope provided a set of work supports for full-time workers—parents and nonparents, men and women—that would lift them out of poverty as well as provide subsidies for essential benefits in the form of health insurance and child care subsidies for people who needed them. If a participant was unable to find a job owing, say, to lack of work experience or a criminal record, the program provided opportunities for temporary community service jobs (CSJs) that paid the minimum wage but still entitled that person to program benefits. All participants had access to help from a caseworker who provided information about jobs, educational opportunities, child care, and other community resources in an atmosphere of respect.

Taken together, New Hope offered a cafeteria of benefits from which participants could choose—a feature that could allow families with diverse needs and circumstances to tailor the program to their own unique situations. In fact, New

Hope benefits were available for any eligible adult, but the New Hope family and child study focused on adults with children aged 1 to 10 living in their household when New Hope started.

Some of the work-support programs developed in the 1990s to support work and reduce poverty, such as New Hope, share some common characteristics (Morris, Huston, Duncan, Crosby, & Bos, 2001). In contrast to such distal policy changes as tax reform or eligibility rules for a program, they engaged directly with low-income adults, with professional staff supporting and monitoring the participants. Some offered a suite of benefits and supports that participants could choose from, rather than being fixed. Program participation and benefits depended on participant actions—in the case of New Hope, working 30 hours or more a week, submitting pay stubs, and maintaining program contact. Also important to some poverty reduction programs, and especially true for New Hope: New Hope's strong focus on making low-wage work "work out" for low-income families made it the most likely to benefit children. Child care and health care benefits are direct examples of such supports, but increased income of course could also benefit children.

At the same time, however, some aspects of the New Hope program might have made it tougher for parents and less beneficial for children. For example, increased work outside the home without available child care might have pressured parents to find care or to leave children at home without other caregivers. The stress of low-wage work could have spilled over into parenting behaviors or further reduced already-fragile and barely sustainable daily routines for these households. The additional income might have gone for purposes other than those directly or indirectly benefiting children. Hence, our study intended to test potential costs as well as benefits for children.

New Hope was relatively generous in its suite of benefits available if participants worked. Other work support programs might offer only help getting a job or only income supplements, for example. A comparison of 10 work support programs showed that those with both employment support and income supplements were more successful in boosting family income and leading to school achievement gains for young children (Morris, Gennetian, & Duncan, 2005). The broader context for these work support programs were proposals to improve existing welfare programs to both support families and children and increase employment and income.

How we initially thought impacts on children might happen is depicted in the logic model shown in Figure 8.1; on balance, we proposed positive impacts. New Hope's work incentive provisions were expected to improve children's resources and contexts in a number of ways. Higher family income was expected to improve children's material well-being by reducing episodes of food insufficiency, improving housing and neighborhood conditions, and enabling parents to buy books and other beneficial forms of cognitive stimulation for their children. Child care subsidies should enable parents to arrange for higher quality child care and participation in community programs. Health care subsidies should increase access to needed health care services. All of these features, plus New Hope's supportive

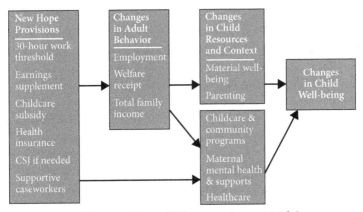

FIGURE 8.1 *New Hope's theory of change (CSJ, community service jobs).*

counselors, were thought likely to improve maternal mental health and parenting. Children could benefit from any of these improvements.

As we planned the evaluation, we considered the model depicted in Figure 8.1 as providing the most promising basis for our conceptual thinking and empirical procedures. We thought that if we could measure the components of adult behavior, child resources and contexts, and child well-being identified in Figure 8.1 and then estimate program impacts on these components and outcomes, we should be able to gauge which of the direct and indirect paths in the model accounted for New Hope's impacts on children. Those calculations might reveal, for example, that most of New Hope's impacts on children came about because of improvements in children's living standards (e.g., less hunger or residential instability) or because of improvements in parents' mental health and parenting beliefs and behaviors. These ideas were consistent with research showing that both family stress and parental investment could potentially be pathways for child impacts, both positive and negative (see McLoyd, Mistry, & Hardaway, Chapter 7).

These kinds of logic models are common in the program evaluation literature. They implicitly assume a prototypic program participant whose attainments and behaviors may change in response to the program and whose actions, in turn, may help (or harm) her children's developmental trajectories. Individual participants may react in different ways to the program's incentives or mandates, but this "treatment heterogeneity" is largely ignored and almost never conceptualized fully or explicitly included in the logic model. Instead of anticipating contextual and individual diversity, most models search for *the* one set of pathways that best account for the program's treatment. This largely implicit presumption of the "averaged, generalized effect" of an intervention and the "average, generalized, normative" subject (e.g., the average parent and child in the analysis) as the focus for research findings is very common in biomedical research, as well as in social evaluation programs.

We proposed that the imagined average subjects who would be so affected, and the homogenous, main-effect model that explains why, are, in reality, exceptional.

Useful for analytic purposes? Yes. Useful for full scientific understanding? Very insufficient. Hence our title: the world is not linear or additive or context-independent. It is fair to say that most researchers, policy makers, practitioners, and participants alike all know this. Yet this is too seldom an integral part of our research in the poverty field and many other areas covered in this volume as well. Modeling and providing evidence for these complex factors could improve our theory and policy/practice alike. Fortunately, for being able to address these issues, it is relatively well understood how heterogeneous the poor and working-poor populations are in the United States today and still more so how diverse they are from an international, European, or global, cross-cultural perspective (Brown, Larson, & Saraswathi, 2002; Rainwater & Smeeding, 2003; Sutcliffe, 2001; UNICEF, 2012).

Our mixed-method investigation of New Hope led us to embrace rather than ignore program treatment heterogeneity. At every step, we discovered a story of diverse pathways rather than unsullied main effects leading to the hoped-for program outcomes. We describe several such ways in which even strong, well-implemented interventions like New Hope might expect a range of pathways from program launch to long-term follow-up impacts.

These surprises began with participants' take-up of the New Hope program itself. What low-income family *would not* take up New Hope's $5,000 worth of annual earnings supplements, health care and child care supplements, and assistance from program specialists? As it turned out, lots of them. Although the vast majority of families eligible for New Hope's benefit package took up at least some of the benefits at least once during their 3-year eligibility period, less than one-third could be considered persistent program participants. We describe how the prior experiences and current lives of New Hope participants affected New Hope program use, and why spells of program use and nonuse did not translate directly into the times in which children may have benefited from the program.

More generally, we highlight the empirical findings of diverse pathways from New Hope program to New Hope outcomes because uncovering such findings are the exceptions rather than the rule in evaluation research. This has significant implications for the ability of further demonstration studies to build on their results. Many successful programs have the potential to be expanded or scaled up in other communities, agencies, cities, counties, states, or nationally. Yet actual instances of scale-up based on programs with strong evidence followed by fidelity of subsequent scale-up are rare. Understanding what happens in the "black box" of a program—the intervention, community responses, households and families, employers, classrooms, and so forth—is essential for knowing how to extend it to the next site, as well as replication on a larger scale (i.e., across multiple sites or nationwide). Granger, Tseng and Wilcox (Chapter 13) point out that practitioners who do want to use the results of research look for such contextually informed evidence, not simply averaged, generalized, decontextualized results. The New Hope program and research team attempted to find out what actually happened when the New Hope intervention engaged with participants, their families, and their households. Our efforts to so do supported our scientific understanding of the study findings, led to possible revisions in our theory and logic model, and even suggested analyses to discover how the program was working.

New Hope's Evaluation

Evidence of New Hope's effectiveness comes from a random-assignment evaluation commissioned by the New Hope Board and conducted by the nonprofit policy evaluation firm MDRC. One-half of the 1,357 individuals who applied for the program were randomly selected to participate in New Hope for 3 years ($n = 678$); the remaining half formed a comparison group that was excluded from New Hope ($n = 679$). Potential applicants were told about the program and then offered the chance to be in a lottery with a 50–50 chance of being in New Hope. Most agreed and became the 1,357 study individuals. All lived in Milwaukee's two poorest zip codes and continued to be eligible for all other federal, state, and local programs (and to be subject to the rules of those programs) during a period of rapidly changing welfare and poverty policies in Wisconsin and across the nation. Both groups enjoyed the fruits of Milwaukee's strong economy in the mid-1990s, and both could claim the increasingly generous federal and state Earned Income Tax Credit (EITC) that supplements the earnings of low-income workers.

With work, poverty, and welfare dominating the public debate over welfare reform at the time, the New Hope research team monitored the implementation of the program and tracked patterns of employment, earnings, and receipt of Food Stamps and cash assistance through administrative records (Brock, Doolitte, Fellerath, & Wiseman, 1997). Two, five, and eight years after participants entered the program, adult participants, school-aged children, and their teachers were surveyed about a variety of topics, including job histories, family changes, economic circumstances, mental health, and child well-being.

For a close-up view of how the program was affecting families, part of the evaluation team conducted in-depth interviews during 3 years of periodic family visits to a representative group of 44 parents and their children, selected at random from both the program and control groups. An additional visit was made 5 years after the program ended (i.e., 8 years after baseline). In all, an average of seven home visits were conducted with each family; most visits involved conversations about the study topics, using the ecocultural family interview (EFI) (Weisner, 2011b), as part of a focused, family-level ethnography (Weisner, Gibson, Lowe, & Romich, 2002).

The conversational format EFI interview takes the parent through his or her daily routine of activities, focusing on the features of each key activity and its importance for the participant (Bernheimer & Weisner, 2007). The EFI is a guided conversation rather than a question-response format, as in a survey instrument. Prompts around topics important to our study, as well as those identified as important to the participant, were used to guide the conversation. There were no false negatives: if a participant did not bring up a topic, the EFI prompted the participant about that topic. For example, if an informant did not bring up her children's fathers or the roles of fathers in their lives, we raised the topic. Fieldworkers also took field notes following each visit, and sometimes took parents and children to lunch or shopping. Several of our fieldwork team members also were involved in the analysis of the quantitative data and assisted in the integration of quantitative and qualitative evidence. Data analysis was facilitated through use of the web-based qualitative software, Dedoose.com, that enabled all team members access to the field notes and interviews, and to index and code them online (Lieber, Weisner, & Presley, 2003; Lieber & Weisner, 2010).

For each part of the New Hope story, we were able to draw on the qualitative data from our 44 families to help us understand the story of the program and how participants experienced New Hope in the contexts of work and family life. Weisner (2012) points out the rapid growth of mixed-methods research in anthropology and throughout the social sciences, and Yoshikawa, Weisner, Kalil, and Way (2008) review the use of such methods and designs specifically for human development and intervention studies.

In the case of New Hope, we used these qualitative data in a variety of ways. We discovered patterns in the lives of the qualitative family sample that then led to analyses using the full quantitative/survey sample. Findings from the analyses of the full quantitative study were sometimes puzzling, did not turn out as anticipated, or showed impacts that were not easy to explain. We turned to the qualitative family stories to explicate these results. We used exemplar families to illustrate findings from the full study in full holistic context—describing what the parents and children and households were like who fell into different outcome patterns. We also analyzed the qualitative data on its own: How did parents deal with budgeting? What did they do with household members with disabilities and health problems? What were their experiences with job discrimination, or having to work nonstandard hours? What were their stated goals and values around the work–family well-being balance in their lives? We talked to the children at the 8-year follow-up (when they were between ages 9 and 19) as well, asking them about family, school, work and other goals, and things they liked and did not like. In the following sections, we provide examples of these kinds of mixed-methods analyses, along with the overall New Hope impact story.

Summary of Program Impacts

New Hope's impacts were assessed through comparisons of outcomes between New Hope families and children in the experimental group and those families and children in the control group. New Hope's random assignment design enabled us to attribute any program–control group differences we observed in child and family well-being to the effects of the New Hope program rather than to individual, family, or other local factors.

Averaged across the first 3 years of program operation, New Hope increased employment for program group parents relative to controls by about 5 percentage points and annual earnings by about $500. New Hope attracted both nonworkers and full-time workers, and employment impacts varied accordingly. For adults who were working less than full time when they signed up for the program, New Hope boosted payroll-based employment by 7 percentage points and annual earnings by about $1,000. New Hope's community service jobs played an important role in these impacts, accounting for about a third of the gains in employment while the program was in operation because many adults were ready for employment and, once there, could access the New Hope benefits. For those already working full time when they enrolled, the program generally sustained employment, although fewer New Hope participants than members of the control group worked more than 50 hours per week, which suggests that some full-time workers used program benefits to finance reductions in overtime or multiple jobs. This finding provides a valuable example of how to select and interpret our outcomes from interventions like New Hope. If the focal outcome is increased work hours and earnings, then full-time workers in New Hope show a negative program impact. But if we recognize that work–family balance for low-wage workers, as for all workers, is important, and if workers themselves describe their intentions in this way, then a reduction of work hours can be understood as a positive result for this group of participants (Bos, Huston, Granger, Duncan, Brock, & McLoyd, 1999).

Based on administrative information on earnings and transfer income, poverty rates were dramatically lower for New Hope than for control families with young children—17 percentage points lower in the first year, 12 points lower in the second and third years, and 8 points lower in the 2 years after New Hope benefits stopped (Huston et al., 2003). Although New Hope failed to eliminate poverty among all of its families, it was clearly more successful in lifting families out of poverty than were the collection of programs available in Wisconsin in the mid-1990s. Poverty reduction was perhaps the most important goal for New Hope's designers.

Arguably, New Hope's greatest success was its positive impact on school achievement and positive behavior among children, especially boys. Expressed in SAT-type standard deviation units, teachers ranked the average child in a New Hope family 25 points higher in achievement than the average child in a comparison family after 2 years of program operation. The impact on boys' achievement (+33 points) was considerably larger than the impact for girls (+12 points). Teachers also rated the boys in New Hope families much more favorably than boys in control families on such indicators of social competence as obeying rules in school, being admired and well-liked by other students, and being self-reliant. They reported fewer disciplinary problems and less frequent behavior problems—less arguing, disturbing others, social withdrawal, or sadness. Impacts for girls were often smaller than those observed for boys and not statistically significant; indeed, teachers rated New Hope girls as somewhat more disobedient and aggressive than girls in control families. Notably, the teachers who provided these evaluations of children in their classrooms were unaware of which children were in the New Hope program or control group (Huston et al., 2001, 2005).

At the point of the 8-year follow-up, some 5 years after the end of the program, New Hope children outperformed control group children in terms of social skills, parent-child and peer relationships, and emotional well-being; however, there were no enduring impacts on delinquency or problem behavior (Huston et al., 2011). New Hope youth viewed work more favorably and were more optimistic about their educational and occupational prospects. They were also more likely than control group youth to be gainfully employed and learning the rudiments of money management (e.g., by having a bank account; McLoyd, Kaplan, Purtell, & Huston, 2011).

Despite these generally positive results, New Hope's impacts were, in fact, selective: it assisted some parents and children, but not others, and those it assisted were helped in different ways. The New Hope benefits were also selectively taken up and used by participants, even though all had access to a full complement of fairly substantial benefits (as intended by the designers of the program). One might have thought that the cost-benefit calculation from program participation would have led many more parents to fully participate in New Hope. However, many did not, and our analyses looked for reasons why.

These and other results from the New Hope study were often unexpected and surprising. Expressed as averaged, generalized program impacts on averaged, generalized normative participants, New Hope did well and showed that it could operate in the real world of work and poverty programs in Wisconsin. But a closer look at which groups benefited from which elements of New Hope tells a far more nuanced, nonlinear, and nonadditive story. The discovery of what happened in New Hope, and understanding how and why it affected families, depended on a strong study design that integrated qualitative and quantitative methods and considered the meanings, ways of reasoning, and everyday practices of the parents and children in the assessment and their understanding of the program (Duncan et al., 2007; Yoshikawa, Weisner, & Lowe, 2006; Lowe & Weisner 2004; Weisner, 2005).

Findings from Integrating Qualitative and Quantitative Evidence Both Complicates and Helps Explain the New Hope Experiment

Figure 8.2 illustrates a combination of impact analyses, correlational outcomes, and qualitative, mixed-methods findings from our study. Although we are not able to detail all 10 findings in this chapter, Duncan et al. (2007) and Yoshikawa et al.

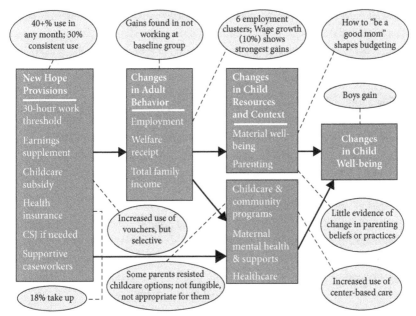

FIGURE 8.2 *New Hope's theory of change with some study findings added (CSJ, community service jobs).*

(2006) present these and other findings, placing the overall successful impacts of the New Hope experiment in context.

- In any given month during the intervention, only 40% to 45% of participants were using any New Hope benefits, and those who did were not using them all. About 30% used New Hope fairly consistently, but even this group did not typically use all of the benefits or use New Hope during the full period it was operating (Gibson & Weisner, 2002). About 15% had lives too troubled and chaotic to take up New Hope, and about 20% did not understand the program clearly. Another 35% or so were strategic users, and the remaining 30% tried to use New Hope regularly.
- New Hope had the greatest employment impacts on adults who were not working when New Hope started, at baseline, but then used the supports to obtain and sustain work. New Hope parents employed full time when the program began actually reduced their work hours relative to their control group counterparts. Our interviews with the treatment and control families in the ethnographic sample helped suggest why. Parents working full time at baseline sometimes used New Hope supports to cut back from working two jobs or working overtime in order to stay home more with their children or for other personal reasons, and to spend more time in other activities that mattered to them a great deal, such as church and family. Some already had benefits at their jobs and so did not

need New Hope benefits, and others working nonstandard hours (nights, swing shifts, weekends) decided to do so less often.

- Fieldworkers noticed that families with one or two circumstances keeping them from working seemed to be more likely to take up New Hope and sustain employment. Barriers to sustaining work included not having a high school diploma, having criminal justice system records, having several young children to care for, having children in their household with developmental or other troubles requiring extra care and attention (Bernheimer, Weisner, & Lowe, 2003), and having little work experience. Katherine Magnuson, then a fieldworker and graduate student at Northwestern University, created a set of indicators identifying work barriers and used the survey data on families to confirm that those with one such barrier were the most likely to use New Hope and demonstrate gains from the program, compared with those with no barriers or more than two barriers (Magnuson, 1999). Those with many work barriers struggled to get and keep employment, which of course is part of New Hope's social contract with participants, and many also needed supports that New Hope could not itself provide. Those with no work barriers sustained work without needing New Hope supports in many cases.

- Parents selectively used the available child care vouchers (Lowe, Weisner, Geis, & Huston, 2005). Some did not feel they could or should leave their younger children (Hispanic parents were more likely to say this in our qualitative conversations). Looking to the far lower right of Figure 8.2, however, shows that there was more use of center-based child care for those parents who started off using the vouchers. New Hope participation significantly increased the use of center-based child care from 29% to 44%. Many told us that they now were more likely to use such care and, in fact, did so in our longitudinal follow-ups.

- There were diverse trajectories of employment over time—the six employment clusters shown in one of the circles in Figure 8.2 include about 10% who not only kept employed but were in jobs in which their wages rose. But another 10% rapidly cycled from one job to another for only a few months at a time without wage growth. Even larger groups kept full-time work but wages remained below average, others kept stable work, and still others worked part time off and on. Younger, better educated adults with cars available were more likely to show wage growth and stable work (Yoshikawa et al., 2006).

- Mistry and colleagues (Mistry & Lowe, 2006; Mistry, Lowe, Benner, & Chien, 2008) explored how parents' budgeting for their households and particularly spending for children was motivated by their need to meet monthly bills, but also by cultural and identity issues. Parents sometimes wanted to be good enough parents in part by being able to take their kids out to restaurants once in a while, go to the malls or on other shopping trips together, and buy them clothes and toys that they believed mattered. This is what some parents described as what a "good mom" does in America. Doing these things often meant deferring other expenses (phone, gas and home heating services, repairs) that might seem more important to an outsider for the ongoing conditions of everyday life and therefore more pressing, but which to parents fit with their preferences.

- It was gratifying to see that some children whose parents were in the New Hope group showed school achievement and behavior gains. It was surprising, however, to find that New Hope led to increased engagement in school and higher aspirations for boys, although not for girls (Duncan et al., 2007; Huston et al., 2003). Our qualitative interviews suggested some of the likely reasons for this. Parents expressed more fears for their sons' safety and progress in school and saw more danger in their neighborhoods for them. Parents were somewhat more likely to invest resources in boys, put them in after-school programs, and monitor them. A number of parents appeared to make different investments in boys and girls based on their unfortunately well-founded concerns about the dangerous neighborhood and peer contexts facing their boys. These differences in risks for boys (and the relative gains for boys whose parents had been in New Hope) persisted into adolescence, well after the New Hope program ended.

Conclusion

Our mixed-method work led us to rethink the logic model depicted in Figure 8.1, at least for this population and this program. Some of the paths anticipated in Figure 8.1 did not matter. The parenting path, for instance, proposed that New Hope participation would have a direct effect on parents, which then might benefit children indirectly. We had expected that parents might feel more positive about their work experiences or more effective or empowered as regular wage earners, and this might lead to more positive parenting. Conversely, we also thought parents might be more stressed and have less time for their children due to increased work hours, work hassles, nonstandard hours required for their work, and so forth, and so New Hope participation could lead to more negative consequences. Yet, neither pathway was found in New Hope; there was little evidence that mothers in the New Hope program group, even that subgroup with increased work hours and program participation, changed their parenting beliefs to any extent compared with control mothers. More broadly, the work, family, and other goals and values we asked parents about did not vary a great deal and did not determine program outcomes in and of themselves, when taken out of context. As more than one mother said about the kinds of jobs they hoped for and family goals they had, "I just want what everyone wants" (Weisner, 2006).

Figure 8.2 suggests what a revised pathway model would need to incorporate—and this only includes the selected findings we have mentioned in this chapter—there are more! Furthermore, if we dimmed down the quantitative associations that were not confirmed and added other pathways that were found, a different version of Figure 8.2 would emerge. This is, after all, our research goal—namely, to look not only for the impacts of a program like New Hope but to enhance and revise the theory and conceptual framework based on the research, to better anticipate and understand work-family-parenting-human development connections going forward.

New Hope's designers, its funders, many participants, and the New Hope research team wanted New Hope to be a success. We all shared the goals of reducing poverty in working-poor households and bringing the strongest suite of methods and analyses we could to the study. The moral core of New Hope "contained the principle that a full-time working mother should not be poor, uninsured, or forced to entrust young children to unsafe or uncaring child-care providers because she cannot afford to pay for better child care" (Duncan et al., 2007, p. 66). We shared a commitment to answer two common questions: Could New Hope reduce poverty and improve family and child well-being and, if so, how? Integrating qualitative and quantitative evidence helped answer these common questions. Because the world we hope to better represent is not linear nor additive nor independent of context, an integrated mixed-methods approach using quantitative and qualitative data is likely to better represent that world and so advance our scientific understanding.

References

Bernheimer, L. P., & Weisner, T. S. (2007). "Let me just tell you what I do all day...": The family story at the center of intervention research and practice. *Infants and Young Children, 20,* 192–201.

Bernheimer, L. P., Weisner, T. S., & Lowe, E. D. (2003). Impacts of children with troubles on working poor families: Mixed-methods and experimental evidence. *Mental Retardation, 41,* 403–419.

Bos, J., Huston, A., Granger, R., Duncan, G., Brock, T., & McLoyd, V. (1999). *New Hope for people with low incomes: Two-year results of a program to reduce poverty and reform welfare.* New York: MDRC.

Bos, J. M., Duncan, G. J. Gennetian, L. A., & Hill, H. D. (2007). *New Hope: Fulfilling America's promise to "make work pay."* Washington DC: The Brookings Institution, The Hamilton Project.

Brock, T., Doolittle, F. Fellerath, V., & Wiseman, M. (1997). *Creating New Hope: Implementation of a program to reduce poverty and reform welfare.* New York: MDRC.

Brown, B. B., Larson, R. W., & Saraswathi, T. S. (2002). *The world's youth: Adolescence in eight regions of the globe.* Cambridge: Cambridge University Press.

Duncan, G. J., Huston, A. C., & Weisner, T. S. (2007). *Higher ground: New Hope for the working poor and their children.* New York: Russell Sage Foundation.

Gibson, C. M., & Weisner, T. S. (2002). "Rational" and ecocultural circumstances of program take-up among low-income working parents. *Human Organization, 61,* 154–166.

Huston, A. C., Duncan, G. J., Granger, R., Bos, J., McLoyd, V. C., Mistry, R., & Ventura, A. (2001). Work-based anti-poverty programs for parents can enhance the school performance and social behavior of children. *Child Development, 72,* 318–336.

Huston, A. C., Duncan, G. J., McLoyd, V. C., Crosby, D. A., Ripke, M. N., Weisner, T. S., & Eldred, C. A. (2005). Impacts on children of a policy to promote employment and reduce poverty: New Hope after five years. *Developmental Psychology, 41,* 902–918.

Huston, A. C., Gupta, A. E., Walker, J. T., Dowsett, C. J., Epps, S., R., Imes, A. E., & McLoyd, V. C. (2011). The long-term effects on children and adolescents of a policy providing work supports for low-income parents. *Journal of Policy Analysis and Management, 30,* 729–754.

Huston, A. C., Miller, C., Richburg-Hayes, L., Duncan, G. J., Eldred, C. A., Weisner, T. S., et al. (2003). *New Hope for families and children: Five-year results of a program to reduce poverty and reform welfare.* New York: MDRC.

Lieber, E., & Weisner, T. S. (2010). Meeting the practical challenges of mixed methods research. In C. Teddlie & A. Tashakkori (Eds.), *Methods in social and behavioral research* (pp. 559–579). Thousand Oaks, CA: Sage.

Lieber, E., Weisner, T. S., & Presley, M. (2003). EthnoNotes: An internet-based field note management tool. *Field Methods, 15,* 405–425.

Lowe, E. D., & Weisner, T. S. (2004). "You have to push it—who's gonna raise your kids?": Situating child care in the daily routines of low-income families. *Children and Youth Services Review, 25,* 225–261.

Lowe, E. Weisner, T. S., Geis, S., & Huston, A. C. (2005). Child care instability and the effort to sustain a working daily routine: Evidence from the New Hope ethnographic study of low-income families. In C. Cooper, C. Garcia Coll, T. Bartko, H. Davis, & C. Chatman (Eds.), *Hills of gold: Diverse pathways through middle childhood* (pp. 121–144). Mahwah, NJ: Erlbaum.

Magnuson, K. (1999). "Appendix K—The barrier indicator index." In J. Bos, A. C. Huston, R. Granger, G. J. Duncan, T. Brock, & V. C. McLoyd (Eds.), *New Hope for people with low incomes: Two-year results of a program to reduce poverty and reform welfare* (pp. 346–355). New York: MDRC.

McLoyd, V. C., Kaplan, R., Purtell, K. M., & Huston, A. C. (2011). Assessing the effects of a work-based antipoverty program for parents on youths' future orientation and employment experiences. *Child Development, 82,* 113–132.

Mistry, R. S., & Lowe, E. D. (2006). What earnings and income buy. The "basics" plus "a little extra": Implications for family and child well-being. In H. Yoshikawa, T. S. Weisner, & E. D. Lowe (Eds.), *Making it work: Low-wage employment, family life, and child development* (pp. 173–205). New York: Russell Sage Foundation.

Mistry, R. S., Lowe, E. D., Benner, A. D., & Chien N. (2008). Expanding the family economic stress model: Insights from a mixed-methods approach. *Journal of Marriage and Family, 70,* 196–209.

Morris, P. A., Gennetian, L. A., & Duncan, G. J. (2005). Effects of welfare and employment policies on young children: New findings on policy experiments conducted in the early 1990's. *SRCD Social Policy Report,19*(2), 3–18.

Morris, P. A., Huston, A. C., Duncan, G. J., Crosby, D. A., & Bos, J. M. (2001). *How welfare and work policies affect children: A synthesis of research.* New York: MDRC.

Rainwater, L., & Smeeding, T. M. (2003). *Poor kids in a rich country: America's children in comparative perspective*. New York: Russell Sage.

Sutcliffe, B. (2001). *100 ways of seeing an unequal world*. London: Zed Books.

UNICEF. (2012). *Measuring child poverty: New league tables of child poverty in the world's rich countries. Innocenti Report Card, No. 10*. Florence, Italy: Innocenti Research Center.

Weisner, T. S. (Ed.). (2005). *Discovering successful pathways in children's development: Mixed methods in the study of childhood and family life*. Chicago: University of Chicago Press.

Weisner, T. S. (2011a). "If you work in this country you should not be poor, and your kids should be doing better": Bringing mixed methods and theory in psychological anthropology to improve research in policy and practice. *Ethos, 39*, 455–476.

Weisner, T. S. (2011b). The Ecocultural Family Interview: New conceptualizations and uses for the study of illness. In S. Bonchini & M. R. Baroni (Eds.), *Sviluppo e salute del bambino: Fattori individuali, sociali e cultuari. In ricordo di Vanna Axia [Child Development and Health: Individual, Social and Cultural Factors. In Memory of Vanna Axia.]Padua, Italy: CLEUP*

Weisner, T. S. (2012). Mixed methods should be a valued practice in anthropology. *Anthropology News, 53*(5), 3–4.

Weisner, T. S., Gibson, C., Lowe, E. D., & Romich, J. (2002). Understanding working poor families in the New Hope program. *Poverty Research Newsletter, 6*, 3–5.

Weisner, T. S., Yoshikawa, H., Lowe, E. D., & Carter, F. (2006). "I want what everybody wants": Goals, values, and work in the lives of New Hope families. In H. Yoshikawa, T. S. Weisner, & E. D. Lowe (Eds.), *Making it work: Low-wage employment, family life and child development* (pp. 147–172). New York: Russell Sage Press.

Yoshikawa, H., Lowe, E. D., Weisner, T. S., Hsueh, J., Enchautegui-de-Jesus, N., Gassman-Pines, A., et al. (2006). Pathways through low-wage work. In H. Yoshikawa, T. S. Weisner, & E. D. Lowe (Eds.), *Making it work: Low-wage employment, family life, and child development* (pp. 27–57). New York: Russell Sage Press.

Yoshikawa, H., Weisner, T. S., Kalil, A., & Way, N. (2008). Mixing qualitative and quantitative research in developmental science: Uses and methodological choices. *Developmental Psychology, 44*, 344–354.

Yoshikawa, H., Weisner, T. S., & Lowe, E. D. (Eds.). (2006). *Making it work: Low-wage employment, family life and child development*. New York: Russell Sage.

Schools and Neighborhoods

THE MICROCOSMS OF CHILDHOOD

9

Neighborhood and School Contexts in the Lives of Children

Elizabeth T. Gershoff and Aprile D. Benner

Perhaps the most salient of the contexts of children's lives outside the home are the neighborhoods in which they live. Neighborhoods determine the quality and variety of physical environments in children's daily lives, the peers with whom children will play, the adults they will have as role models, the amount of violence and chaos to which they will be exposed, and, often, the schools that they will attend. Indeed, the majority of U.S. school-aged children (73%) attend "neighborhood schools" (National Center for Education Statistics [NCES], 2009), revealing that neighborhoods and schools are inextricably linked for the majority of children. This chapter explores several parallel aspects of neighborhoods and schools that are known to affect how children grow and develop, namely the quality and climate of these contexts, exposure to violence within these contexts, and transitions within and mobility between contexts. Our focus is on school-aged children from elementary through high school. Throughout, we pay particular attention to what is known about how each of these contexts changes over time and how these changes relate to children's development.

Neighborhoods as Contexts of Development

The study of neighborhood influences on individuals began as an effort by sociologists to understand social problems that were observed to cluster at the neighborhood level, particularly poverty and crime. The first major study of neighborhood effects by Shaw and McKay (1942) proposed a social disorganization theory to explain why crime tended to cluster in a few communities. They found that concentrations of crime were situated in neighborhoods with high levels of economic hardship, residential instability, and race and ethnic heterogeneity, characteristics that they argued undermined community social ties and community-based social controls, thereby making crime more likely. The notion that social connections among neighborhood residents determine its quality would carry forward through the next several decades of research. Indeed, the next highly influential work on neighborhoods, Wilson's (1987) *The Truly Disadvantaged*, argued that residents of neighborhoods with concentrations of poverty and disadvantage experience isolation from the social norms, resources, opportunities, and role models available to residents in nonpoor neighborhoods. This social isolation, in turn, is responsible, Wilson argued, for the increased rates of antisocial behaviors and risk behaviors in disadvantaged communities. In their reviews of research on poor neighborhoods, Jencks and Mayer (1990) and Leventhal and Brooks-Gunn (2000) identified several mechanisms by which living in a poor neighborhood might affect children, including a lack of role models, poor monitoring and supervision, negative peer influences, inferior or scarce institutional resources, and the competition and deprivation that are a result of scarce resources.

In the years since these investigators spearheaded the study of neighborhood effects on children and families, research has focused on a few key aspects. We discuss three such aspects in this chapter, namely neighborhood climate, violence, and instability.

NEIGHBORHOOD QUALITY AND CLIMATE

The most salient aspect of neighborhood quality is the physical state of the neighborhood. Most research in this regard has focused on negative aspects of neighborhoods, under the assumption that, to paraphrase Tolstoy, happy neighborhoods are all alike, but unhappy neighborhoods are unhappy in their own ways. Raudenbush (2003) has noted that some negative neighborhood characteristics are problematic from a public health perspective (e.g., garbage, drug paraphernalia, broken glass), whereas others are of concern because they may facilitate criminal behavior (e.g., vacant buildings, broken streetlights, lack of police presence, loitering). Although not noted by Raudenbush (2003), living in run-down neighborhoods can be discouraging and depressing, which take an emotional toll on the families living in them.

Efforts to link objective neighborhood quality (as opposed to perceived quality, which will be discussed later) to developmental outcomes have increased in recent years. Evans (2006), in particular, has focused attention on several harmful aspects of the physical environment that affect children's development, including noise, crowding, and pollution. Methods for characterizing physical neighborhoods have included intensive ones that involve videotaping and coding every city block (Sampson & Raudenbush, 1999) to modern methods that code the street-view pictures of blocks in Google (Odgers, Caspi, Bates, Sampson, & Moffitt, 2012). Using such methods, Odgers and colleagues (2012) found that observed neighborhood disorder, decay, and dangerousness were associated with higher child antisocial behavior whereas positive neighborhood features, such as safety and recreational space, were associated with healthy weight and prosocial behaviors in children.

In contrast to the physical environment and resources of a neighborhood that are objective characteristics, perceived *climate* is the subjective experience of living in a particular neighborhood and typically refers to interactions among neighborhood residents. Of particular interest has been the level of neighborhood social cohesion, or the strength of the social bonds among individuals in a community. Because children in socially cohesive neighborhoods feel they can trust and rely on their neighbors, they may be more likely to spend time outside their homes engaging in positive activities. Indeed, youth engage in more frequent physical activity when they live in socially cohesive neighborhoods, over and above other neighborhood and individual-level characteristics (Cradock, Kawachi, Colditz, Gortmaker, & Buka, 2009). Also, elementary school children in socially cohesive neighborhoods display higher verbal ability and fewer behavior problems as mediated through positive parenting, over and above the neighborhood socioeconomic characteristics (Kohen, Leventhal, Dahinten, & McIntosh, 2008).

A neighborhood construct closely related to social cohesion is that of *collective efficacy* or *social control*, which refers to levels of monitoring and social pressure exerted by members of a community to achieve shared goals (Sampson, Raudenbush, & Earls, 1997). Collective efficacy can affect youth both directly, by discouraging delinquent or socially inappropriate behavior, and indirectly, by ensuring that neighborhoods are safe places for them to spend time. Levels of social control have been linked with child and youth outcomes. One study that included objective measures of neighborhood disadvantage (e.g., percent of residents in a tract who are poor) along with measures of collective efficacy and mothers' perceptions of neighborhood quality (e.g., "My neighborhood is clean and attractive") found that both objective and subjective neighborhood indicators were only indirectly associated with youth internalizing problems through their associations with family cohesion and parent-child conflict (Deng et al., 2006). Living in neighborhoods with high collective efficacy has also been shown to buffer children against other risks in their lives. High neighborhood collective efficacy moderates the association of maternal hostility with child externalizing problems (Silk, Sessa, Morris, Steinberg, & Avenevoli, 2004), the association of early neglect with later externalizing behavior problems (Yonas et al., 2010), and the association of local alcohol retailers and sales on underage drinking (Maimon & Browning, 2012).

NEIGHBORHOOD VIOLENCE

Exposure to violence is a frighteningly common experience in the lives of American children. A recent national survey revealed that 61% of all children have been exposed to some form of violence, with 37% having been directly assaulted and 19% having witnessed an assault in their neighborhoods (Finkelhor, Turner, Ormrod, Hamby, & Kracke, 2009). Neighborhood violence can affect children indirectly by straining social ties, forcing children indoors, and creating a climate of danger and mistrust, or directly by exposing children to violence as either witnesses or victims. The majority of research on neighborhood violence has, understandably, been focused on its direct impacts on children and youth.

Two of the main ways that neighborhood violence exposure directly impacts youth are by causing emotional stress and trauma that can affect long-term mental health and by negatively biasing their processing of social information and thereby increasing the likelihood that they engage in aggressive and antisocial behavior (Gershoff & Aber, 2006). Accordingly, a large literature has linked exposure to violence with children's mental health and an increased likelihood of engaging in aggressive and antisocial behavior (e.g., Aber, Gershoff, Ware, & Kotler, 2004; Lynch, 2003; Margolin, Vickerman, Oliver, & Gordis, 2010). Exposure to neighborhood violence has also been linked with physical problems, such as higher levels of somatic complaints (e.g., headache; Jones, Foster, Forehand, & O'Connell, 2005) and reduced levels of academic achievement (Milam, Furr-Holden, & Leaf, 2010).

Despite this focus on direct effects of neighborhood violence in the literature, some effort has also been made to establish indirect links between neighborhood-level rates of violence to individual child outcomes. One study using a national dataset (Add Health) found that high aggregate neighborhood-level violence, over and above individual-level violence exposure, predicted lower rates of high school graduation and higher rates of teenage pregnancy (Harding, 2009). Another study linked neighborhood measures of violence, operationalized as recent homicides in Chicago neighborhoods, to children's academic test scores, but without controls for individual-level violence exposure (Sharkey, 2010). However, a third study of more than 700 youth in New York City found that although the associations between direct violence exposure (youth-reported) and youth depression and conduct disorder symptoms were consistent, neighborhood-level violence (city-reported rates of violent crimes, youth arrests, youth deaths, and child abuse) did not predict youth mental health over and above direct violence exposure (Gershoff, Gilster, & Aber, 2012). Given these inconsistent findings, more studies are needed to clarify whether merely living in a neighborhood characterized by daily violence has the potential to indirectly impact children and adolescents.

NEIGHBORHOOD MOBILITY

"Moving on up" from a lower income, lower resource neighborhood to a higher income, higher resource neighborhood has long been part of the American dream. Unfortunately, many moves are precipitated by declines in family economic circumstances and as such involve either downward or at least lateral mobility. In a test of the differential impacts of upward versus lateral mobility, Sharkey and Sampson (2010) compared the violence experiences of youth in Chicago whose families voluntarily moved within the city (lateral mobility) with youth whose families moved from the city to the suburbs (upward mobility). They found clear differences, with moves within the city predicting increased risk for violent behavior, violence exposure, and violent victimization, and moves outside the city predicting reductions in violent behavior and exposure to violence.

As with much research seeking to attribute causal influences to neighborhoods (Duncan & Raudenbush, 1999; Sampson, Morenoff, & Gannon-Rowley, 2002), selection bias is inherent in studies of neighborhood mobility impacts. Because families do not move at random but rather do so based on a set of socioeconomic characteristics (e.g., parent education), family economic conditions (e.g., parent's job promotion), and values (e.g., importance of child going to a better-resourced school), the effects of neighborhood moves cannot be divorced from the effects of these other aspects of children's and youth's lives. The true test of whether a move to a better neighborhood is beneficial would in fact be to make it random—in other words, to randomly assign families that are otherwise equal in socioeconomic characteristics and prospects to move or not. The Moving to Opportunity (MTO) project, sponsored by the U.S. Department of Housing and Urban Development, was just such an experiment. MTO is discussed at length in the chapter by Crosnoe and Leventhal (Chapter 10), but the take-away was that moving low-income families to low-poverty neighborhoods had minimal impacts on youth mental health and no effects on education, health, and risk behavior.

Regardless of the reason for moves or the type of moves (upward, downward, or lateral), high neighborhood mobility can be a disruptive experience in children's lives because it involves separation from familiar social networks and settings, including schools. In support of the role social networks play in mediating the influence of residential mobility on children and youth, adolescents who experienced residential mobility between school years were found to report diminished intimacy with close friends, although they rebounded to levels similar to nonmovers by within a year of the move (Vernberg, Greenhoot, & Biggs, 2006). Several aspects of child and youth behavior have thus been linked with residential mobility. The number of residential moves has been linked with lower academic performance as well as to higher rates of risk behavior, including increased likelihood of engaging in violence (Hagan, MacMillan, & Wheaton, 1996; Haynie & South, 2005; Pribesh & Downey, 1999). These negative impacts appear to stretch across the life course, with the number of childhood moves being associated with lower levels of psychological well-being in adulthood (Shigehiro & Schimmack, 2010).

Schools as Contexts of Development

Moving to the school context, we review three lines of research concerning the effects of schools on the lives of young people. Specifically, parallel to the neighborhood research just reviewed, we provide an overview of the extant literature on school climate, violence in schools, and school transitions and student mobility. For each area, we identify the influences of schools' structural characteristics—features such as school size, race/ethnic composition, or the wealth/poverty of the students served—as well as how each facet is linked to the academic and socioemotional development of children and adolescents.

SCHOOL CLIMATE

Since the beginning of the 20th century, scholars have been interested in how schools as communities of learners and educators influence students' academic and psychosocial development (Cohen, McCabe, Michelli, & Pickeral, 2009). Although there is general consensus that school climates have repercussions for young people's development across domains, variation exists in ideas about exactly what school climate comprises. For the purposes of this chapter, we use the broad view provided by Cohen and colleagues that defines school climate as "the quality and character of school life…reflect[ing] norms, goals, and values" of those in the school community (Cohen et al., 2009, p. 182). We view school climate as multidimensional in nature, tapping into students' feelings of connectedness and belonging to their schools, the fairness of rules, and the interpersonal relationships formed within the school walls.

How the structural characteristics of schools impact the various aspects of school climate is an area of recent study. Particular emphasis has been placed on how the size of the student body influences students' perceptions of school climate, under the assumption that larger schools should be more impersonal, bureaucratic, and difficult for students to navigate. Yet, across elementary and secondary schools, it appears that school size is of little consequence for students' feelings of belonging, perceptions of rule fairness, or the quality of student-teacher relationships (Fan, Williams, & Corkin, 2011; Koth, Bradshaw, & Leaf, 2008). More limited attention has been placed on how the socioeconomic composition of the student body might influence students' perceptions of school climate. Although attending school with more affluent peers may hold limited benefits for students' sense of school belonging and connectedness (Battistich, Solomon, Watson, & Schaps, 1997), such benefits do not seem to extend to perceptions of other aspects of the school climate (Koth et al., 2008).

The implications of school climate for young people's well-being are well-established, particularly in relation to academic achievement and educational progress. Students who feel as if they belong to their schools, who deem school rules fair and discipline strategies as reasonable, and who report positive relationships with their teachers generally express stronger engagement in school, exhibit greater academic motivation and earn higher grades (Hopson & Lee, 2011; Jia et al., 2009). Moreover, those students who express more positive views of their school's climate are more likely to persist in school and less likely to drop out (Reyes, Gillock, Kobus, & Sanchez, 2000). The impacts of positive school climates extend beyond the academic realm. For example, studies using nationally representative data on

U.S. secondary students from the Add Health study find that positive perceptions of school climate are tied to fewer mental health challenges and lower levels of substance use and other risky health behaviors (Anderman, 2002; Blum, McNeely, & Nonnemaker, 2002). Similar benefits for socioemotional well-being are observed at the elementary level (Battistich et al., 1997).

SCHOOL VIOLENCE

When Americans think about school violence, they typically think of rare, high-profile incidents, such as the school shootings at Columbine, or of gang-related assaults that are fairly restricted to high-poverty, underresourced urban schools. Yet, it is a sad fact that violence in schools is more frequent and widespread and, as a result, more mundane than most Americans are aware. Bullying remains common in school, with over a quarter (28%) of all 12- to 18-year-olds reporting that they had been bullied in the 2009–10 school year (Robers, Zhang, Truman, & Snyder, 2012). Levels of severe violence, which include physical assaults, assaults with weapons, sexual assaults, and robbery with weapons, are also disturbingly common at 4% (translating into an estimated 2 million student victims of severe violence at school; Robers et al., 2012). The majority of schools across the country report problems with violence; in the 2009–10 school year, 64% of all public elementary schools and 91% each of both middle and high schools reported at least one serious violent incident (Robers et al., 2012). The school context is the setting for much of the violence to which children are exposed; in a recent national survey of children and youth, 61% of all peer victimization, including assaults and property victimization, occurred in schools (Turner, Finkelhor, Hamby, Shattuck, & Omrod, 2011).

As with community violence, exposure to school violence, including both bullying and more severe incidents, either as a witness or a victim, can exact a toll on students' mental health. Among both elementary and secondary students, violence victimization in schools is linked with greater anxiety, depression, posttraumatic stress disorder (PTSD) symptoms, and general trauma, as well as with violent behavior (Turner et al., 2011). School violence also directly impacts students' school performance because students who report that their schools are dangerous have a decreased sense of school-based self-efficacy (Bowen, Richman, Brewster, & Bowen, 1998). Exposure to violence in schools has often been linked with a particular form of anxiety: fear and avoidance of school. In 2009, 4% of students reported that they were afraid of being assaulted at school, and 5% reported they avoided school out of fear of being attacked (Robers et al., 2012); although small as percentages of the population, if these rates from national surveys are extrapolated to the 49 million children in the K–12 education system (NCES, 2009), they translate to an estimated 2 million children fearing assaults at school and 2.5 million children avoiding school out of such fear.

TRANSITIONS AND MOBILITY

The U.S. K–12 educational system contains three basic levels—elementary, middle, and high school—and is characterized by structured transitions into and out of each. Although these transitions are normative (i.e., these school moves are expected and are generally consistently timed across American schools), they can still be disruptive for young people. Of the three transitions characterizing the K–12 system, the transition to middle school has received extensive attention, both due to its concurrent timing with the physical transition of puberty and common perceptions regarding the wide-ranging differences between U.S. elementary and middle schools (Eccles, 2004). It was only 25 years ago that Simmons and Blyth's groundbreaking work documented that, although moving into adolescence was disruptive to youth, the transition from elementary to middle school itself was the driving force in explaining early adolescents' declines in educational performance and socioemotional well-being. Subsequent work further supports those initial findings, highlighting declines in grades, school engagement, and feelings of self-worth as students move from elementary to middle school (e.g., Gutman & Midgley, 2000).

Compared to the extensive research based on the transition to middle school, the high school transition remains a relatively understudied phenomenon. A recent review of the extant literature suggests that, like its earlier timed counterpart, the move from middle to high school can be quite disruptive for students' school performance, and it can leave students feeling more anxious and depressed (Benner, 2011). A recent study of students in southern California found that, although students seem to bounce back from transition challenges as they gain more experience in their middle schools, the decreases in mental health and school performance emerging after the high school transition tend to persist (Benner & Graham, 2009). Similar findings were observed in a study examining a cohort of Philadelphia public school students, such that students who experienced greater academic challenges across the high school transition were at particular risk for later school dropout (Neild, Stoner-Eby, & Furstenberg, 2008).

Although school transitions are normative experiences for young people as they move through the K–12 system, non-normative school moves are becoming increasingly common for American youth. By the end of middle school, approximately one-third of U.S. students have changed schools two times, and a similar percentage (31%) have changed schools three times or more (Government Accounting Office [GAO], 2010). Parallel to motivations for neighborhood mobility, school mobility most commonly arises from residential instability tied to economic difficulties, geographic moves tied to parental employment, and family instability linked to parental divorce and/or repartnering (Hanushek, Kain, & Rivkin, 2004). Less common are moves driven by parents' efforts to send their children to higher quality schools or schools that better match their children's individual needs. In looking at who is most likely to be mobile, the GAO (2010) has identified higher mobility rates for children from low-income families, military families, African-American households, and families where English is not the primary language.

These overall patterns, however, mask important variation that links family characteristics to underlying motivations for such school moves. In their study of Texas schools, Hanushek and colleagues (2004) found that mobility across school systems or districts generally involved moving to schools with greater school quality, whereas mobility within school systems did not result in enrollment in higher quality schools. More informative was who moves where: African-American and Latino students and students from low-income families made moves *within* school systems at substantially higher rates than did White students and students from more advantaged families. Similar findings were observed by Alexander and colleagues (1996) in their study of children in the Baltimore public school system.

Because it is less predictable and closely tied to family sociodemographic risk factors, school mobility can disrupt young people's academic performance and educational progress more so than normative school transitions. In their meta-analysis of school mobility during the elementary years, Mehana and Reynolds (2004) found that, on average, mobile students had a 3- to 4-month disadvantage in academic achievement when compared to their nonmobile peers. Two more recent comprehensive examinations of mobility effects during the elementary years (Gruman, Harachi, Abbott, Catalano, & Fleming, 2008) and early adolescence (Ou & Reynolds, 2008) found that school moves were associated with poorer classroom participation, lower academic performance, and poorer educational attainment, even after controlling for sociodemographic characteristics, school-based factors, and the stressful life events that often necessitate such moves (e.g., job loss, divorce). Overall, these findings suggest that although school moves complicated by family stress add an additional layer of difficulty for students as they negotiate their new school settings, the severing of school ties and the tasks of finding one's niche in a new school are challenging above and beyond the underlying reasons for mobility.

Future Directions

Although much has been learned about the influences that neighborhood and school contexts have on children over the past 30 or so years, several gaps remain in our knowledge about how these crucial contexts affect children and about how best to identify and quantify these influences. We thus end our chapter with what we see as three key directions for future research on neighborhoods and schools in children's lives.

THE NEED TO EXAMINE NEIGHBORHOOD AND SCHOOL CONTEXTS SIMULTANEOUSLY

As noted earlier, neighborhoods and schools are typically interdependent, with neighborhoods determining the schools children attend and with schools situated within the physical neighborhoods in which children live. Such physical interdependence between neighborhoods and schools has clear implications for identifying neighborhood or school influences on development. Indeed, it may be impossible to entirely separate their influences, such that there may be no "pure" effect of schools that does not include the influence of the neighborhoods in which the schools are situated.

Limited research has considered neighborhood and school contexts as simultaneous predictors of child and youth outcomes. Among the findings to date are that neighborhood crime and violence are closely linked with levels of violence and crime within schools (Bowen & Van Dorn, 2002; Sheley, McGee, & Wright, 1992) and that school characteristics, such as perceived safety or behavioral norms, can disrupt links between neighborhood characteristics and youths' risky behaviors, such as substance use and sexual initiation (Ennett, Flewelling, Lindrooth, & Norton 1997; Teitler & Weiss, 2000). Cook and colleagues (2002) found neighborhood and school quality to be closely associated but independently influential for children's academic success. More appropriate modeling of multiple contexts using such methods as cross-classified multilevel models (Luo & Kwok, 2009; Meyers & Beretvas, 2006) is found in two studies examining neighborhood and school influences. The first found that the between-school variation in the proportion of sexually active youth was greater than the between-neighborhood variation and that there was virtually no added contribution of neighborhood once school effects were included (Teitler & Weiss, 2000). The second found few school- or neighborhood-level influences on youth mental health over and above individual rates of violence exposure (Gershoff et al., 2012).

THE NEED FOR MORE RESEARCH ON HOW CONTEXTS CHANGE AROUND CHILDREN

In the preceding review, we focused on mobility and children's transitions among contexts as important issues for both neighborhood and school influences on development. Yet, it is also true that neighborhoods and schools are not static; they change around the children who live and learn within them. Throughout the country, urban neighborhoods are transforming through processes of urban renewal or gentrification, while the charter school movement and the strictures of the No Child Left Behind law that require "reorganization" of underperforming campuses have led to radical change in many public K–12 schools. The full impact of these transformations has yet to be appreciated and deserves significant research attention. Although a few attempts have been made to document the existence of change in both neighborhood (Jackson & Mare, 2007; Timberlake, 2009) and school (Saunders & Goldenberg, 2005; Woodside-Jiron & Gehsmann, 2009) contexts, there are very few attempts to link these changes to the welfare of children and youth. Understanding how neighborhood and school transformations affect the children and families within them is an important future direction for research on neighborhood and school effects.

THE NEED FOR MORE MIXED-METHODS APPROACHES

The field's reliance on administrative data to characterize neighborhood and school contexts has meant that much of the influence of these contexts is assumed to be indirect rather than directly experienced. Children may live in an objectively violent neighborhood, but they may have parents who structure their days to protect them from direct exposure to violence. Alternatively, young people may attend schools that are outwardly nonviolent, but they may be the target of incessant bullying. In both cases, individual experiences will differ dramatically from the administrative aggregate data. These mismatches between administrative characterizations of neighborhoods and individuals' own lived experience can lead to an inaccurate estimation of the influence that contexts have on children and youth.

One solution would be to incorporate both individual perspectives and administrative characterizations of neighborhoods and schools simultaneously, an approach often referred to as "mixed-methods" research (see Chapter 8 for an in-depth example of a mixed-methods approach). In their recent call for mixing qualitative and quantitative methods in developmental science, Yoshikawa, Weisner, Kalil, and Way (2008) noted that such mixed-methods approaches are best able to provide a comprehensive understanding of how contexts influence the lives of children and youth. Approaches that follow-up quantitative analyses of neighborhoods and schools with qualitative analyses of individual perspectives garnered through in-depth interviews or focus groups are needed to characterize neighborhood and school influences in children's lives in the most ecologically valid and comprehensive ways possible.

Conclusion

As this chapter illustrates, there has been an exciting focus on understanding the neighborhood and school contexts in which children develop, and much has been learned about how these contexts do, or do not, influence individual development. Yet there is still more work to do in identifying which aspects of neighborhoods and schools are most important for children's development and the processes by which they do so in order to inform interventions in, and reforms of, these two essential contexts of childhood and adolescence.

References

Aber, J. L., Gershoff, E. T., Ware, A., & Kotler, J. A. (2004). Estimating the effects of September 11th and other forms of violence on the mental health and social development of New York City's youth: A matter of context. *Applied Developmental Science, 8,* 111–129.

Alexander, K. L., Entwisle, D. R., & Dauber, S. L. (1996). Children in motion: School transfers and elementary school performance. *The Journal of Educational Research, 90*, 3–12.

Anderman, E. M. (2002). School effects on psychological outcomes during adolescence. *Journal of Educational Psychology, 94*, 795–809.

Battistich, V., Solomon, D., Watson, S., & Schaps, E. (1997). Caring school communities. *Educational Psychologist, 32*, 137–151.

Benner, A. D. (2011). The transition to high school: Current knowledge, future directions. *Educational Psychology Review, 23*, 299–328.

Benner, A. D., & Graham, S. (2009). The transition to high school as a developmental process among multiethnic urban youth. *Child Development, 80*, 356–376.

Blum, R. W., McNeely, C., & Nonnemaker, J. (2002). Vulnerability, risk, and protection. *Journal of Adolescent Health, 31*(S), 28–39.

Bowen, G. L., Richman, J. M., Brewster, A., & Bowen, N. (1998). Sense of school coherence, perceptions of danger at school, and teacher support among youth at risk of school failure. *Child and Adolescent Social Work Journal, 15*, 273–286.

Bowen, G. L., & Van Dorn, R. A. (2002). Community violent crime rates and school danger. *Children & Schools, 24*, 90–104.

Cohen, J., McCabe, E. M., Michelli, N. M., & Pickeral, T. (2009). School climate: Research, policy, practice, and teacher education. *Teachers College Record, 111*, 180–213.

Cook, T. D., Herman, M. R., Phillips, M., & Settersten, R. A., Jr. (2002). Some ways in which neighborhoods, nuclear families, friendship groups, and schools jointly affect changes in early adolescent development. *Child Development, 73*, 1283–1309.

Cradock, A. L., Kawachi, I., Colditz, G. A., Gortmaker, S. L., & Buka, S. L. (2009). Neighborhood social cohesion and youth participation in physical activity in Chicago. *Social Science & Medicine, 68*, 427–435.

Deng, S., Lopez, V., Roosa, M. W., Ryu, E., Burrell, G. L., Tein, J., & Crowder, S. (2006). Family processes mediating the relationship of neighborhood disadvantage to early adolescent internalizing problems. *Journal of Early Adolescence, 26*, 206–231.

Duncan, G. J., & Raudenbush, S. W. (1999). Assessing the effects of context in studies of child and youth development. *Educational Psychologist, 34*, 29–41.

Eccles, J. S. (2004). Schools, academic motivation, and stage-environment fit. In R. M. Lerner & L. Steinberg (Eds.), *Handbook of adolescent psychology* (pp. 125–153). Hoboken, NJ: John Wiley & Sons.

Ennett, S. T., Flewelling, R. L., Lindrooth, R. C., & Norton, E. C. (1997). School and neighborhood characteristics associated with school rates of alcohol, cigarette, and marijuana use. *Journal of Health and Social Behavior, 38*, 55–71.

Evans, G. W. (2006). Child development and the physical environment. *Annual Review of Psychology, 57*, 423–451.

Fan, W., Williams, C. M., & Corkin, D. M. (2011). A multilevel analysis of student perceptions of school climate: The effect of social and academic risk factors. *Psychology in the Schools, 48*, 632–647.

Finkelhor, D., Turner, H., Ormrod, R., Hamby, S., & Kracke, K. (2009, October). *Children's exposure to violence: A comprehensive national survey. OJJDP Juvenile Justice Bulletin.* Retrieved from: https://www.ncjrs.gov/pdffiles1/ojjdp/227744.pdf

Gershoff, E. T., & Aber, J. L. (2006). Neighborhood and school contexts of the mental health and risk behaviors of children and youth. In L. Balter & C. Tamis-LeMonda

(Eds.), *Child psychology: A handbook of contemporary issues* (2nd ed., pp. 611–645). New York: Psychology Press/Taylor & Francis.

Gershoff, E. T., Gilster, M. E., & Aber, J. L. (2012). Identifying home neighborhood, school neighborhood, and school context effects on youth mental health and behavior problems: A cross-classified random effects multilevel approach. *Manuscript under review*

Government Accounting Office. (2010). *K–12 education: Many challenges arise in educating students who change schools frequently.* Washington DC: GAO.

Gruman, D. H., Harachi, T. W., Abbott, R. D., Catalano, R. F., & Fleming, C. B. (2008). Longitudinal effects of student mobility on three dimensions of elementary school engagement. *Child Development, 79*, 1833–1852.

Gutman, L. M., & Midgley, C. (2000). The role of protective factors in supporting the academic achievement of poor African American students during the middle school transition. *Journal of Youth and Adolescence, 29*(2), 223–248.

Hagan, J., MacMillan, R., & Wheaton, B. (1996). New kid in town: Social capital and the life course effects of family migration on children. *American Sociological Review, 61*, 368–385.

Hanushek, E. A., Kain, J. F., & Rivkin, S. G. (2004). Disruption versus Tiebout improvement: The costs and benefits of switching schools. *Journal of Public Economics, 88*, 1721–1746.

Harding, D. J. (2009). Collateral consequences of violence in disadvantaged neighborhoods. *Social Forces, 88*, 757–784.

Haynie, D. L., & South, S. J. (2005). Residential mobility and adolescent violence. *Social Forces, 84*, 361–374.

Hopson, L. M., & Lee, E. (2011). Mitigating the effect of family poverty on academic and behavioral outcomes: The role of school climate in middle and high school. *Children and Youth Services Review, 33*, 2221–2229.

Jackson, M. I., & Mare, R. D. (2007). Cross-sectional and longitudinal measurements of neighborhood experience and their effects on children. *Social Science Research, 36*, 590–610.

Jencks, C., & Mayer, S. (1990). The social consequences of growing up in a poor neighborhood. In L. Lynn & Mc-Geary (Eds.), *Inner-city poverty in the United States* (pp. 111–186). Washington, DC: National Academy Press.

Jia, Y., Way, N., Ling, G., Yoshikawa, H., Chen, X., Hughes, D., et al. (2009). The influence of student perceptions of school climate on socioemotional and academic adjustment: A comparison of Chinese and American adolescents. *Child Development, 80*(5), 1514–1530.

Jones, D. J., Foster, S., Forehand, G., & O'Connell, C. (2005). Neighborhood violence and psychosocial adjustment in low-income urban African American children: Physical symptoms as a marker of child adjustment. *Journal of Child and Family Studies, 14*, 237–249.

Kohen, D. E., Leventhal, T., Dahinten, V. S., & McIntosh, C. N. (2008). Neighborhood disadvantage: Pathways of effects for young children. *Child Development, 79*, 156–169.

Koth, C. W., Bradshaw, C. P., & Leaf, P. J. (2008). A multilevel study of predictors of student perceptions of school climate: The effect of classroom level factors. *Journal of Educational Psychology, 100*, 96–104.

Leventhal, T., & Brooks-Gunn, J. (2000). The neighborhoods they live in: The effects of neighborhood residence on child and adolescent outcomes. *Psychological Bulletin, 126*, 309–337.

Luo, W., & Kwok, O. (2009). The impacts of ignoring a crossed factor in analyzing cross-classified data. *Multivariate Behavioral Research, 44*, 182–212.

Lynch, M. (2003). Consequences of children's exposure to community violence. *Clinical Child and Family Psychology Review, 6*, 265–274.

Maimon, D., & Browning, C. R. (2012). Underage drinking, alcohol sales and collective efficacy: Informal control and opportunity in the study of alcohol use. *Social Science Research, 41*, 977–990.

Margolin, G., Vickerman, K. A., Oliver, P. H., & Gordis, E. B. (2010). Violence exposure in multiple interpersonal domains: Cumulative and differential effects. *Journal of Adolescent Health, 47*, 198–205.

Mehana, M., & Reynolds, A. J. (2004). School mobility and achievement: A meta-analysis. *Children and Youth Services Review, 26*, 93–119.

Meyers, J. L., & Beretvas, S. N. (2006). The impact of inappropriate modeling of cross-classified data structures. *Multivariate Behavioral Research, 41*, 473–497.

Milam, A. J., Furr-Holden, C. D. M., & Leaf, P. J. (2010). Perceived school and neighbour-hood safety, neighborhood violence and academic achievement in urban school children. *Urban Review, 42*, 458–467.

National Center for Education Statistics, U.S. Department of Education. (2009). *The Condition of Education 2009 (NCES 2009-081)*. Retrieved from:

Neild, R. C., Stoner-Eby, S., & Furstenberg, F. (2008). Connecting entrance and departure: The transition to ninth grade and high school dropout. *Education and Urban Society, 40*, 543–569.

Odgers, C. L., Caspi, A., Bates, C. J., Sampson, R. J., & Moffitt, T. E. (2012), Systematic social observation of children's neighborhoods using Google Street View: a reliable and cost-effective method *Journal of Child Psychology and Psychiatry, 53*, 1009–1017.

Ou, S.-R., & Reynolds, A. J. (2008). Predictors of educational attainment in the Chicago Longitudinal Study. *School Psychology Quarterly, 23*, 199–229.

Pribesh, S., & Downey, D. B. (1999). Why are residential and school moves associated with poor school performance? *Demography, 36*, 521–534.

Raudenbush, S. W. (2003). The quantitative assessment of neighborhood social environments. In I. Kawachi & L. F. Berkman (Eds.), *Neighborhoods and health* (pp. 112–131). New York: Oxford.

Reyes, O., Gillock, K. L., Kobus, K., & Sanchez, B. (2000). A longitudinal examination of the transition into senior high school for adolescents from urban, low-income status, and predominantly minority backgrounds. *American Journal of Community Psychology, 28*(4), 519–536.

Robers, S., Zhang, J., Truman, J., & Snyder, T. (2012). Indicators of School Crime and Safety: 2011 (NCES 2012-002/NCJ 236021). National Center for Education Statistics, U.S. Department of Education, and Bureau of Justice Statistics, Office of Justice Programs, U.S. Department of Justice. Washington, DC.

Sampson, R. J., Morenoff, J. D., & Gannon-Rowley, T. (2002). Assessing "neighborhood effects": Social processes and new directions in research. *Annual Review of Sociology, 28*, 443–478.

Sampson, R. J., & Raudenbush, S. W. (1999). Systematic social observation of public spaces: A new look at disorder in urban neighborhoods. *American Journal of Sociology, 105*, 603–651.

Sampson, R. J., Raudenbush, S. W., & Earls, F. (1997). Neighborhoods and violent crime: A multilevel study of collective efficacy. *Science, 277,* 918–924.

Saunders, W. M., & Goldenberg, C. N. (2005). The contribution of settings to school improvement and school change: A case study. In C. R. O'Donnell & L. Yamauchi (Eds.), *Culture and context in human behavior change: Theory, research, and applications* (pp. 127–150). New York: Peter Lang.

Sharkey, P. (2010). The acute effect of local homicides on children's cognitive performance. *Proceedings of the National Academy of Sciences, 107,* 11733–11738.

Sharkey, P., & Sampson, R. J. (2010). Destination effects: Residential mobility and trajectories of adolescent violence in a stratified metropolis. *Criminology, 48,* 639–681.

Shaw, C., & McKay, H. D. (1942). *Juvenile Delinquency and Urban Areas.* Chicago: University of Chicago Press.

Sheley, J. F., McGee, Z. T., & Wright, J. D. (1992). Gun-related violence in and around inner-city schools. *American Journal of Diseases of Children, 146,* 677–682.

Shigehiro, O., & Schimmack, U. (2010). Residential mobility, well-being, and mortality *Journal of Personality and Social Psychology, 98,* 980–994.

Silk, J. S., Sessa, F. M., Morris, A. S., Steinberg, L., & Avenevoli, S. (2004). Neighborhood cohesion as a buffer against hostile maternal parenting. *Journal of Family Psychology, 18,* 125–146.

Simmons, R. G., & Blyth, D. A. (1987). *Moving into adolescence: The impact of pubertal change and school context.* Hawthorn: Aldine.

Teitler, J. O., & Weiss, C. C. (2000). Effects of neighborhood and school environments on transitions to first sexual intercourse. *Sociology of Education, 73,* 112–132.

Timberlake, J. M. (2009). "Scratchin' and surviving" or "movin' on up?" Two sources of change in children's neighborhood SES. *Population Research and Policy Review, 28,* 195–219.

Turner, H. A., Finkelhor, D., Hamby, S. L., Shattuck, A., & Omrod, R. K. (2011). Specifying the type and location of peer victimization in a national sample of children and youth. *Journal of Youth and Adolescence, 40,* 1052–1067.

Vernberg, E. M., Greenhoot, A. F., & Biggs, B. K. (2006). Intercommunity relocation and adolescent friendships: Who struggles and why? *Journal of Consulting and Clinical Psychology, 74,* 511–523.

Wilson, W. J. (1987). *The truly disadvantaged: The inner city, the underclass, and public policy.* Chicago: University of Chicago Press.

Woodside-Jiron, H., & Gehsmann, K. M. (2009). Peeling back the layers of policy and school reform: Revealing the structural and social complexities within. *International Journal of Disability, Development and Education, 56,* 49–72.

Yonas, M. A., Lewis, T., Hussey, J. M., Thompson, R., Newton, R., English, D., & Dubowitz, H. (2010). Perceptions of neighborhood collective efficacy moderate the impact of maltreatment on aggression. *Child Maltreatment, 15,* 37–47.

Yoshikawa, H., Weisner, T. S., Kalil, A., & Way, N. (2008). Mixing qualitative and quantitative research in developmental science: Uses and methodological choices. *Developmental Psychology, 44,* 344–354.

10

School- and Neighborhood-Based Interventions to Improve the Lives of Disadvantaged Children

Robert Crosnoe and Tama Leventhal

Schools and neighborhoods share many similarities. They typically include large and diverse assortments of people. They influence and are influenced by the political, economic, and cultural systems in which they are embedded. They are, at their core, physical spaces in which people go about everyday life. At the same time, schools and neighborhoods also differ in important ways. Schools are more physically bounded than neighborhoods, with concrete borders and well-defined spaces, and they are both age-specific (i.e., serving particular age groups) and age-stratified (i.e., divided internally by age). Neighborhoods, because they are more diffuse and serve a broader and often undifferentiated population are, consequently, harder to define. Unlike schools, they also represent the interests and experiences of families as opposed to children themselves (Arum, 2000; Sampson, Morenoff, & Gannon-Rowley, 2002). Because of their similarities and differences, as well as their interdependence, discussing schools and neighborhoods together can be enlightening. In particular, doing so helps to illustrate the promise and peril of connecting research and policy (DeLuca & Dayton, 2009).

Not only have schools and neighborhoods been studied extensively (see Gershoff & Benner, Chapter 9), they also offer numerous examples of small- and large-scale policy interventions in children's lives. Importantly, these interventions have often revealed the complexity of policy interventions aiming to improve the lives of young people and how even research-grounded actions can produce unintended consequences. In this chapter, we delve into this complexity by focusing on a class of school and neighborhood interventions that share the same general spirit: altering the socioeconomic composition of some setting as a means of improving the future prospects of children from economically disadvantaged backgrounds. This topic serves a useful purpose because it represents conceptually parallel policy efforts across settings that have yielded some of the same insights and led to some of the same challenges.

Schools as Contexts for Intervention

From the earliest origins of state-sponsored schooling in the United States, educators have recognized that whom children attend school with matters. Historically, tinkering with school composition has been a fundamental component of managing the education of young people while also serving the broader public interest (Labaree, 1997).

At the societal level, school composition has been viewed as a tool for improving social stability and economic productivity. Here, we discuss composition in socioeconomic terms, but race and ethnicity are also important. The significance of school composition is typified by the "common school" philosophy, the idea that democratic societies should support schools that educate children from diverse walks of life under one roof. Many early architects of the public school system in the United States argued that common schools would enhance society by promoting social cohesion among different segments of the population, thus producing a better educated populace to engage in civic institutions, a better trained labor force, and a meritocratic hierarchy of achievement (Coleman & Hoffer, 1987). On the individual level, school composition has been viewed as a tool for raising the achievement of children from disadvantaged backgrounds. The argument is that redistributing such children across schools serving more advantaged populations will give them more opportunities and resources to pursue their education, offer them entry into more demanding curricula with better instruction, and expose them to sources of cultural and social capital (Arum, 2000; Grant, 2009; Kahlenberg, 2001).

Thus, school diversity serves the interests of students and society, and creating common schools by manipulating the composition of enrollees is a way for the state to achieve these goals. What constitutes diversity and what makes a common school, however, have varied over the years. When the common school philosophy was gaining steam as the public school system was designed and implemented in the 19th century, socioeconomic diversity was prioritized, not racial and ethnic diversity (and, indeed, African-American youth were largely excluded from public schools). Over time, race and ethnicity became the focal point of discussions of school diversity. With the *Brown v. Board of Education* decision by the Supreme Court in 1954, which made racial desegregation of the schools the law of the land, racial (and later ethnic) diversity became the driving force in policy targeting school composition. Decades of court-ordered racial and ethnic desegregation followed, helping to increase interracial interaction and reduce racial and ethnic achievement disparities but also generating social and political conflict in the process (Coleman, Kelly, & Moore, 1976; Cottrol, Diamond, & Ware, 2003; Schofield, 1995).

This conflict culminated in another Supreme Court decision in 2007, *Parents Involved in Community Schools v. Seattle*, which effectively curtailed the use of race and ethnicity as a factor in public school assignment. The justices' opinion high-lighted a return to socioeconomic status (SES) as the primary means of achieving common schools (Bazelon, 2008). This Supreme Court action tapped into wide-spread perceptions that socioeconomic diversity—and achieving it through state action—was less a political hot potato and more a legitimate goal in general than was racial and ethnic diversity. As such, it increased attention to an educational policy movement that had been building for some time: the socioeconomic desegregation of public schools (Clotfelter, Ladd, & Vigdor, 2005; Reardon, Yun, & Eitle, 2001).

Echoing the common school philosophy, the argument behind the socioeco-nomic desegregation movement was that diverse schools would be good for youth and society—they expose students to different groups, address issues of resource equity by educating groups within the same schools, and target the socioeconomic achievement gap as a means of building a meritocracy. At the same time, socio-economic desegregation has the bonus of offering a way to create racial and eth-nic diversity within and across schools without explicitly using race or ethnicity as criteria, given the significant overlap among racial, ethnic, and socioeconomic stratification in the United States. If schools were diverse on SES, the thought was, they would be diverse on race and ethnicity while avoiding the conflicts and ten-sions that often come with focusing on race and ethnicity in educational policy (Grant, 2009; Kahlenberg, 2001; Rothstein, 2004).

WHAT WE KNOW ABOUT THE SOCIOECONOMIC COMPOSITION OF SCHOOLS

The extant evidence base on school composition supports the basic premise of the socioeconomic desegregation movement: namely, that children from more socio-economically disadvantaged backgrounds do better academically when attend-ing schools with more socioeconomically advantaged student bodies. In short, the aggregate SES of the student body (in terms of income, parent education, or other indicators) consistently predicts a variety of academic indicators, includ-ing students' performance on standardized tests (Chubb & Moe, 1990; Rothstein, 2004; Rusk & Mosley, 1996). Although this pattern has been reported by multiple sources, much of the evidence comes from the National Educational Longitudinal Study (NELS), a nationally representative sample of eighth graders in 1988 fol-lowed for more than a decade (Lee, Smith, & Croninger, 1997; Rumberger & Palardy, 2005; Sui-Chu & Willms, 1996).

The general consensus is that this evidence reflects three advantages that can be accrued by children from socioeconomically disadvantaged families who attend more socioeconomically advantaged schools. They will gain access to (1) peers who, because of histories of greater cognitive stimulation and learning supports, will have greater vocabulary, academic skills, and engagement patterns; (2) class-rooms that are better organized and have more enriched curricula, lower student/teacher turnover, more intensive instruction, and more resources; and (3) parent communities with higher levels of involvement, broader networks with more social and cultural capital, and greater capacities to raise funds, demand action, and enforce accountability. These resources allow children from socioeconomically disadvantaged backgrounds to make up some of the achievement gap with their more socioeconomically advantaged peers that precedes even the beginning of school (Coleman & Hoffer, 1987; Kahlenberg, 2001; Mayer, 2002).

As compelling as this evidence base is, it also has limitations. To begin, much of the evidence is based on correlational patterns in survey data. Although informative, such patterns are not strong on causal inference. The possibility that they merely reflect unobserved differences between children from socioeconomically disadvantaged families who select into more advantaged schools and those who do not—an important issue raised in the Gershoff and Benner chapter—is difficult to determine (Crosnoe, 2009; Reardon, Yun, & Kurlaender, 2006).

Studies with causally informed designs (e.g., instrumental variables) suggest that much of the achievement impact of peer SES in socioeconomically diverse schools is not the product of peer SES itself but instead the higher peer achievement that goes along with having more socioeconomically advantaged peers. In other words, what matters is being surrounded by high-achieving students, regardless of their SES. Because socioeconomically advantaged students tend to be higher achieving, their presence can lead to the observation of benefits of having socioeconomically advantaged peers even when that is not the case (Hoxby & Weingarth, 2005).

When the lens is widened to multiple outcomes, studies have revealed that students from socioeconomically disadvantaged families often have worse socioemotional functioning and lower level coursework in schools serving socioeconomically advantaged populations (Crosnoe, 2009). Thus, any achievement gains derived from school socioeconomic diversity are likely to be chipped away if socioeconomic desegregation plans do not also attend to the nonacademic problems associated with mixing diverse students within schools.

Finally, parent education is often a more meaningful dimension of family SES than income in terms of the benefits of socioeconomically diverse schools, but income is the most commonly used indicator of SES in actual desegregation plans because low income is easier to verify (e.g., through tax returns) than low parent education (Crosnoe, 2009; Hoxby & Weingarth, 2005). Despite these important limitations, as well as other issues (e.g., inattention to the mechanisms of observed effects, lack of clarity about critical thresholds or interactive effects), the relevant literature does provide some overall support for the aims of school socioeconomic desegregation. Still, much more needs to be done.

THE SOCIOECONOMIC COMPOSITION OF SCHOOLS AS POLICY

The 2007 *Parents Involved* decision—and its explicit citation of socioeconomic desegregation as an alternative to race- and ethnicity-focused school assignment plans—lent credence to the socioeconomic desegregation movement, but efforts to implement socioeconomic desegregation were already under way before the Supreme Court ruled. In the past two decades, different kinds of socioeconomic desegregation plans have been implemented in several locales, most prominently in Wake County (North Carolina), La Crosse (Wisconsin), Cambridge (Massachusetts), and San Francisco (Flinspach & Banks, 2005; Grant, 2009; Kahlenberg, 2001; Plank, 2000). After the *Parents Involved* decisions, such plans have been pilot-tested in Texas, Kentucky, and Washington (Bazelon, 2008).

The La Crosse and Wake County plans are perhaps the most famous socioeconomic desegregation efforts. In the 1980s, La Crosse was one of the first districts in the nation to implement efforts to increase socioeconomic diversity within its schools, and this plan was made more systematic and extensive a decade later when several new schools were built in the city. The La Crosse plan created explicit representational goals for schools according to the SES of students' families (Plank, 2000). In the early 2000s, the Wake County district began to follow a plan to use busing, magnet programs, and other means to ensure that no school had a proportion of free or reduced lunch-eligible students exceeding 40% of the student body (Grant, 2009).

These plans have received a great deal of attention and, initially at least, were heralded as the future of educational policy in the United States. Yet their implementation did not always go smoothly. Despite the base of research evidence on school compositional benefits for student achievement, the achievement gains realized through these plans were not as large as expected, perhaps reflecting limitations of that research base or the power of nonachievement outcomes of school diversity (e.g., social problems) to interfere with the realization of the final achievement outcomes. At the same time, the plans proved to be highly unpopular over time, with public outcries over the measures used to achieve socioeconomic diversity in schools, the effective loss of neighborhood schools for many, and the uncertainty and fluidity in school assignments from year to year. Tellingly, these complaints came from socioeconomically advantaged parents and socioeconomically disadvantaged parents alike, and they resulted in major turnovers on the local school boards and local governments more generally. Ultimately, public dissatisfaction led to a significant scaling back of the La Crosse plan and to the Wake County plan being overturned (Hoxby & Weingarth, 2005; McCrummen, 2011; Mercer, 2003; Plank, 2000). There is still much to learn about how these plans were sold to and interpreted by the public.

Although not a part of the controversy surrounding the La Crosse and Wake County socioeconomic desegregation plans or others like them, an added complication of increasing socioeconomic diversity in schools goes back to race and ethnicity. Recall that one selling point of socioeconomic desegregation was that the overlap among socioeconomic, racial, and ethnic segregation in the United States would mean that efforts to socioeconomically diversify schools would effectively increase racial and ethnic diversity. Yet this argument has also proven to be too simplistic. Analyses of national data sources, including the U.S. Census, have revealed that racial and ethnic segregation is not entirely overlapping with socioeconomic residential segregation and that the different patterns of each type of segregation (e.g., whether they occur within or across official city boundaries such as school districts) mean that even aggressive socioeconomic desegregation efforts would have only a marginal effect on race and ethnic segregation (Reardon et al., 2006). Thus, although socioeconomic desegregation might have benefits, the "hidden" benefit of increasing racial and ethnic diversity in schools is unlikely to be one.

In sum, interest in the implications of the socioeconomic composition of schools has a long history in research and policy. The combination of a seemingly convincing research base and several political and legal developments led to renewed interest in and action on this issue in recent years. Early momentum, however, seems to have stalled. The socioeconomic composition of schools remains an important topic that warrants continued attention, but this attention needs to do a better job of recognizing the inherent complexities of the issue, both in terms of building a strong foundation of evidence to guide policy action and in terms of recognizing the political and cultural elements that might disrupt even research-grounded actions.

Neighborhoods as Contexts for Intervention

Much like schools, neighborhoods have, for some time, been viewed as potential targets of policy intervention for improving the lives of children and families in the United States. For example, 19th-century social reformers directed their attention to "slum" neighborhoods in which poor, often immigrant, families lived in growing urban industrial centers. These neighborhoods were targeted out of concerns for public health and safety. Despite this early interest in the importance of place, not until the past decade have neighborhoods truly moved to the forefront as a target of intervention for fostering child well-being. This argument is not to discount or ignore the numerous community-based initiatives of the past 50 years (Kubisch, Auspos, Brown, & Dewar, 2010), previous smaller-scale efforts directed at neighborhood composition, or the federal HOPE VI initiative that demolished the most distressed public housing in the poorest neighborhoods to create mixed-income communities (Popkin et al., 2004). Still, a concerted focus on neighborhood composition, child development, and policy action did not come together in any significant way until recently, crystallizing around a 2009 federal initiative, Promise Neighborhoods, to specifically fund place-based change for children and families in poor communities (Komro, Flay, & Biglan, 2011).

The scholarly attention to neighborhood composition discussed by Gershoff and Benner (Chapter 9) in this volume outpaced policy attention during the past century (Sampson & Morenoff, 1997; Sampson et al., 2002). Beginning in the 1920s, Park and Burgess, sociologists at the University of Chicago, studied patterns of urban social changes, which had been sources of concern to urban reformers nearly a decade earlier. They and their successors (e.g., Shaw & McKay, 1942) documented how migration in and out of poor neighborhoods led to socioeconomic conditions that gave rise to related social problems, particularly crime and delinquency. Neighborhood composition—the dimensions of which include high levels of poverty, family disruption, residential instability, and racial and ethnic heterogeneity—was thought to undermine social organization by weakening community institutions and hindering their ability to monitor residents and maintain order, especially in terms of youth peer groups.

Like this early research, contemporary interest in neighborhood socioeconomic composition and its implications for children was fueled by demographic circumstances (Massey & Denton, 1993; Wilson, 1987). With the loss of industrial jobs, rising concentrations of unemployment and poverty and growing segregation in urban centers in the 1970s and 1980s reignited scientific and policy concerns by the 1990s about the consequences of neighborhood composition for children and families (Leventhal & Brooks-Gunn, 2000; Sampson et al., 2002). Much of the focus was and still is on urban neighborhoods that are high in poverty (those with 30% or more of residents living below the poverty threshold) and racial and ethnic minority concentration. Although the field has expanded to consider a wider array of neighborhoods (e.g., suburban) and aspects of socioeconomic composition beyond disadvantage (e.g., affluence), policy attention has remained on poor neighborhoods and, thus, so has the research.

WHAT WE KNOW ABOUT THE SOCIOECONOMIC COMPOSITION OF NEIGHBORHOODS

As with school research, a fair amount of work has addressed how the socioeconomic composition of neighborhoods is associated with children's development. Much of this research has used data collected from the U.S. Decennial Census to examine links between neighborhood socioeconomic composition and a range of child and youth outcomes (controlling for family background characteristics). The census tract (3,000–8,000 residents) or block group (600–3,000 residents) is commonly used to define the neighborhood unit, and the Census provides information on neighborhood sociodemographic characteristics. Separate indicators of disadvantage/poverty (e.g., percentage of poor residents, percentage of female-headed households, percentage of unemployed residents) and advantage/affluence (e.g., median income, percentage of professionals/managers, percentage of residents with college degrees) are frequently examined because the presence of poor or affluent neighbors may have differential associations with child well-being (Jencks & Mayer, 1990). In fact, what this literature indicates is that neighborhood disadvantage places children at risk for adverse social and emotional outcomes, whereas neighborhood advantage is associated with children's favorable schooling outcomes (see Leventhal & Brooks-Gunn, 2000; Leventhal, Dupéré, & Brooks-Gunn, 2009, for reviews; see also Gershoff & Benner, Chapter 9).

The observed links between neighborhood socioeconomic composition and children's development likely operate through mechanisms in other ecologies (e.g., families, peers, schools), many of which were reviewed by Gershoff and Benner in their chapter (e.g., Jencks & Mayer, 1990; Leventhal & Brooks-Gunn, 2000, Sampson et al., 2002). Conceptual and empirical support exists for a number of possible pathways, all of which have implications for policy. First, as proposed by sociologists more than a century ago, neighborhood socioeconomic composition may influence the extent of formal (e.g., police) and informal (e.g., community groups) institutions present to monitor residents' behavior and protect against physical threats. Second, neighborhood socioeconomic composition may affect the quantity and quality of institutional resources available to children, such as schools, health and social services, recreational programs, and the like. If resources are scarce, neighbors may compete for them. Third, neighborhood socioeconomic composition may dictate the types of role models (e.g., employed adults) available to children. Fourth, neighborhood composition may influence children's and families' social networks, which play a role in their connections to resources (including information) and support. Fifth, neighborhood composition is thought to contribute to community norms regarding both parents' and children's behavior; for example, involvement in children's schooling and children's educational expectations, respectively.

More research has considered *whether* neighborhood socioeconomic composition matters for children than *how* it matters, which helps to explain the limited policy attention given to neighborhoods relative to schools. Also important to consider is that associations between neighborhood socioeconomic composition and child development are typically small to moderate once family background is taken into account. Uncertainty about the true nature of neighborhood effects also matters. As in school research, findings linking neighborhood factors to child outcomes are robust, having been replicated across national datasets, neighborhood-based studies, and regional and local samples, but remain debatable because so many are correlational. Because families select neighborhoods, any observed neighborhood effects may be due to unobserved family characteristics associated with neighborhood selection that are also associated with child outcomes (e.g., parental motivation; Duncan, Connell, & Klebanov, 1997). A final impediment to policy action may be that the handful of experimental and quasi-experimental studies emanating from policy efforts have yielded mixed results. We discuss those cases next.

THE SOCIOECONOMIC COMPOSITION OF NEIGHBORHOODS AS POLICY

Policy efforts addressing neighborhood socioeconomic composition and its potential impacts on children's development can take two general forms: (1) person-based approaches that move poor families out of poor (often segregated) neighborhoods into nonpoor neighborhoods and (2) placed-based approaches that change the socioeconomic composition of a neighborhood to reduce poverty (and thereby often racial and ethnic concentration). Systematic research on these policy efforts is limited and has produced ambiguous results.

PERSON-BASED APPROACHES TO NEIGHBORHOOD CHANGE

Person-based approaches have provided some of the very limited experimental and quasi-experimental evidence of neighborhood compositional effects. All of these studies are limited to poor, often racial and ethnic minority families receiving housing assistance who volunteered to participate in mobility programs; like school-based interventions, most programs have emanated from lawsuits. The Gautreaux Program, the oldest such program, was enacted following a 1976 court order to desegregate Chicago's public housing. During its operation from 1976 to 1998, more than 7,000 families were given housing vouchers (or rent subsidies) that were to be used in low-poverty, racially integrated neighborhoods, with a majority of families to be placed outside of the city limits (Rubinowitz & Rosenbaum, 2000). Because of limited housing availability at times, families were placed inside and outside of the city based on housing availability that was presumably random. A study following about 350 of these families found that, 10 years after relocating, poor youth who moved to private housing in affluent suburban neighborhoods were less likely to drop out of high school and more likely to enroll in college preparatory classes and attend college than were youth who moved to private housing in poor urban neighborhoods. Recent work following a larger sample of families through administrative data sources reports that, 15 years later, youth who moved to the suburbs had established their own households in less poor and segregated neighborhoods than did their peers who stayed in the city (Keels, Duncan, Deluca, Mendenhall, & Rosenbaum, 2005). The long-term impacts on educational and economic attainment, however, are unknown, particularly for the larger, more representative sample.

Another court-ordered desegregation effort in Yonkers, New York, in 1985, took a different and more controversial approach. Prior to the decree, the majority of the city's residents were middle-class and White, except for the residents in Southwest Yonkers, where the city's public housing was located. As a response to the court mandate, 200 units of low-rise publicly funded townhouses were constructed in eight primarily White middle-class areas of the city. The construction of the new housing was met with strong public contention among White middle-class residents; however, this opposition eventually abated over time. Residents' initial concerns about potential drops in property values were not borne out (Briggs, Darden, & Aidala, 1999). Unlike the Gautreaux results, a quasi-experimental study following approximately 220 families 7 years after relocating found uniformly unfavorable outcomes in both the schooling and behavioral domains for youth who moved to the new housing compared with their peers from the old neighborhood, about half of whom had families who were on the waitlist for the new public housing (Fauth, Leventhal, & Brooks-Gunn, 2007).

The most recent, well-known, and only true experimental study of neighborhood mobility is the Moving to Opportunity for Fair Housing Program (MTO), which began in 1994. In this study, which Gershoff and Benner also highlighted in their chapter, approximately 4,600 families in public housing in high-poverty neighborhoods (poverty rates of 40% or higher in Baltimore, Boston, Chicago, Los Angeles, and New York City) were randomly assigned to one of three groups: (1) an experimental group whose members received housing vouchers along with special assistance to move into private housing in low-poverty neighborhoods (poverty rates of 10% or lower); (2) a comparison group whose members received housing vouchers to move into private housing in neighborhoods of their choice (i.e., no restrictions on neighborhood poverty rates); or (3) a control group whose members remained in place in public housing in high-poverty neighborhoods (Goering & Feins, 2003). Notably, race was explicitly left out of the mobility criteria, in large part to avoid public controversy, echoing trends in school policy. A 10-year evaluation of MTO revealed that adolescent girls, but not boys, who moved to low-poverty neighborhoods reported better mental health than their peers who remained in public housing in high-poverty neighborhoods. Generally, no program effects on youths' education, crime, or physical health were reported (Sanbonmatsu et al., 2011).

We again draw some parallels to the school research, given the rather mixed results to emerge from these mobility programs. Before doing so, however, we should acknowledge that all of the mobility programs were successful at achieving their goal of moving families to lower poverty neighborhoods. A number of factors may contribute to the mixed results, but the underlying reasons likely vary somewhat across the programs. To begin, moving likely disrupted youths' existing social networks, which could have offset any benefits associated with more advantaged neighborhoods. For example, qualitative work on MTO suggests that boys' access to fathers and father-figures was curtailed by moving, which might account for the minimal program effects seen for boys (Clampet-Lundquist, Edin, Kling, & Duncan, 2011). In addition, boys were more likely than girls to return to their old neighborhoods to access social networks. Both factors might have mitigated the benefits of more advantaged neighborhoods for boys.

At the same time, income and racial and ethnic differences between mover youth and their new neighbors may have been a source of tension. These differences may have precluded the formation of close ties, subjected movers to experiences of racism and discrimination, and engendered resentment because of feelings of relative deprivation. For instance, families who moved to less poor neighborhoods were more likely to report experiences with discrimination in Gautreaux and less informal socializing with neighbors in Yonkers, at least in the short term, than were their respective counterparts in higher poverty neighborhoods (Fauth, Leventhal, & Brooks-Gunn, 2004; Rubinowitz & Rosenbaum, 2000).

Another factor explaining the mixed results centers on schools. If school quality was not improved by moving, educational benefits were unlikely to accrue.

For example, in Yonkers, children remained in the same city and school district. In MTO, the situation was more complex. Families who moved to low-poverty neighborhoods remained in urban areas and in predominately racial and ethnic minority neighborhoods (i.e., did not move to the more affluent suburbs, as in Gautreaux). As such, children often remained in the same urban school districts as prior to the move, and many even attended the same schools because of school choice policies allowing them to do so. This issue speaks to the need for research and policy to better reflect the overlap among neighborhood and school influences in the United States, which was highlighted by Gershoff and Benner in Chapter 9.

Finally, we should note that, in all of the programs, families remained poor despite their improved neighborhood conditions. Many economic, social, and personal challenges that children and their families faced—beyond neighborhood poverty and related conditions such as safety—likely remained in place after they moved and may have been heightened or made more salient with the move to a more advantaged neighborhood. These mixed results are perhaps not surprising, given that mobility programs do not directly target child outcomes and given that neighborhood socioeconomic composition influences children's development largely indirectly.

PLACE-BASED APPROACHES TO NEIGHBORHOOD CHANGE

Place-based strategies, which seek to alter the socioeconomic composition of poor neighborhoods to reduce concentrated poverty, offer a potentially wider reaching and more consistently favorable approach to addressing poverty concentration than do mobility programs. These efforts may involve government intervention, private investment, or some combination of the two (Kubisch et al., 2002). Reductions in neighborhood socioeconomic disadvantage also may occur naturally through the in-migration of nonpoor families or through changes in the socioeconomic circumstances of current residents and possibly their out-migration.

In contrast to housing mobility programs, very limited research exists on how neighborhood socioeconomic transformation is associated with children's development (Briggs, 2003; Leventhal & Brooks-Gunn, 2001). Rather, most research on this policy approach has focused on "gentrification" or the spontaneously occurring decrease in socioeconomic disadvantage in urban areas (rather than as a result of public or private investment). Of concern has been whether existing residents, who are presumably poor, are displaced. Several rigorously conducted studies find converging evidence that poor residents are no more likely to leave gentrifying neighborhoods than nongentrifying neighborhoods and may even be more likely to stay in gentrifying neighborhoods. The limited research exploring the impacts of neighborhood gentrification—or reductions in socioeconomic disadvantage more broadly—on children has also yielded conflicting results. One study reported that African-American youth benefitted with respect to their adult economic attainment (Sharkey, 2012), but another reported that boys were harmed in terms of their social and emotional functioning (Leventhal & Brooks-Gunn, 2011). In early stages, gentrification may have unfavorable consequences for children because of the instability that it creates, but benefits may accrue over time as the process takes hold (Kreager, Lyons, & Hays, 2011).

Despite more community-based initiatives in recent years (Kubisch et al., 2010), we still know little about how they affect children. One reason may be that most prior initiatives have focused heavily on community development, which entails economic and housing development (Kubisch et al., 2002). These efforts are clearly more adult- than child-focused. Even the large-scale HOPE VI initiative to demolish some public housing to promote mixed-income communities has not been systematically examined with respect to how redevelopment efforts have influenced children (Popkin et al., 2004). One notable exception has been the Harlem Children's Zone (HCZ), which is the most well-known example of a place-based intervention and is the inspiration for the current federal Promise Neighborhoods initiative.

The HCZ encompasses 97 blocks in a poor, largely African-American community (Tough, 2008). To change the lives of children in large numbers and eliminate the socioeconomic achievement gap, it provides an array of services to children and families from birth through adulthood, conceived of as a pipeline or conveyor belt of support. These services include family services, early education, charter schools, health and dental care, job training and placement, and community development. One evaluation found achievement test score gains for children, which appear largely attributable to the charter school (Dobbie & Fryer, 2011). Based on these results and the high profile of the HCZ, President Barack Obama codified place-based approaches as a federal strategy for improving the lives of families in the most distressed neighborhoods with the Promise Neighborhoods initiative. To date, this effort has entailed 36 one-year planning awards and five implementation grants to organizations that will attempt to achieve place-based change through the integration and coordination of existing systems within communities, as well as the development of tools to track and evaluate progress. As a bridge to existing research, researchers involved in Promise Neighborhoods have developed "a framework for creating nurturing environments" that draws on work documenting potential pathways of neighborhood socioeconomic influences to help guide these efforts (Komro et al., 2011).

Given that Promise Neighborhoods are just getting off the ground, we cannot yet forecast what their effects and problems may be. There appears to be widespread enthusiasm, but some concerns remain about the ability to replicate the success of the HCZ, particularly without the large influx of private resources that have been used to build and sustain the HCZ. Researchers and policy makers alike will be watching these initiatives closely to see how things unfold.

Conclusion

Efforts to address social inequalities—economic, racial, or both—in schools and neighborhoods are likely to engender controversy and produce mixed results. The judicial system has been the governing body to play the largest role in policy here, one that is often overlooked by researchers in the social policy arena. In many, but not all cases, any controversy related to the redistribution of children across schools or of families across neighborhoods subsided over time. Public outcry in response to such policies can often be appeased with information, especially if framed in terms of benefits. We need additional research on how setting-level change affects children and families who are not the direct targets of the policy. Such information may be useful in quelling (or possibly fueling) concerns at the outset.

Policies targeting children from disadvantaged families are often guided by the overarching goal of improving their future prospects—almost always conceptualized as their educational and economic attainment. Lack of consideration of social and emotional functioning is a major oversight, one that may account for the mixed results across setting-level policy efforts. Without attention to children's developmental needs across interrelated domains—social, emotional, and cognitive—future policies and programs are not likely to achieve their full potential.

Almost all of the policies and programs reviewed here had mixed results. The hypothesized pathways, as laid out in the research on schools and neighborhoods described in the Gershoff and Benner chapter, are often quite complex, and there are multiple routes to action. Most policies and programs do not directly target these underlying pathways, nor do they jointly target schools and neighborhoods, despite their close connections. Perhaps this next generation of policies and programs, as exemplified by Promise Neighborhoods, will do a better job of bridging research and policy and of affecting both schools and neighborhoods. Future research needs to track program effects on children's development in the short- and long-term, to consider impacts on indirect mechanisms through which programs are thought to work, to do so in a rigorous manner, and to replicate findings across initiatives.

Acknowledgments

Direct correspondence to the first author at Department of Sociology and Population Research Center, University of Texas at Austin, 1 University Station A1700, Austin, TX 78712 (crosnoe@austin.utexas.edu). The authors acknowledge the support of grants from the William T. Grant Foundation (PI: Robert Crosnoe, Co-PI: Tama Leventhal), the National Institute of Child Health and Human Development (R01 HD055359-01, PI: Robert Crosnoe; R24 HD42849, PI: Mark Hayward) to the Population Research Center, University of Texas at Austin, and the Foundation for Child Development (PI: Tama Leventhal). Opinions reflect those of the authors and not necessarily those of the granting agencies.

References

Arum, R. (2000). Schools and communities: Ecological and institutional dimensions. *Annual Review of Sociology, 26,* 395–418.

Bazelon, E. (2008). The next kind of integration. *New York Times magazine.* July 20, 2008.

Belkin, L. (1999). *Show me a hero: A tale of murder, suicide, race, and redemption.* Boston: Little, Brown, and Company.

Briggs, X. (2003). *Traps and stepping stones: Neighborhood dynamics and family well-being* Cambridge, MA: Harvard University.

Briggs, X., Darden, J. T., & Aidala, A. (1999). In the wake of desegregation: Early impacts of scattered-site public housing on neighborhoods in Yonkers, New York. *Journal of the American Planning Association, 65,* 27–49.

Chubb, J. E., & Moe, T. M. (1990). *Politics, markets, and American schools.* Washington, DC: Brookings Institution.

Clampet-Lundquist, S., Edin, K., Kling, J., & Duncan, G. (2011). Moving teenagers out of high-risk neighborhoods: How girls fare better than boys. *American Journal of Sociology, 116*(4), 1154–1189.

Clotfelter, C. T., Ladd, H. F., & Vigdor, J. L. (2005). *Federal oversight, local control, and the specter of "resegregation" in southern schools. National Bureau of Economic Research Working Paper Series 11086.*

Coleman, J. S., & Hoffer, T. (1987). *Public and private schools: The impact of communities.* New York: Basic Books.

Coleman J. S., Kelly, S. D., & Moore, J A. (1976). *Trends in school desegregation, 1968–73.* Washington DC: The Urban Institute.

Cottrol, R. J., Diamond, R., & Ware, L. B. (2003). *Brown v. Board of Education: Caste, culture, and the Constitution.* Lawrence: University Press of Kansas.

Crosnoe, R. (2009). Low-income students and the socioeconomic composition of public high schools. *American Sociological Review, 74,* 709–730.

DeLuca, S., & Dayton, E. (2009). Switching social contexts: The effects of housing mobility and school choice programs on youth outcomes. *Annual Review of Sociology, 35,* 457–491.

Dobbie, W., & Fryer, R. G., Jr. (2011). Are high-quality schools enough to increase achievement among the poor? Evidence from the Harlem Children's Zone. *American Economic Journal: Applied Economics, 3,* 158–187.

Duncan, G. J., Connell, J. P., & Klebanov, P. K. (1997). Conceptual and methodological issues in estimating causal effects of neighborhoods and family conditions on individual development. In J. Brooks-Gunn, G. J. Duncan & J. L. Aber (Eds.), *Neighborhood poverty: Vol. 1. Context and consequences for children* (pp. 219–250). New York: Russell Sage Foundation.

Fauth, R. C., Leventhal, T., & Brooks-Gunn, J. (2004). Short-term effects of moving from public housing in poor to middle-class neighborhoods on low-income, minority adults' outcomes. *Social Science and Medicine, 59*(11), 2271–2284.

Fauth, R. C., Leventhal, T., & Brooks-Gunn, J. (2007). Welcome to the neighborhood? Long-term impacts of moving to low-poverty neighborhoods on poor children's and adolescents' outcomes. *Journal of Research on Adolescence, 17*(2), 249–284.

Flinspach, S. E., & Banks, K. E. (2005). Moving beyond race: Socioeconomic diversity as a race-neutral approach to desegregation in the Wake County schools. In J. C. Borger & G. Orfield (Eds.), *School segregation: Must the south turn back?* (pp. 261–280). Chapel Hill: University of North Carolina Press.

Freeman, L. (2005). Displacement or succession? Residential mobility in gentrifying neighborhoods. *Urban Affairs Review, 40*(4), 463–491.

Freeman, L., & Braconi, F. (2004). Gentrification and displacement: New York City in the 1990s. *Journal of the American Planning Association, 70*(1), 39–52.

Goering, J., & Feins, J. (Eds.) (2003). *Choosing a better life? Evaluating the Moving to Opportunity social experiment.* Washington, DC: Urban Institute Press.

Grant, G. (2009). *Hope and despair in the American city: Why there are no bad schools in Raleigh?* Cambridge: Harvard University Press.

Hoxby, C., & Weingarth, G. (2005). *Taking race out of the equation: School reassignment and the structure of peer effects.* Harvard University Department of Economics Working Paper.

Jencks, C., & Mayer, S. (1990). The social consequences of growing up in a poor neighborhood. In L. Lynn & M. McGeary (Eds.), *Inner-city poverty in the United States* (pp. 111–186). Washington, DC: National Academy Press.

Kahlenberg, R. (2001). *All together now: Creating middle class schools through public choice.* Washington, DC: Brookings Institution.

Keels, M., Duncan, G. J., Deluca, S., Mendenhall, R., & Rosenbaum, J. (2005). Fifteen years later: Can residential mobility programs provide a long-term escape from neighborhood segregation, crime, and poverty? *Demography, 42*(1), 51–73.

Komro, K. A., Flay, B. R., & Biglan, A. (2011). Creating nurturing environments: A science-based framework for promoting child health and development within high-poverty neighborhoods. *Clinical Child and Family Psychology Review, 14*, 111–134.

Kreager, D. A., Lyons, C. J., & Hays, Z. (2011). Urban revitalization and Seattle crime, 1982–2000. *Social Problems, 58, 615–639.*

Kubisch, A. C., Auspos, P., Brown, P., Chaskin, R., Fulbright-Anderson, K., & Hamilton, R. (2002). *Voices from the field II: Reflections on comprehensive community change.* Washington, DC: Aspen Institute.

Kubisch, A. C., Auspos, P., Brown, P., & Dewar, T. (2010). *Voices from the field III: Lessons and challenges from two decades of community change efforts.* Washington, DC: Aspen Institute.

Labaree, D. F. (1997). Public goods, private goods: The American struggle over educational goals. *American Educational Research Journal, 34*, 39–81.

Lee, V., Smith, J., & Croninger, R. (1997). How high school organization influences the equitable distribution of learning in mathematics and science. *Sociology of Education, 70*, 128–150.

Leventhal, T., & Brooks-Gunn, J. (2000). The neighborhoods they live in: Effects of neighborhood residence upon child and adolescent outcomes *Psychological Bulletin, 126*, 309–337.

Leventhal, T., & Brooks-Gunn, J. (2001). Changing neighborhoods and child well-being: Understanding how children may be affected in the coming century *Advances in Life Course Research, 6*, 263–301.

Leventhal, T., & Brooks-Gunn, J. (2011). Changes in neighborhood poverty from 1990 to 2000 and youth's problem behaviors. *Developmental Psychology, 47*(6), 1680–1698.

Leventhal, T., Dupéré, V., & Brooks-Gunn J. (2009). Neighborhood influences on adolescent development. In R. M. Lerner & L. Steinberg (Eds.), *Handbook of adolescent psychology* (3rd ed., pp. 411–443). Hoboken, NJ: Wiley.

Massey, D. S., & Denton, N. A. (1993). *American apartheid: Segregation and the making of the underclass.* Cambridge, MA: Harvard University Press.

Mayer, S. E. (2002). How economic segregation affects children's educational attainment. *Social Forces, 81,* 153–186.

McCrummen, S. (2011). *Republican school board in N.C. backed by tea party abolishes integration policy. Washington Post,* January 12, 2011.

McKinnish, T., Walsh, R., & White, T. K. (2010). Who gentrifies low-income neighborhoods? *Journal of Urban Economics, 67*(2), 180–193.

Mercer, A. (2003). Socioeconomic balance: School board to consider the issue that divided community a decade ago. *LaCrosse Tribune.* January 19, 2003.

Plank, S. (2000). *Finding one's place: Teaching styles and peer relations in diverse classrooms.* New York: Teachers College Press.

Popkin, S. J., Katz., B., Cunningham, M. K., Brown, K. D., Gustafson, J., & Turner, M. A. (2004). *A decade of HOPE VI: Research findings and policy challenges.* Washington, DC: The Urban Institute.

Reardon, S. F., Yun, J. T., & Eitle, T. M. (2001). The changing structure of school segregation: Measurement and evidence of multiracial metropolitan-area school segregation, 1989–1995. *Demography, 37,* 351–364.

Reardon, S. F., Yun, J. T., & Kurlaender, M. (2006). Implications of income-based school assignment policies for racial school segregation. *Educational Evaluation and Policy Analysis, 28,* 49–75.

Rothstein, R. (2004). *Class and schools: Using social, economic, and educational reform to close the black-white achievement gap.* Washington DC: Economic Policy Institute.

Rubinowitz, L. S., & Rosenbaum, J. E. (2000). *Crossing the class and color lines: From public housing to white suburbia* Chicago: University of Chicago Press.

Rumberger, R. W., & Palardy, G. J. (2005). Does segregation still matter? The impact of social composition on academic achievement in high school. *Teachers College Record, 107,* 1999–2045.

Rusk, D., & Mosley, J. (1996). *The academic performance of public housing children: Does living in middle class neighborhoods and attending middle class schools make a difference?* Washington, DC: Urban Institute.

Sampson, R. J., & Morenoff, J. D. (1997). Ecological perspectives on the neighborhood context of urban poverty. In J. Brooks-Gunn, G. J. Duncan, & J. L. Aber (Eds.), *Neighborhood poverty: Policy implications in studying neighborhoods* (pp. 1–22). New York: Russell Sage.

Sampson, R. J., Morenoff, J. D., & Gannon-Rowley, T. (2002). Assessing "neighborhood effects": Social processes and new directions in research. *Annual Review of Sociology, 28,* 443–478.

Sanbonmatsu, L., Ludwig, L., Katz, L. F., Gennetian, L. A., Duncan, G. J., Kessler, R. C., et al. (2011). *Moving to Opportunity for Fair Housing Demonstration Program: Final impacts evaluation.* Washington: U.S. Department of Housing and Urban Development, Office of Policy Development and Research.

Schofield, J. W. (1995). Review of research on school desegregation's impact on elementary and secondary students. In J. A. Banks (Ed.), *Handbook of research on multicultural education* (pp. 597–616). New York: Macmillan.

Sharkey, P. (2012). An alternative approach to addressing selection into and out of social settings: Neighborhood change and African American children's economic outcomes. *Sociological Methods & Research, 41*, 251–293.

Shaw, C. R., & McKay, H. D. (1942). *Juvenile delinquency and urban areas.* Chicago: University of Chicago Press.

Sui-Chu, E. H., & Willms, J. D. (1996). Effects of parental involvement on eighth-grade achievement. *Sociology of Education, 69*, 126–141.

Tough, P. (2008). *Whatever it takes.* New York: Houghton Mifflin Company.

Vigdor, J. (2002). Does gentrification harm the poor? In W. G. Gale & J. R. Pack (Eds.), *Brookings-Wharton papers on urban affairs.* Washington, DC: Brookings Institution.

Wilson, W. J. (1987). *The truly disadvantaged: The inner city, the underclass, and public policy.* Chicago: University of Chicago Press.

Development in the Context of Omnipresent Media

{ 11 }

Children and Electronic Media

Sandra L. Calvert and Ellen A. Wartella

The glow of electronic screens is an increasing part of the backdrop of children's lives in the 21st century. Some parents and adults are proponents, while others are opponents, of these images and sounds that infuse the daily lives of our children. Regardless of perspective, however, electronic media are here to stay. What is life like for children and adolescents in this emerging digital space? How do they learn, communicate, and act in this digital world? These kinds of questions are the focus of this chapter.

Media Use and Exposure Patterns

The major source of information about U.S. children's media consumption in the past decade comes from the Kaiser Family Foundation, which conducted multiple cross-sectional studies with nationally representative samples of children 6 months to 6 years of age and of youth 8 to 18 years of age. More recently, Common Sense Media examined media use patterns of children who were 6 months to 8 years old. Over the years, four main trends emerged. The first involves a major increase in children's use of all kinds of media. The second is the creation and use of media designed for very young children, ages 2 and under. Multitasking, in which more than one medium is used at a time, such as texting on a cell phone while watching television, is a third trend. This multitasking pattern led to a separation of media use, which considers the amount of time media are used (regardless of how many different media are used at a given time) from media exposure, which adds more time into the equation when more than one medium is used simultaneously (Roberts, Foehr, & Rideout, 2005). The final trend is the creation and use of media platforms, such as the smartphone, that are digital, interactive, and easily transportable (Rideout, Foehr, & Roberts, 2010). Media platforms made media use so ubiquitous that youth can now be connected even when they are walking down the street.

EARLY MEDIA USE PATTERNS

From the beginnings of life, children grow up and develop with media as a major developmental context. According to data from Common Sense Media (2011), a young child's (6-months to age 8) typical day involves some media exposure. Specifically, about 65% of young children watch television, 58% read or are read to from print books, 25% watch DVDs, 14% use a computer, 9% play console video games, and 8% use handheld game players, mobile phones, iPods, or iPads to access games, apps, or video. Media exposure for all platforms increases from ages 0–1 to 2–4 to 5–8, except for a decline in DVD use from ages 5–8 when compared to ages 2–4.

In light of the American Academy of Pediatrics' (AAP) 1999 recommendation that children have no screen exposure before age 2 and its 2010 recommendation that parents "avoid" screen media for very young children (American Academy of Pediatrics [AAP], 1999, 2010), it is noteworthy that most parents do not follow the AAP guidelines. Common Sense Media (2011) reported that 66% of children under age 2 had been exposed to television content at some point in time and that 37% of children under age 2 are exposed to screen media on a daily basis. Thirty percent of 6-month- to 2-year-old children had a television set in their bedroom (Common Sense Media, 2011), suggesting that very young children often view video content alone.

Not all screen media are alike, however. That is, parents perceive different screen media differently, believing, for instance, that computers are a gateway to their young child's future but that video games are harmful. In particular, 69% of parents think that computers mostly help their children's learning compared to 38% who view television favorably and only 17% who perceive video games favorably. Because both computers and video games are interactive media, it is likely that parental beliefs about the value of different media emerge partly because of differences in the content typically embedded in different platforms. For instance, focus group interviews revealed that parents thought that computers got their children to think whereas video games were likely to expose children to violent content (Rideout & Hamel, 2006).

Data collected in the 2003 Kaiser Family early media use survey revealed age differences in computer use. Parents of 21% of children under age 2, 58% of those with 3- and 4-year-olds, and 77% of those with 5- and 6-year-olds reported computer use by their children (Calvert, Rideout, Woolard, Barr, & Strouse, 2005). Children's first use of a computer tended to occur in their second year, typically from a parent's lap, with independent computer use increasing across the first 6 years of life (Calvert et al., 2005).

A recent survey by Common Sense Media (2011) revealed that mobile media are rapidly becoming part of children's worlds. More than half of the households in their nationally representative sample of 0- to 8-year-olds had a mobile phone, a tablet such as an iPad, or an iPod or similar device. An "app gap" emerged, with high-income children having more access to this kind of experience than did low-income children. Overall, though, racial and ethnic minority children, who tend to come from families with lower incomes, spent more time with media than White children did. Specifically, the average media use (including screen media, music, reading) of Black children was 4 hours, 27 minutes, followed by 3 hours, 28 minutes among Hispanic children, and 2 hours, 51 minutes by White children.

OLDER CHILDREN'S MEDIA USE PATTERNS

Media use explodes among 8- to 18-year-old youths. According to the most recent nationally representative Kaiser Family Foundation surveys of media use (Rideout et al., 2010), 8- to 18- year-old youth spend an average of 7 hours, 38 minutes per day using media; this estimate increases to 10 hours, 45 minutes per day of overall exposure when multitasking (i.e., the use of more than one medium at a time) is considered. For media use, television content continues to dominate youth's time, with youth reporting watching an average of 4 hours 29 minutes per day as compared with 2 hours, 31 minutes per day listening to music and other audio media, 1 hour, 29 minutes using the computer, 1 hour, 13 minutes playing video games, 38 minutes engaged in print use, and 25 minutes viewing movies. Increases for this recent 2009 cohort over prior cohorts from 2004 and 1999 occurred in the amount of time youth spent using television, music/audio, computers, and video games. When cohorts from 1999 and 2009 were compared, the use of print media significantly declined and exposure to movies significantly increased.

Owning mobile devices, such as iPods that are used primarily for listening to music, fueled the increase in music exposure, with 79% of a nationally representative sample of 12- to 17-year-old U.S. teens reporting ownership of digital musical devices (Lenhart, Ling, Campbell, & Purcell, 2010). The ownership of cell phones by 8- to 18- year-old youth also increased from 39% in 2004 to 66% in 2009 and of laptops from 12% in 2004 to 29% in 2009 (Rideout et al., 2010). Mobile devices now include cameras, apps, and Internet access, making them an increasingly important player in the lives of U.S. youth, giving them 24/7 access to content and content creation, virtually anytime, anywhere.

Media exposure rates also differ substantially across racial and ethnic youth. Specifically, 8- to 18-year-old Black youth are exposed to 13 hours of media per day and Hispanic youth to 12 hours, 59 minutes per day, whereas White youth are exposed to "only" 8 hours, 36 minutes per day (Rideout et al., 2010). The difference between racial and ethnic minority and White youth is mainly attributed to heavier exposure to television content by racial and ethnic minority youth. Specifically, Black youth were exposed to television content 5 hours, 54 minutes per day, Hispanic youth to 5 hours, 21 minutes per day, and White youth to 3 hours, 36 minutes per day in 2009 (Rideout et al., 2010). The implication is that media, particularly television programs, provide a context for the development of racial and ethnic minority youth even more so than for White youth.

How Do Young Children Learn from Media?

Early research on children and the media conducted during the 1970s and 1980s, such as that spearheaded by Huston, Wright, and Anderson, focused on children's attention to and comprehension of television programs (D. Anderson & Levin, 1976; D. Anderson, Lorch, Field Collins & Nathan, 1986; D. Anderson, Lorch, Field & Sanders, 1981; Calvert, Huston, Watkins, & Wright, 1982; Wright, et al., 1984). When children watched television in laboratory or naturalistic studies in which they could do other activities, such as play with toys or talk to other people, looking at television was typically intermittent, although the amount of time spent looking at the screen dramatically increased with age from infancy through the preschool and grade school years (D. Anderson & Levin, 1976; D. Anderson et al., 1986; D. Anderson et al., 1981; Calvert et al., 1982; Wright, et al., 1984). With the existence of media now specifically designed for the very young, infants pay substantially greater attention to videos than was the case in the past (Frankenfield et al., 2004).

Two complementary theories have been particularly influential in explaining the development of attention to television during the infancy, preschool, and middle childhood years (D. Anderson & Lorch, 1983; Frankenfield et al., 2004; Gola & Calvert, 2011; Huston & Wright, 1983). One theory focused on the comprehensibility of the content (D. Anderson & Lorch, 1983) and the other on the formal production features, particularly perceptually salient features such as rapid action and sound effects, used to present the content (Huston & Wright, 1983).

These theories parallel general theories that invoke two major systems underlying the development of sustained attention (e.g., Ruff & Rothbart, 1996; Wright & Vlietstra, 1975). One early-developing attentional system involves responsiveness to stimulus change and repetition, producing orienting responses and habituation. The general assumption is that perceptually salient surface stimulus features somewhat reflexively drive the attentional system (Wright & Vlietstra, 1975). If the current stimulus presents novel stimulus features, orienting occurs and attention is initiated, maintained, or intensified. If the current stimulus contains recently experienced stimulus features and little novelty, then attention is diminished. The second later-developing attentional system is driven by plans, goals, and comprehension schemes and is under much greater voluntary control. In general, early attention to a stimulus, such as that presented by videos, is expected to be driven predominantly by the orienting-habituation system with increasing control by the second system as the child grows older.

When these theories are applied to screen-based media, at some early age, children pay attention *only* because the orienting system has been activated. The child's cognitive and neural maturation, particularly during infancy, is not sufficient to have plans, goals, or video comprehension schemas. Sustained looking occurs because there is an optimal pacing of novel visual and auditory features. As the child matures and gains experience with media, especially during the toddler and preschool years, comprehension schemas begin to form, ultimately leading to content expectations, the ability to create connections between parts of a narrative or exposition (D. Anderson & Lorch, 1983; see Truglio & Kotler, Chapter 12), and eventually complex understanding of program plots (Calvert et al., 1982). With experience, the child also comes to understand that many features of videos have general significance, both as predictors of content and conveyors of meaning (Calvert et al., 1982). For example, animation is a useful indicator that the content is for children. By contrast, a dreamy dissolve between shots usually conveys that a significant shift in time and place, such as a flashback in time, has taken place in a narrative (Calvert, 1988). The child uses these *formal features* to cue attention and comprehension (Calvert et al., 1982).

The emerging literature suggests that, until about 12 months of age, attention is primarily driven by visual and auditory novelty and change (i.e., perceptual salience; Gola & Calvert, 2011), but then research demonstrates increasing interest in comprehensible, meaningful video by 18- and 24-month-olds (Richards & Cronise, 2000). A 24-month-old will also pay more attention to a comprehensible version of *Sesame Street* than to the same program if the shots are put in random order or if the dialogue is backwards or in a foreign language (D. Anderson et al., 1981), a finding that also holds true for 18- and 24-month-olds who view comprehensible and incomprehensible versions of *Teletubbies* (Frankenfield et al., 2004).

THE VIDEO DEFICIT

Although children's attention starts to be guided by comprehensible content around12 months of age, indicating cognitive processing rather than simple orienting responses, they have difficulty understanding what they view at this age. That is, although children under age 2.5 show competent performance when exposed to live information, they show poor performance when exposed to the same information on video, a finding that became known as the *video deficit* (D. Anderson and Pempek, 2005). For example, infants are less likely to imitate actions performed with a puppet if they see the actions demonstrated on video rather than in a live presentation (Barr & Hayne, 1999). Only with numerous repetitions, including repetitions using sound effects, does imitation from video reach the level found with a single live presentation (Barr, Muentener, Garcia, Fujimoto, & Chavez, 2007). As another example, 24-month-olds were also poorer at retrieving a hidden toy if they saw it hidden via video as compared to seeing it hidden as they looked through a window (Suddendorf, 2003; Troseth & DeLoache, 1998). Although very young children appear to comprehend language when it is presented by video (e.g., Hirsch-Pasek & Golinkoff, 1996), language learning is also substantially less when it is compared to learning from equivalent live experiences (Krcmar, Grela, & Lin, 2007; Kuhl, Tsao, & Liu, 2003). In a study of 30- to 42- month-old children, younger children learned verbs from video only when learning was supported by live social interactions, but the oldest children were able to learn verbs solely from video (Roseberry, Hirsh-Pasek, Parish-Morris, & Golinkoff, 2009).

Troseth, Saylor, and Archer (2006) argued that infants initially treat video portrayals as if they are real events. With experience, the lack of social responsiveness between child actions and contingent replies from television programs produces the video deficit. Indeed, 6-month-old infants demonstrated no video deficit in an imitation task, but 12-month-old infants did (Barr, Muentener, & Garcia, 2007). In a very real sense, the older infant's responses are reasonable, given that the content onscreen does not reply contingently to his or her actions. Not surprisingly, then, the video deficit can be eliminated when the content is socially relevant, such as addressing a child by name on a video and responding contingently to a child's actions via close-circuit television (Troseth et al., 2006).

Krcmar (2010) separated the concept of social relevance into two distinct components: social meaningfulness and social contingency. *Social meaningfulness* involves a relationship with an onscreen character. *Social contingency* involves a media character who engages a child in a conversation, such as asking questions of a child, waiting for a reply, and then acting as if the child's responses have been heard (Calvert, 2006). Programs created for preschool-aged children use both meaningful characters and attempt to create the perception of social contingency in their productions. Fred Rogers pioneered these techniques in his program *Mister Rogers' Neighborhood*, producing the popular and meaningful character of Mr. Rogers. Producers subsequently had other characters adopt these practices in children's educational programs such as *Blue's Clues* and *Dora the Explorer*.

The social meaningfulness of onscreen characters can improve early learning. For instance, Krcmar (2010) found that toddlers' imitation was superior when their mother rather than an unfamiliar adult presented the same content. Similarly, 21-month-old toddlers learned to seriate a group of objects when Elmo, a meaningful media character, presented the task rather than when DoDo, a popular Taiwanese character unknown in the United States, presented the same task. The Elmo group also performed better than a baseline control group, but the DoDo group did not (Lauricella, Gola, & Calvert, 2011). Taken together, these results suggest that young children can develop meaningful social relationships with media characters, also referred to as *parasocial relationships* (Hoffner, 2008; Horton & Wohl, 1956), that can improve their learning.

Socially contingent interactions that occur between a child and a computer or between a child and a television character can also increase subsequent learning. In a study of *Dora the Explorer*, for example, 4-year-old children who participated when the character asked them to do an action (e.g., pretend like they were climbing a ladder) or who interacted with the content by responding to prompts embedded in the computer program to advance the story line, learned more of the important story content than did those who simply observed the same program with an adult when there were no program prompts (Calvert, Strong, Jacobs, & Conger, 2007). Girls were also more motivated by the Dora program, as indexed by how much fun they thought the experience was, and they perceived themselves as being more like the female character than did boys; perceiving oneself as being more like Dora also predicted more divergent, creative responses (Calvert et al., 2007).

Similarly, a computer program created for toddlers about the *Curious Buddies* characters was adapted such that 30- to 36-month-old children either played an interactive hide-and-seek game in which characters popped up when the child touched the keyboard, observed the game in which characters popped up without any action by the child, or observed an adult through a one-way mirror as she hid the characters in an adjacent playroom (Lauricella, Pempek, Barr, & Calvert, 2010). Children who observed the live adult or who interacted with the computer program subsequently found more characters in the adjacent playroom than did those who only observed the characters onscreen. Overall, then, both social meaningfulness and social contingency in media presentations can improve early screen-based learning.

Media Effects During Middle Childhood and Adolescence

Although television use continues to dominate the time that youth spend with media during middle childhood and adolescence, youth increasingly use interactive media (Rideout et al., 2010). Children's developmental needs remain a constant in driving children's experiences in this ever-changing media landscape.

SOCIAL MEDIA INFLUENCES

A critical hallmark of middle childhood and adolescence is having friends, getting along with one's peers, and creating a mature identity, which requires them to interact and to communicate with their friends and peers. Advancements in computer technology made it possible for children and youth to interact with friends at social networking sites rather than with strangers in chatrooms (Pempek, Yermolayeva, & Calvert, 2009). Thus, the face-to-face interactions that children enjoyed everyday could continue into their online experiences.

For effective communications to take place, language systems emerged that enabled youth to communicate quickly and efficiently with one another. More specifically, abbreviated, coded language conventions such as u (you), ur (you are), lol (laughing out loud) became common linguistic practices that emerged during early online conversations, allowing written conversations to take place at about the speed of an oral conversation (Greenfield & Subrahmanyam, 2003). Coded language initially appeared in three main venues, namely chatrooms, where youth "talked" with others about various topics in online public forums (Greenfield & Subramanyam, 2003); multiuser domains (MUDs), in which youth often engaged in online role play (which was initially textual and later became visual and textual; Calvert, Mahler, Zehnder, Jenkins, & Lee, 2003; Turkle, 1995); and in instant messaging programs, in which youth chatted with one another during computer applications (Greenfield & Subramanyam, 2003). Although these particular applications are less common now, coded language continues, particularly in phone texts.

Although online applications such as chatrooms were once thought to create a color-blind and gender-blind online culture, that did not happen. Instead, teens often used language codes, such as a/s/l, which asked and told other users about their age, sex, and location (Tynes, Reynolds, & Greenfield, 2004), and 55% of users of a typical chatroom identified themselves (Subrahmanyam, Smahel, & Greenfield, 2006). The communication styles used during middle childhood also varied by gender. Specifically, boys were more likely to utilize action and rapid pacing to communicate whereas girls were more likely to use written dialogue to communicate in their MUD play (Calvert et al., 2003). In short, chatrooms and MUDs became additional spaces where middle childhood and adolescent youth communicated in ways and expressed themselves about issues that were important to them, such as race and gender, which were indicators of their identity (Calvert, 2002).

Personal websites called *blogs* (abbreviated from "web logs") are another kind of application that was once popular with youth, allowing them to express their personal identity (Gola & Calvert, 2012). Huffaker and Calvert (2005) found that adolescents who maintained online blogs often made honest comments about themselves, such as disclosing their sexual identity, their names, their ages, and the locations in which they lived. These kinds of online experiences also allowed youth to reach out to others who were similar to them, which is of particular importance for those who may feel socially isolated.

Faster Internet connections enabled the development of more recent applications, such as social media like Facebook.com and Myspace.com, which allow youth to describe themselves and build a network of friends. Approximately 75% of U.S. adolescents and emerging adults (late teen years through mid-20s) are members of social networking sites (Mazur & Richards, 2009). These social media also address the developmental needs of youth, such as creating, interacting with, and maintaining friends during the adolescent and emerging adulthood years. For example, Pempek and colleagues (2009) found that college students often had hundreds of "friends" on their Facebook profiles. Youth mainly spent their time on Facebook communicating with those friends, particularly those from their high school years who did not attend their current college.

Although interactive media provide the option to create content, youth spent more time observing what their friends were doing, which is known as "lurking," than they did creating content (Pempek et al., 2009). Even on web sites such as Youtube.com, which allow youth to distribute and view brief videos, youth spend more time lurking to be entertained by others' content rather than creating and distributing their own content (Chau, 2010). Taken together, these behaviors reveal an ongoing interest by youth in observing others, a pattern not unlike that found when youth watch people on a television screen. An important addition made possible by these interactive platforms is the option to view their friends and their friends' content rather than what a traditional broadcaster distributes (Pempek et al., 2009).

Gaming is a popular interactive activity, particularly with boys, whether using gaming consoles or consoles connected to the Internet (Lenhart et al., 2008). Content analyses revealed that 98% of video games with a T rating (for Teens) and 64% of video games rated as E (for Everyone) contained violent content (Haninger & Thompson, 2004; Thompson & Haninger, 2001). Playing these kinds of games can lead to aggressive behaviors. For instance, longitudinal research revealed that third- to fifth-graders who played violent video games increased in physical aggression, verbal aggression, and hostile attributions over a period of 5 months (C. Anderson, Gentile, & Buckley, 2007). Meta-analyses have also linked exposure to aggressive video game content to childhood aggressive actions and hostile feelings (C. Anderson, 2002).

MEDIA INFLUENCES ON COGNITIVE AND EDUCATIONAL OUTCOMES

With the increase in children's media use, there has been growing interest in how such media use affects children's cognitive development. Gaming in particular can have beneficial outcomes on cognitive skills (Calvert, 2005). For example, expert gamers are faster than novices at deploying attentional skills, can improve those attentional strategies with video game practice, and can transfer those attentional skills to other tasks (Green & Bavelier, 2003; Greenfield, deWinstanley et al., 1994). Divided attention requires youth to multitask because they must attend to multiple stimuli in order to succeed at video game play. Spatial skills also improve when children play video games that require visualization of spatial fields (Subramanyam & Greenfield, 1994). Even violent games can advance cognitive skills, such as task switching (Green & Bavelier, 2006), because the player must identify friends and foes quickly during game play to determine who to shoot and to avoid shooting (Green & Bavelier, 2003). Competitive exergame sports play, which requires players to move their bodies as they play video games, have also been associated with increases in adolescents' executive function skills, such as planning and task switching, presumably because competitive activities activate the prefrontal cortex to select strategies to win (Staiano, Abraham, & Calvert, 2012).

Online opportunities can also enrich low-income students' educational attainment. Low-income, predominantly Black adolescents who were given home Internet access subsequently had higher grade point averages (GPAs) and higher standardized reading scores over a 16-month period than did a group who did not receive home Internet access (Jackson et al., 2006). Math scores, however, did not increase over time. The authors speculated that students who spent more time online read more than their peers who were not connected to the Internet. Reading about school projects or about personal interests, they conjectured, could lead to better overall reading scores. Taken together, these findings suggest that certain kinds of electronic game play can cultivate visual spatial and executive function skills, whereas online reading can cultivate better linguistic skills.

Conclusion

Children of the 21st century are digital natives (Prensky, 2001). They talk the talk and they walk the walk of digital natives as they chat on their phones while gliding down the streets of our cities and play video games with others who live on the other side of the world. The vast amount of time devoted by today's youth to digital media is met with concern by educators who find it difficult to compete with these vast and ubiquitous information networks that wire youth into a world wide web of culture. But let us not forget that these same information technologies and networks are framing the economies and workplaces of the 21st century. Youth will lead the way into this new digital landscape, creating new pathways for learning as they face age-old developmental struggles, such as coming to know who they are. Our children's engagement with and use of the ever-changing information technologies of this century remind us that we are living in yet another age when a long-standing truth is played out: the only constant is change.

References

American Academy of Pediatrics, Committee on Public Education. (1999). Media education. *Pediatrics, 104*(2 pt 1), 341–343.

American Academy of Pediatrics, Committee on Public Education. (2010). Policy Statement on Media education. *Pediatrics,* doi: 10.1542/peds.2010-1636.

Anderson, C.A. (2002). Violent video games and aggressive thoughts, feelings, and behaviors. In S. L. Calvert, A. B. Jordan, & R. R. Cocking (Eds.), *Children in the digital age: Influences of electronic media on development (pp. 101–119)* Westport, CT: Praeger.

Anderson, C. A, Gentile, D. A., & Buckley, K. E. (2007). *Violent video games effects on children and adolescents: Theory, research, and public policy.* New York: Oxford University Press.

Anderson, D. R., & Levin, S. R. (1976). Young children's attention to "Sesame Street." *Child Development, 47,* 806–811.

Anderson, D. R., & Lorch, E. P. (1983). Looking at television: Action or reaction? In J. Bryant & D. R. Anderson (Eds.), *Children's understanding of television: Research on attention and comprehension* (pp. 1–33). New York: Academic Press.

Anderson, D. R., Lorch, E. P., Field, D. E., Collins, P. A., & Nathan, J. G. (1986). Television viewing at home: Age trends in visual attention and time with TV. *Child Development, 57,* 1024–1033.

Anderson, D. R., Lorch, E. P., Field, D. E., & Sanders, J. (1981). The effects of TV program comprehensibility on preschool children's visual attention to television. *Child Development, 52*(1), 151–157.

Anderson, D. A., & Pempek, T. A. (2005). Television and very young children. *American Behavioral Scientist, 48,* 505–522.

Barr, R., Muentener, P., & Garcia, A. (2007). Age-related changes in deferred imitation from television by 6- to 18-month-olds. *Developmental Science, 10,* 910–921.

Barr, R., Muentener, R., Garcia, A., Fujimoto, M., & Chavez, V. (2007). The effect of repetition on imitation from television during infancy. *Developmental Psychobiology, 49,* 196–207.

Barr, R., & Hayne, H. (1999). Developmental changes in imitation from television during infancy. *Child Development, 70,* 1067–1081.

Calvert, S. L. (1988). Television production feature effects on children's comprehension of time. *Journal of Applied Developmental Psychology, 9,* 263–273.

Calvert, S. L. (2002). Identity on the Internet. In S. L. Calvert, A. B. Jordan, & R. R. Cocking (Eds.), *Children in the digital age: Influences of electronic media on development (pp. 57–70).* Westport, CT: Praeger.

Calvert, S.L. (2005). Cognitive effects of video games. In J. Goldstein & J. Raessens (Eds.). *Handbook of computer game studies* (pp. 125–131). Cambridge, MA: MIT Press.

Calvert, S. L. (2006). Media and early development. In K. McCartney & D. A. Phillips (Eds.), *Blackwell handbook of early childhood development* (pp. 843–879). Boston, MA: Blackwell.

Calvert, S. L., Huston, A. C., Watkins, B. A, & Wright, J. C. (1982). The relation between selective attention to television forms and children's comprehension of content. *Child Development, 53,* 601–610.

Calvert, S. L., Mahler, B. A., Zehnder, S. M., Jenkins, A., & Lee, M. (2003). Gender differences in preadolescent children's online interactions: Symbolic modes of self-presentation and self-expression. *Journal of Applied Developmental Psychology, 24,* 627–644.

Calvert, S. L., Rideout, V. J., Woolard, J. L., Barr, R. F., & Strouse, G. A. (2005). Age, ethnicity, and socioeconomic patterns in early computer use: A national survey. *American Behavioral Scientist, 48,* 590–607.

Calvert, S. L., Strong, B. L., Jacobs, E. L., & Conger, E. E. (2007). Interaction and participation for young Hispanic and Caucasian girls' and boys' learning of media content. *Media Psychology, 9,* 431–445.

Chau, C. (2010). YouTube as a participatory culture. *New Directions for Youth Development, 128,* 65–74.

Common Sense Media (2011). Zero to Eight. Located at: http://www.commonsensemedia. org/research/zero-eight-childrens-media-use-america/

Frankenfield, A. E., Richards, J. R., Lauricella, A. R., Pempek, T. A., Kirkorian, H. L., & Anderson, D. R. (2004). *Looking at and interacting with comprehensible and incomprehensible Teletubbies* Poster presented at the Biennial International Conference for Infant Studies, Chicago, IL.

Gola, A. A., & Calvert, S. L. (2011). Infants' visual attention to infant DVDs as a function of program pacing. *Infancy, 16,* 295–305.

Gola, A. A., & Calvert, S. L. (2012). Children's and adolescents' internet access, use, and online behaviors. In Y. Zheng (Ed.), *Encyclopedia of cyber behavior (pp. 220–232).* Hershey, PA: IGI Global.

Green, C., & Bavelier, D. (2003). Action video game modifies visual selective attention. *Nature, 423,* 534–537.

Green, C. S., & Bavelier, D. (2006). Effect of action video games on the spatial distribution of visuospatial attention. *Journal of Experimental Psychology: Human Perception and Performance, 32,* 1465–1478.

Greenfield, P. M., deWinstanley, P., Kilpatrick, H., & Kaye, D. (1994). Action video games and informal education: Effects on strategies for dividing visual attention. *Journal of Applied Developmental Psychology, 15,* 105–123.

Greenfield, P. M., & Subrahmanyam, K. (2003). Online discourse in a teen chat room: New codes and new modes of coherence in a visual medium. *Journal of Applied Developmental Psychology, 24,* 713–738.

Haninger, K., & Thompson, K. M. (2004). Content and ratings of teen-rated video games. *Journal of the American Medical Association, 291,* 856–865.

Hirsch-Pasek, K., & Golinkoff, R. M. (1996). *The origins of grammar: Evidence from early language comprehension.* Cambridge, MA: MIT press.

Hoffner, C. (2008). Parasocial and online social relationships. In S. L. Calvert & B. J. Wilson (Eds.), *The handbook of children, media, and development* (pp. 309–333). Malden, MA: Wiley-Blackwell.

Horton, D., & Wohl, R. R. (1956). Mass communication and parasocial interaction, *Psychiatry, 19,* 215–229.

Huffaker, D. A., & Calvert, S. L. (2005). Gender, identity, and language use in teenage blogs. *Journal of Computer-Mediated Communication, 10:* 00. doi: 10.1111/j.1083-6101.2005.tb00238.x

Huston, A. C., & Wright, J. C. (1983). Children's processing of television: The informative functions of formal features. In J. Bryant & D. R. Anderson (Eds.), *Children's understanding of television: Research on attention and comprehension* (pp. 35–68). New York: Academic Press.

Jackson, L. A., von Eye, A., & Biocca, F. A., Barbatsis, G., Zhao, Y., & Fitzgerald, H. (2006). Does home Internet use influence the academic performance of low-income children? *Developmental Psychology, 42,* 429–435.

Krcmar, M. (2010). Can social meaningfulness and repeat exposure help infants and toddler overcome the video deficit. *Media Psychology, 13,* 31–53.

Kremar, M., Grela, B. & Lin, K. (2007). Can toddlers learn vocabulary from television? *Media Psychology, 10,* 41–63.

Kuhl, P. K., Tsao, F., & Lui, H. (2003). Foreign language experience in infancy: Effects of short term exposure and interaction on phonetic learning. *Proceedings of the National Academy of Sciences, 100,* 9096–9101.

Lauricella, A., Gola, A. A., & Calvert, S. L. (2011). Toddlers' learning from socially meaningful video characters. *Media Psychology, 14,* 216-232.

Lauricella, A., Pempek, T., Barr, R., & Calvert, S. L. (2010). Contingent computer interactions for young children's object retrieval success. *Journal of Applied Developmental Psychology, 31,* 362–369.

Lenhart, A. L., Kahne, J., Middaugh, E., Macgill, A. R., Evans, C., & Vitak, J. (2008). *Teens, video games, and civics. Pew Internet and American Life Project, September* 2008 Retrieved from http://www.pewinternet.org/Reports/2008/Teens-Video-Games-and-Civics.aspx

Lenhart, A., Ling, R., Campbell, S., & Purcell, K. (2010). *Teens and mobile phones.* Pew Internet and American Life Project, Washington, D.C.

Mazur, E., & Richards, L. (2009). Adolescents' and emerging adults' social networking online: Homophily or diversity? *Journal of Applied Developmental Psychology, 32,* 180–188.

Pempek, T., Yermolayeva, Y., & Calvert, S. L. (2009). College students social networking experiences on Facebook. *Journal of Applied Developmental Psychology, 30,* 227–238.

Prensky, M. (2001). Digital natives, digital immigrants, Part 1. *On the Horizon, 9,* 1–6.

Richards, J. E., & Cronise, K. (2000). Extended visual fixation in the early preschool years: Look duration, heart rate changes, and attentional inertia. *Child Development, 71,* 602–620.

Rideout, V., Foehr, U. G., & Roberts, D. F. (2010). *Generation M2: Media in the lives of 8-18-year-olds. A Kaiser Family Foundation Study, January 2010.* Retrieved from http://www.kff.org/entmedia/mh012010pkg.cfm

Rideout, V., & Hamel, E. (2006). *The media family: Electronic media in the lives of infants, toddlers, preschoolers, and their parents. A Kaiser Family Foundation Study, May 2006.* Retrieved from http://www.kff.org/entmedia/7500.cfm.

Roberts, D., Foehr, U., & Rideout, V. (2005). *Generation M: Media in the lives of 8-18-year-olds.* Menlo Park, CA: Kaiser Family Foundation.

Roseberry, S., Hirsh-Pasek, K. Parish-Morris, J., & Golinkoff, R. (2009). Live action: Can children learn verbs from video? *Child Development, 80,* 360–375.

Ruff, H. A., & Rothbart, M. K. (1996). *Attention in early development: Themes and variations.* New York: Oxford University Press.

Staiano, A. E., Abraham, A., & Calvert, S. L. (2012). Competitive versus cooperative exergame play for African American adolescents' executive functioning skills. *Developmental Psychology, 48,* 337–342.

Subramanyam, K., & Greenfield, P. M. (1994). Effects of video game practice on spatial skills in girls and boys. *Journal of Applied Developmental Psychology, 15,* 13–32.

Subrahmanyam, K., Smahel, D., & Greenfield, P. (2006). Connecting developmental constructions to the Internet: Identity presentation and sexual exploration in online teen chat rooms. *Developmental Psychology, 42,* 395–406.

Suddendorf, T. (2003). Early representational insight: Twenty-four month-olds can use a photo to find an object in the world. *Child Development, 74,* 896–904.

Thompson, K. M., & Haninger, K. (2001). Violence in E-rated video games. *Journal of the American Medical Association, 286,* 591–598.

Troseth G. L., & DeLoache J. S. (1998). The medium can obscure the message: Young children's understanding of video. *Child Development, 69,* 950–965.

Troseth, G. L., Saylor, M. M., & Archer, A. H. (2006). Young children's use of video as a source of socially relevant information. *Child Development, 77,* 786–799.

Turkle, S. (1995). *Life on the screen* New York: Simon and Schuster.

Tynes, B., Reynolds, L., & Greenfield, P. M. (2004). Adolescence, race, and ethnicity on the Internet: A comparison of discourse in monitored vs. unmonitored chat rooms. *Journal of Applied Developmental Psychology, 25,* 667–684.

Wright, J. C., Huston, A. C., Ross, R. P., Calvert, S. L., Rolandelli, D., Weeks, L. A., et al. (1984). Pace and continuity of television programs: Effects on children's attention and comprehension. *Developmental Psychology, 20,* 653–666.

Wright, J. C., & Vlietstra, A. G. (1975). The development of selective attention: From perceptual exploration to logical search. In H. W. Reese (Ed.), *Advances in child development and behavior* (Vol. 10, pp. 195–254). New York: Academic Press.

Language, Literacy, and Media

WHAT'S THE WORD ON *SESAME STREET?*

Rosemarie T. Truglio and Jennifer A. Kotler

Media in general, and television and videos in particular, are pervasive aspects of children's lives in the 21st century (see Calvert & Wartella, Chapter 12). This is especially true for preschool children, who spend about 2 hours per day watching television or videos (Common Sense Media, 2011) despite the American Academy of Pediatrics advisement of limiting screen time. Numerous studies on the effects of media on children have led a number of researchers and policy makers to make recommendations about what is best for children. Many conclude that the content of what is watched or used, along with the context in which content is being experienced and the characteristics of the viewer and consumer, all contribute to the effects of exposure (cf. Guernsey, 2007; Kirkorian, Wartella, & Anderson, 2008).

This chapter focuses on content and how quality educational media can enhance educational outcomes. Using the example of *Sesame Street*, the most well-known and well-researched preschool television show, evidence of effectiveness, particularly around vocabulary and oral language, and theories of influence will be highlighted. From its inception, the developers of *Sesame Street* appreciated the potential for television to serve as an educational platform for young children in general and for low-income children in particular, whose access to school readiness experiences was limited.

A Brief Historical View of *Sesame Street*

The 1960s brought many social, economic, and educational initiatives to the forefront of American life. Head Start was developed to provide preschool experiences to children living in disadvantaged socioeconomic conditions so that they could enter formal schooling with the skills and knowledge of peers from more affluent families. At the same time, more families were buying television sets and spending hours in front of the screen watching advertising and programming (almost all of which was not made for young children).

Noting the allure of television and the particular need for improving the school readiness skills of young children from disadvantaged communities, Joan Ganz Cooney, a public affairs producer for the New York public television station, and Lloyd Morrisett, vice president of the Carnegie Foundation, decided in 1966 to produce a television show that brought the best in educational foundations together with the engaging features of television. They named the show *Sesame Street*, and it debuted on November 10, 1969. The product of grants by the Carnegie Foundation, the Ford Foundation, and the Corporation for Public Broadcasting, *Sesame Street* was seen as an experiment, one that that was meticulously planned and heavily researched both as the show was in development (formative research) and at the conclusion of the first season once the show aired (summative research).

The results of the first season's evaluation were highly positive and found strong evidence that the show taught children important school readiness skills. The Educational Testing Service (ETS) evaluated children's skills before and after exposure to 26 weeks of *Sesame Street* compared to children who were not encouraged to view the show. The researchers found that children's learning increased in relation to the amount of time they viewed the show and that the skills emphasized most on the show were those that children learned best. For many of the skills highlighted (e.g., the alphabet and letter sounds, numbers, classification, and shapes), frequent viewers had dramatic increases in those skills (Ball & Bogatz, 1970). The second season's evaluation was also positive (Bogatz & Ball, 1971), and the show garnered critical acclaim and a large audience of preschool fans.

More than 40 years later, *Sesame Street* is the longest "street" in the world, with original or dubbed co-productions in more than 150 countries. The original *Sesame Street* model, which brought together producers, writers, educators, and researchers, still exists today. Each season is still approached as an experimental season (i.e., trying and testing new ideas) and driven by a whole-child curriculum (academic skills such as literacy, mathematics, and science; social and emotional development; and health). Formative research remains integral to the production process, and results are used to ensure that the content is engaging, relevant, and comprehensible to a preschool audience. The core mission of *Sesame Street* (formerly known as Children's Television Workshop), to help children from economically disadvantaged backgrounds and families prepare for school and reach their highest potential, still remains. To address the critical needs of children and to incorporate the latest research in child development and educational practices into content development, a specific curriculum focus is identified and a curriculum is developed and later evaluated for its educational effectiveness as it is implemented in content across media platforms.

Effectiveness of *Sesame Street* as a Teaching Tool

Numerous research studies have demonstrated *Sesame Street*'s effectiveness across a wide range of cognitive, emotional, social, and physical domains (see Fisch & Truglio [2001] for a review). For example, the Early Window Study demonstrated that children who were regular viewers of *Sesame Street* at age 2 scored higher on reading, math, vocabulary, and school readiness tests at age 5 and also spent more time reading or looking at books as compared with nonviewers, even when controlling for maternal education, the quality of the home environment, and the child's primary home language (Wright, Huston, Scantlin, & Kotler, 2001). A second study demonstrated that regular *Sesame Street* viewers at age 3 had greater vocabulary knowledge at age 5, controlling for other factors also associated with greater vocabulary development as just noted (Rice, Huston, Truglio, & Wright, 1990), and that those who watched the show regularly at age 4 were more likely than nonviewers to have higher emergent literacy skills, have greater ability to read storybooks on their own, and have fewer reading problems in first or second grade (Zill, Davies, & Daly, 1994). Lemish and Rice (1986) noted that parents who co-view *Sesame Street* with their children tended to use techniques similar to those used when reading with children such as labeling, questioning, commenting, and using descriptive language to describe events. Such supports are critical in helping to encourage children's language development (Whitehurst & Lonigan, 1998).

Findings from a more recent long-term study found that greater exposure to *Sesame Street* in the preschool years was related to higher academic achievement scores during the high school years. Specifically, children who viewed *Sesame Street* content regularly in the preschool years attained better grades in English, math, and science in high school as compared with nonviewers or less frequent viewers. *Sesame Street* viewers also had higher grade point averages, read more frequently, reported higher levels of academic self-esteem, and expressed greater appreciation for the value of educational achievement as compared with nonviewers and those who viewed less frequently. These effects were maintained even after controlling for variables related to both viewing and educational outcomes, such as mother's education, the quality of the home environment, and the child's primary home language (Anderson, Huston, Schmitt, Linebarger, & Wright, 2001).

In contrast, several recent studies have questioned the use of educational television as a learning tool, especially for children aged 2 and younger, and one study in particular found that viewing *Sesame Street* was associated with slower growth in vocabulary as compared with the vocabulary trajectories of nonviewers (Linebarger & Walker, 2005). A possible explanation for these results may be an artifact of the magazine-style format of *Sesame Street* as compared with the more story-driven format of shows such as *Dora the Explorer* and *Blue's Clues*. Specifically, *Sesame Street*'s original format involved a main storyline that was woven throughout the hour instead of being shown as a noninterruptible linear story. In 2001, *Sesame Street* redesigned the show format so that the main "street" story is shown as a noninterruptible narrative at the top of the hour, thereby lending itself to a more cohesive viewing experience. Indeed, in a follow-up study, researchers found that children who viewed *Sesame Street* videos (which are designed as a cohesive story driven by a singular theme) had higher vocabulary growth than did children who did not watch *Sesame Street* videos (Linebarger, 2005).

Theoretical Basis

A variety of cognitive and social psychological theories have been applied to understand *Sesame Street*'s success in improving young children's school readiness skills and what it is about good quality educational media that contributes to effective teaching practices. First, information processing models suggest that people learn better with multiple sensory inputs, such as charts, diagrams, and moving pictures, than with a singular input (Mayer, 2001). In fact, Paivio (2006) posits that people process visual and audio information through multiple channels and store the processed information differently. The synergy of the two or more representations in memory allow for more efficient retrieval of information. A capacity model of processing suggests that children process educational information woven explicitly into stories more efficiently than educational information conveyed in alternate formats because they have a well-developed schema of story understanding that facilitates comprehension and storage of the story content (Fisch, 2000). When the educational content is embedded into the arc of the story, people will have an easier time processing the educational content than if it is tangential to the plotline. For example, a recent study examining the effectiveness of *The Electric Company* on children's learning found that children learned educational content that was embedded in the main storyline better than educational content that was included in short bits in between segments that did not advance the larger story line (Garrity, Piotrowski, McMenamin, & Linebarger, 2010).

Second, social learning theories (e.g. Bandura, 1977) speak more to specific character actions and portrayals and the effects those characters have on viewers or users of media. Furthermore, social learning perspectives place value on the characteristics of the media users themselves and the qualities they bring to the experience. *Parasocial relationships*, or the relationships that users develop with beloved characters, exert powerful influences on viewers' attitudes, knowledge, and behavior. Evidence suggests that children learn more from and are more likely to behave in ways that are similar to those of their favorite characters (Kotler, Schiffman, & Hanson, 2012; Lauricella, Gola, & Calvert, 2011). For example, children were more likely to choose healthy foods when a sticker of a liked character (e.g., Elmo) was used to promote it as compared with when a sticker of an unknown character was used to promote the healthy food or when no sticker was placed on the food item (Kotler et al., 2012; Wansink, Just, & Payne, 2012). Similarly, toddlers were more likely to learn a math task (seriation) when an Elmo puppet was shown modeling the task as compared with when an unknown puppet was used to model the same task (Lauricella et al., 2011).

Taken together, theoretical and empirical evidence suggests that television programs for children can be powerful educators because of their multiple sensory inputs, their relevant and engaging storylines that encourage children to remain focused on the plotline, and their characters whom children admire and want to emulate. Given the rich conversations that characters have with each other on *Sesame Street*, an emphasis on vocabulary development was included as part of the literacy curriculum focus for Season 38 (2006–2007) to address our nation's literacy crisis. The next section focuses specifically on how *Sesame Street* utilized the power of the show's characters and a new segment entitled "Word on the Street" to expose children to rich vocabulary and, through repetition across contexts, to deepen their understanding of these words and concepts.

Supporting Young Children's Oral Language and Vocabulary Development

Children's vocabulary and oral language comprehension during the preschool years play an essential role in their long-term academic success (Cunningham & Stanovich, 1997; Hart & Risley, 1995; Stahl & Nagy, 2006). Extensive research indicates that vocabulary, conceptual knowledge, and comprehension are inextricably related (Biemiller, 2006) and central to comprehension in elementary school and beyond (Cunningham & Stanovich, 1997; Scarborough, 2001). Research also informs us of the significant gap in words preschool-aged children are exposed to and use across children from low-income families and those from middle- and upper-class families (Hart & Risley, 2003). Furthermore, over time, children who enter school with limited vocabulary knowledge fall further behind those who initially have greater word knowledge and language skills (Biemiller & Slonim, 2001).

Given the differential trajectories in school achievement between those who enter school already behind and those who enter at level, researchers have highlighted the critical importance of vocabulary interventions to increase knowledge and accelerate learning for children most at risk of school failure (Maroulis & Neuman, 2010). Effective vocabulary instruction provides clear instructions regarding word learning, is systematic and explicit, and provides children with plenty of opportunities to use words in a variety of contexts (Neuman & Dwyer, 2009; Pressley, 2001).

What's the *Word on the Street*?

The newly created *Word on the Street* segment features Murray, a new muppet who interviews various children and adults about one targeted word each day. Every show begins with Murray on the streets of New York City introducing the word of the day. Children and adults describe the targeted word in various ways, through actions, visuals, and verbal descriptions. To reinforce learning, the targeted word is repeated and defined in the context of the "street story," a 10- to 15-minute narrative story toward the beginning of the program and in a subsequent segment featuring a celebrity and a muppet character. The use of celebrities on the show invites the adult co-viewer to extend the learning of these words.

EVALUATION OF WORD ON THE STREET

To assess the effectiveness of these segments in increasing children's knowledge of the target vocabulary words, we worked with children ($N = 112$) in six early childhood centers located across New York City that served children from predominantly low-income backgrounds. Three centers served as the experimental group, and three centers served as the control group. The centers were comparable across demographics. The experimental group received eight abridged *Sesame Street* episodes (approximately 20 minutes each) containing the targeted vocabulary word in each episode. The words were *ballet, squid, pumpernickel, pretend, gigantic, amazing, tricycle,* and *lazy.* Teachers in the experimental group centers were asked to show two assigned episodes two times per week over the course of 4 weeks. During the final week of the study, teachers were asked to show all eight episodes, two on each of four days. The procedure for the control group was the same as the experimental group except that the eight episodes viewed by the children were designed around health and nutrition, discussed different types of foods, and did not include any literacy- or vocabulary-based messages. Teachers in the control group were given the same instructions as those in the experimental group in terms of the frequency of viewing.

Although standardized measures of vocabulary might be ideal for assessing change in children's vocabulary development pre- and post-intervention, we did not believe such an assessment would be sensitive enough to capture the change produced by a brief intervention. Indeed, the National Reading Panel notes that standardized measures are often not sensitive enough to detect change in vocabulary knowledge as a function of various interventions (Maroulis & Neuman, 2010). Consequently, we developed a more proximal measure to assess whether children learned the targeted vocabulary words shown in the episodes. This approach is consistent with that taken in a recent study by Coyne and colleagues (e.g., Coyne, McCoach, & Kapp, 2007).

Children were pre-tested via a multiple-choice picture test on the eight target words, two alternative words on the street from episodes not shown to either group, and an additional five foods mentioned in the control group episodes but not highlighted by a *Word on the Street* segment. Assignment of the six early child care centers to either the experimental or control group conditions was informed by the pre-test scores. We attempted to ensure that the average pre-test scores of the schools to each condition were matched to the average pre-test scores of the others.

After each week of viewing, children were tested on the two words on the street that were highlighted for that week in the experimental condition, as well as on one of the foods that were mentioned in the control videos. In these weekly post-tests, children were asked in an open-ended manner to produce the meaning of each word (e.g., What is pumpernickel?). They also were given pictorial multiple-choice options (e.g., Which one of these pictures shows a tricycle?). After the fifth viewing week, children were retested on all of the 15 pre-test words with multiple-choice options. Results demonstrated differences in knowledge across the experimental and control group conditions at pre-test. However, as shown in Figure 12.1, children who viewed the *Word on the Street* episodes (i.e., assigned to the experimental condition) knew an average of two more word meanings at post-test, approximately 1 week after the study was completed, as compared with the children who viewed the control episodes.

Children were more likely to identify the words highlighted on *Sesame Street* after viewing. The content increased children's word knowledge with little intervention from the teachers to encourage discussion about the words. These promising results occurred with words that were related to the particular street story for each episode, but were unrelated to each other. Based on these findings, *Sesame Street* decided to continue with the *Word on the Street* format to expose preschoolers to both general vocabulary and domain-specific vocabulary to support a science curriculum (a curriculum focus to address science, technology, engineering, and math [STEM] education) in subsequent seasons.

EVALUATION OF WORLDS OF WORDS

As researchers have noted, children are likely to learn words faster and more efficiently if they learn them through understanding the superordinate categories into

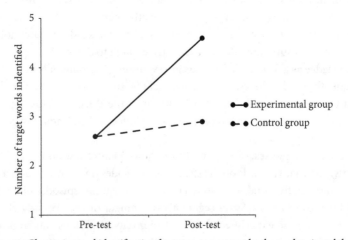

FIGURE 12.1 *Change in word identification from pre- to post-test by those who viewed the Word on the Street episodes (experimental) versus those who watched alternative episodes (control).*

which they fit. In other words, children learn words better in taxonomies, which are groupings of items with particular characteristics (see Neuman, Newman, & Dwyer, 2010). Susan Neuman has developed a language-rich curriculum called "Worlds of Words (WOW)." The WOW curriculum, aligned with national pre-K standards, supports children's literacy through a variety of exercises that help develop knowledge and vocabulary in academic subjects such as math, health, and social studies. The goal of this experimental pilot curriculum was to foster growth in vocabulary and conceptual knowledge among 3- and 4-year-old children from economically disadvantaged backgrounds and families. The curriculum integrated selected segments from *Sesame Street* to support the concepts being taught. Books, cards, and other activities are also part of this 12-minute daily supplemental curriculum (Neuman et al., 2010).

A recent evaluation of the WOW curriculum was conducted in two phases. In the first phase, Head Start classrooms were randomly assigned to an experimental group that received the WOW curriculum or a control group that was given an alternative supplemental literacy curriculum. In the second phase, a sample of children from middle- to high-income preschool centers were given tests of expressive language, receptive language, and knowledge of categories and concepts that children who received the WOW curriculum were also tested on to assess the degree to which WOW narrowed a potential achievement gap. Results indicated that the children in the Head Start centers who received the WOW curriculum consistently outperformed their Head Start peers who received the alternative curriculum. Moreover, children in Head Start classrooms that received the WOW curriculum in some instances scored on par with children sampled from the middle- to high-income preschool centers who did not receive the curriculum (Neuman et al., 2010). This study demonstrated further empirical support that *Sesame Street* content could improve vocabulary knowledge.

THE *WORD ON THE STREET* IS . . . SCIENCE

Given the importance of domain knowledge, the findings from our own study of *Word on the Street*, and Susan Neuman's evaluation of *Worlds of Words,* we sought to examine the effect of our science curriculum in Seasons 40 and 41 (which launched in the fall of 2009 and 2010, respectively) on children's knowledge of scientific vocabulary. The goal of *Sesame Street*'s 40th season was to foster children's sense of wonder and exploration of the natural world, addressing topics such as bees and pollination, camping and outdoors, gardens, and amphibians. In Season 41, *Sesame Street* expanded the science curriculum to emphasize scientific investigation and inquiry skills, addressing such topics as gravity, wind, and camouflage.

To assess the show's impact on science domain vocabulary and concept comprehension, two studies were conducted using methodology similar to the initial *Word on the Street* study. More than 600 children participated across the two studies. The children were 3-, 4-, and 5-year-olds from lower- and middle-income households in the urban northeast and suburban Midwest. Participating children were randomly assigned either to a control group, which viewed health and nutrition videos, or an experimental group, which viewed science and nature videos. Children in the experimental group classrooms and centers watched seven 15-minute *Sesame Street* clips two to three times a week for 4 weeks, for a total of 20 viewings. Children were tested on science knowledge before and after the 4-week viewing period. Teachers were instructed not to supplement the video instruction between the pre- and post-tests.

In the first study, covering Season 40, children were given two assessments. One was a free-response question in which children were asked to describe a concept presented in the video, such as metamorphosis. The second assessment was a 22-item multiple-choice test in which children chose one of four pictures to answer a specific scientific question. Results indicated that children in the experimental group scored significantly higher than the control group on their knowledge of nature on the post-test, compared with the pre-test on both free responses (see Figure 12.2) and multiple-choice questions (see Figure 12.3). Furthermore, they showed evidence of learning about topics such as pollination, hibernation, and habitats (Brooks, Kotler, & Truglio, 2011).

The second study, based on Season 41, was similar to the first, but focused on different and more challenging scientific concepts. Given the successful results from Season 40, we assessed whether *Sesame Street* content could extend beyond teaching scientific facts into scientific process skills. In addition to free-response and multiple-choice questions, children's story comprehension skills were also assessed.

Results were similar to the earlier study assessing children's learning of science-related terms included in Season 40; children in the experimental group scored significantly higher than children in the control group after watching the videos

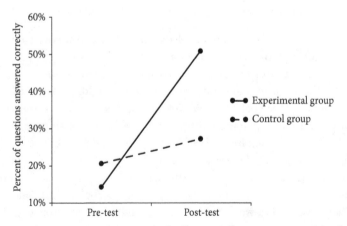

FIGURE 12.2 *Average correct response rates for Season 40 free-response questions about meaning of science words.*

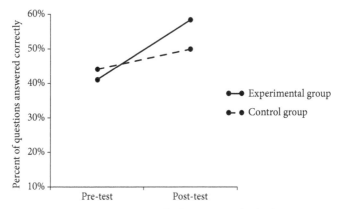

FIGURE 12.3 *Average correct response rates for Season 40 multiple-choice questions about meaning of science words.*

(Brooks, Kotler, Gartner, & Truglio, 2012). In fact, children's scores on the free-response questions were 100% greater at post-test for children in the experimental condition (see Figure 12.4). Increases were also found for the multiple-choice questions (see Figure 12.5).

As a part of this study, educators were asked not to discuss the program with children during the research phase, to avoid contaminating the results through the additional benefit of supplementary conversation or support. Given that most children who view such programs would likely be doing so at home and may not have access to an adult who could or would be able to elaborate on the programming, we believed it necessary to test the effectiveness of the lessons and scaffolding embedded in the media on their own. We heard from educators, however, that they and the children were indeed interested in continuing conversations from what they had learned and that the shows were a springboard for classroom activities. Consequently, we are currently working on projects that would integrate

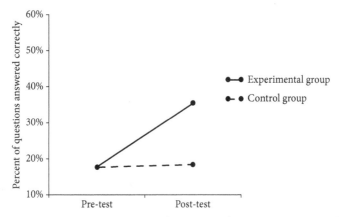

FIGURE 12.4 *Average correct response rates for Season 41 free-response questions about meaning of scientific process words.*

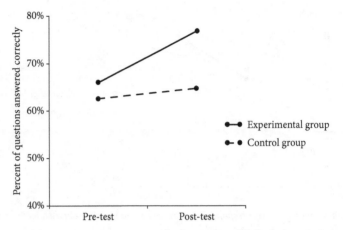

FIGURE 12.5 *Average correct response rates for Season 41 multiple-choice questions about meaning of scientific process words.*

Sesame Street digital assets into classroom lessons so that teachers can extend the learning from media with in-depth discussions and classroom activities.

One example of using *Sesame Street* and other digital assets embedded within a classroom curriculum was developed by the Center for Children and Technology division of the Education Development Center (EDC) in partnership with SRI International. Video clips and interactive web and computer games from several educational media properties, including *Sesame Street*, were included in a 10-week literacy-rich curriculum. A randomized experimental study, implemented in low-income preschools in New York and California, evaluated the effectiveness of the multiple-media curriculum as compared with an alternative curriculum. The results indicated that children who were exposed to the multiple-media literacy intervention showed greater gains in their scores on a variety of literacy measures (i.e., naming letters, knowledge of letter sounds, concepts of stories and print) relative to the control group (Penuel et al., 2009). This study further supports the role of *Sesame Street* in making a significant contribution to literacy interventions.

Sesame Street on the Go

As more media are developed for use on mobile devices, educators and researchers have begun to think about the ways in which educational content can be developed to capitalize on the unique features of these new technologies. One innovative project entitled *Learning Letters with Elmo* provided parents with a smartphone to help support children's literacy skills (Horowitz et al., 2006). Given the importance of parental involvement in children's reading skills (Sénéchal & LeFevre, 2002), the idea of this project was to provide parents with simple, "everyday moments" suggestions for how to support children's letter and word knowledge using smartphones as a tool to do so. Four times a week over the course of 8 weeks, 79 parents received a text message that reminded them that content was ready for them. Parents were asked to access the available content through their mobile phone and were provided with literacy tips through a recording by one of the *Sesame Street* human cast members. The tips focused on how parents can incorporate letter recognition and letter sounds activities into their everyday routines. For example, parents were told that the letter of the day was "*c*" and the message suggested that they talk to their children about all of the items in their home that begin with the letter *c*. Parents were then asked to hand their phone to their child to watch a segment with Elmo introducing the letter of the day, followed by a short video about the letter. Parents were asked to stream a new letter set (the parent tips and the video) several times a week.

Participants were surveyed before and after receiving the text messages about activities around letters and their children's knowledge of the alphabet. Findings indicated that participants reported statistically significant pre-post changes on literacy activities targeted by the intervention. Parents reported an increase in how often they asked their children to look for letters on signs or on printed materials around the house. Moreover, more than three-fourths of participants believed to a *good extent* or *great extent* that a cell phone used in this way can be an effective learning tool (Horowitz et al., 2006).

Although there was no control group, results of this study indicate the potential that mobile phones may have for learning, particularly as they become more ubiquitous in families with children. To this end, Sesame Workshop has created free podcasts around *Word on the Street* that can be downloaded on a variety of mobile devices. These podcasts contain parent tips as well as video content to be viewed by parents, children, caregivers, or anyone else who wants to view or listen to them, and they are available for free on iTunes. We are currently working on an initiative that would deliver podcasts via mobile phones to parents of preschoolers with tips and activities that would help their children transition to kindergarten.

Conclusion

Various media initiatives involving *Sesame Street* content and characters have been associated with increased literacy skills for children. There are several theoretical reasons for these positive effects, and most of them focus on the content of the messages, the techniques used to deliver the content, the extent to which children identify with the characters, and the contexts of use (i.e., using media as a tool for a teachable learning moment between a parent and child).

Future Sesame Workshop initiatives will continue to focus on the use of new media platforms for educating children. Given the explosion in the new media landscape and the near universality of mobile technology that will potentially be seen within the new decade, the use of media content will likely be transformed. Individualized content and the ability to use media anytime, anywhere has begun to shape new conversations about the effects of digital media on children. The evidence base for the influence of such technologies is relatively nascent, but the Education and Research Department at Sesame Workshop has been spending time with children as they play and use a variety of new digital media platforms. The focus of this research is on how age-appropriate content can be placed on a range of media platforms to help children develop foundational literacy skills to better prepare them for kindergarten.

Sesame Street exists in a larger universe of educational media content and a much larger societal context. However, given that it is the longest running educational children's program, there are clearly some elements of the show's success that have implications for developing educational media and policies around young children's use of media. First, the attention to research (basic, formative, and summative) and the process of refining content based on the results of testing has resulted in quality educational content that is developmentally appropriate. Second, by identifying critical needs of children and developing the age-appropriate curriculum that addresses these needs across media platforms, we have been able to reach, engage, and teach children important school readiness skills and life lessons. And third, the strong collaborative working relationships within a cross-disciplinary team (e.g., producers, writers, performers, animators, educators, researchers) is the cornerstone of Sesame Workshop's success in providing access to quality early childhood education to all children, especially those who have the least access to help them reach their full potential.

References

Anderson, D. R., Huston, A. C., Schmitt, K. L., Linebarger, D. L., & Wright, J. C. (2001). Early childhood television viewing and adolescent behavior: The Recontact Study. *Monographs of the Society for Research in Child Development 68*(1), 1–143.

Ball, S., & Bogatz, G. A. (1970). *The first year of Sesame Street: An evaluation* Princeton, NJ: Educational Testing Service.

Bandura, A. (1977). *Social learning theory*. New York: General Learning Press.

Biemiller, A. (2006). Vocabulary development and instruction: A prerequisite for school learning. In D. K. Dickinson & S. B. Neuman (Eds.), *Handbook of early literacy research* (Vol. 2, pp. 41–51). New York: Guilford Press.

Biemiller, A., & Slonim, N. (2001). Estimating root word vocabulary growth in normative and advantaged populations: Evidence for a common sequence of vocabulary acquisition. *Journal of Educational Psychology, 93*(3), 498–520.

Bogatz, G. A., & Ball, S. (1971). *The second year of Sesame Street: A continuing evaluation.* Princeton, NJ: Educational Testing Service.

Brooks, M. K., Kotler, J. A., Gartner, T., & Truglio, R. T. (2012). *The words on the street are nature and science: An evaluation of Sesame Street's curriculum.* Paper presented at the annual meeting of the International Communication Association, Phoenix, Arizona.

Brooks, M. K., Kotler, J. A., & Truglio, R. T. (2011). The Influence of Sesame Street on children's understanding of nature and the environment. *Poster presented at the biennial meeting of the Society for Research in Child Development,* Montreal, QC, Canada.

Common Sense Media. (2011). *Zero to eight: Children's media use in America.* San Francisco, CA: Common Sense Media.

Coyne, M. D., McCoach, D. B., & Kapp, S. (2007). Vocabulary intervention for kindergarten students: Comparing extended instruction with embedded instruction and incidental exposure. *Learning Disabilities Quarterly, 30,* 74–88

Cunningham, A. E., & Stanovich, K. E. (1997). Early reading acquisition and its relation to reading experience and ability 10 years later. *Developmental Psychology, 33,* 934–945.

Fisch, S. M. (2000). A capacity model of children's comprehension of educational content on television. *Media Psychology, 2,* 63–91.

Fisch, S. M., & Truglio, R. T. (2001). *"G" is for growing.* Mahwah, NJ: Lawrence Erlbaum Associates.

Garrity, K. M., Piotrowski, J. T., McMenamin, K., & Linebarger, D. L. (2010). *A summative evaluation of The Electric Company. A report prepared for the Corporation for Public Broadcasting* Philadelphia, PA: Annenberg School for Communication, University of Pennsylvania.

Guernsey, L. (2007). *Screen time: How electronic media—From baby videos to educational software—Affects your young children.* New York: Basic Books.

Hart, B., & Risley, T. (1995). *Meaningful differences in the everyday experience of young American children.* Baltimore: Paul H. Brookes Publishing

Hart, B., & Risley, T. (2003). The early catastrophe: The 30 million word gap. *American Educator, 27,* 4–9.

Horowitz, J. E., Sosenko, L. D., Hoffman, J. L. S., Ziobrowski, J., Tafoya, A., Haagenson, A., & Hahn, S. (2006). *Evaluation of the PBS Ready to Learn Cell Phone Study: Learning letters with Elmo.* A report prepared for the PBS Ready to Learn Grant.

Kirkorian, H. L., Wartella, E. A., & Anderson, D. R. (2008). Media and young children's learning. *The Future of Children, 18,* 39–61.

Kotler, J. A., Schiffman, J. M., & Hanson, K. G. (2012). The influence of media characters on children's food choices. *Journal of Health Communication, 17*(8), 886–898.

Lauricella, A. R., Gola, A. A. H., & Calvert, S. L. (2011). Toddlers' learning from socially meaningful video characters. *Media Psychology, 14* (2), 216–232.

Lemish, D., & Rice M. (1986). Television as a talking picture book: A prop for language acquisition. *Journal of Child Language, 13,* 251–274.

Linebarger, D. L. (2005). *Infants' and toddlers' video and on-air viewing and language development.* Paper presented at the biennial meeting of the Society for Research on Child Development, Atlanta, GA.

Linebarger, D. L., & Walker, D. (2005). Infants' and toddlers' television viewing and language outcomes. *American Behavioral Scientist, 48,* 624–645.

Maroulis, L., & Neuman, S. (2010). The effects of vocabulary intervention on young children's word learning: A meta-analysis. *Review of Educational Research, 80* (3), 300–335.

Mayer, R. E. (2001). *Multimedia learning.* Cambridge: Cambridge University Press.

Neuman, S. B., & Dwyer, J. (2009). Missing in action: Vocabulary instruction in pre-K. *The Reading Teacher, 62,* 384–392.

Neuman, S. B., Newman, E. H., & Dwyer, J. (2010). *Educational effects of an embedded multimedia vocabulary intervention for economically disadvantaged pre-K children: A randomized trial.* A report prepared for the Corporation for Public Broadcasting. Ann Arbor: University of Michigan.

Paivio, A. (2006). *Mind and its evolution; A dual coding theoretical interpretation*, Mahwah, NJ: Lawrence Erlbaum Associates, Inc.

Penuel, W. R., Pasnik, S., Bates, L., Townsend, E., Gallagher, L. P., Llorente, C., & Hupert, N. (2009). *Preschool teachers can use a media-rich curriculum to prepare low-income children for school success: Results of a randomized controlled trial.* New York and Menlo Park, CA: Education Development Center, Inc., and SRI International.

Pressley, M. (2001). *Effective beginning reading instruction.* Executive Summary and Paper Commissioned by the National Reading Conference. Chicago, IL: National Reading Conference.

Rice, M. L., Huston, A. C., Truglio, R., & Wright, J. C. (1990). Words from 'Sesame Street': Learning vocabulary while viewing. *Developmental Psychology, 26,* 421–428.

Scarborough, H. (2001). Connecting early language and literacy to later reading (dis)abilities: Evidence, theory, and practice. In S. B. Neuman & D. Dickinson (Eds.), *Handbook of early literacy research* (pp. 97–110). New York: Guilford.

Sénéchal, M., & LeFevre, J. (2002). Parental involvement in the development of children's reading skill: A five-year longitudinal study. *Child Development, 73,* 445–460.

Stahl, S., & Nagy, W. (2006). *Teaching word meanings.* Mahwah, NJ: Lawrence Erlbaum.

Wansink, B., Just, D. R., & Payne, C. R. (2012). Can branding improve school lunches? *Preventive Medicine, 166*(10): 967–968

Whitehurst, G., & Lonigan, C. (1998). Child development and emergent literacy. *Child Development, 69,* 848–872.

Wright, J. C., Huston, A. C., Scantlin, R. M., & Kotler, J. A. (2001). The Early Window Project: Sesame Street prepares children for school (pp. 97–114). In S. Fisch & R. Truglio (Eds.), *"G" is for "growing": Thirty years of research on Sesame Street.* Mahwah, NJ: Lawrence Erlbaum Associates.

Zill, N., Davies, E., & Daly, M. (1994). *Viewing of Sesame Street by preschool children and its relationship to school readiness.* Report prepared for Children's Television Workshop. Rockville, MD: Westat.

Programs and Policies as Contextual Opportunities for Improving Children's Lives

{ 13 }

Connecting Research and Practice

Robert C. Granger, Vivian Tseng, and Brian L. Wilcox

There is a common model—shared by many researchers and funders—that describes how applied developmental science is used to improve young people's lives. Researchers do rigorous studies, develop important findings, and clearly communicate those findings to policy makers and practitioners, who in turn use them to shape policy and practice to improve the lives of young people. Given the significant changes over the past 30 years in how research is conducted and disseminated, we should expect to see accompanying improvements in child and youth outcomes. There are, however, few examples of research informing policy or practice and improving youth outcomes on a broad scale (Granger, 2011).

In 2009, the National Academies of Science noted this problem, issuing a report that summarized what had been learned in the prior 15 years about the factors that protect young people from risk—or place them at risk—for mental, emotional, and behavioral disorders. The report identified a number of thoroughly studied programs that had reduced risk or prevented problems. It went on to state, "thus far, however, prevention interventions have generally not been widely implemented in schools and communities and have done little to reduce behavioral health problems in American communities" (O'Connell, Boat, & Warner, 2009, p. 297).

As senior staff at the William T. Grant Foundation—an institution whose mission is "supporting research to improve the lives of young people"—we are concerned about the disconnection between research and practice. We have come to believe that the steps researchers have taken to improve their work—better methodologies, syntheses, and the like—are important but insufficient. The Foundation has begun to explore the gaps between research, policy, and (particularly) practice, looking for ways that practitioners and researchers can work together to productively inform each other's efforts. As part of this examination, we are supporting studies of how policy makers and practitioners acquire, interpret, and use research evidence.

Early impressions from this work challenge the wisdom of many of the existing approaches for facilitating research use. Consistent with the common model, we and other researchers have too often approached the problem from our own perspective, focusing on producing more reliable and accurate findings and writing about those findings in clear, short documents. What we have failed to emphasize, until more recently, are the intended research users and the organizational and other forces that shape their work. For example, recent studies of the use of research evidence funded by the Foundation find that practitioners define evidence more broadly than researchers. When it comes to "what works," they are focused on the relevance of evidence-based programs or practices to their local situation and the ease, procedures, and cost of implementing such innovations. Research and evaluation studies seldom provide information on these issues. Moreover, practitioners often prefer to get their information from their networks of trusted peers and intermediaries, rather than from researchers whom they do not know or policy makers whom they often mistrust. Researchers and policy makers fail to capitalize on these networks in their dissemination activities. If these early impressions are durable, they open up fresh ways to think about research–practice connections.

We frame our discussion around three reasons why research and practice are poorly connected:

1. Differences in areas such as language, norms, and incentives separate researchers and practitioners and lead to differing definitions of what counts as evidence;
2. Practitioners do not trust the relevance of research findings or the motives behind many interpretations of findings; and
3. Research evidence is not readily accessible or easily interpreted.

In developing our analysis, we draw on research studies as well as on conceptual and exploratory work we commissioned in the past few years (Coburn, Penuel, & Geil, 2012; Davies & Nutley, 2008; Nelson, Leffler, & Hansen, 2009) and a framework we developed for guiding our grant making in this area (Tseng, 2012b). These sources consider the processes by which practitioners and policy makers define, acquire, interpret, and use research evidence. In general, we are less focused on the individual actors and more on how their social networks, organizational settings, and political, policy, and service contexts affect such processes.

We support researchers who draw on theory and methods from a wide range of disciplines. Most are conducting in-depth case studies in a small number of sites in order to uncover promising ideas that could lead to more robust theories and testable hypotheses. Investigators have chosen a sample of cases that contrast with each other in ways presumed to matter for the acquisition, interpretation, and/or use of research. The investigators are collecting and integrating multiple sources of data on the same activities, going beyond prior studies that relied solely on interviews and surveys. For example, some teams are observing meetings at which people deliberate over issues and make decisions, interviewing participants to understand their perceptions of what occurred and the research discussed, and collecting and coding relevant documents. Most of the studies are prospective and longitudinal, which helps mitigate the problems of recall bias and post-hoc rationalization of events. Several are also incorporating social network analyses in order to rigorously examine the role of relationships.

Because most of the research projects are still in the field, our impressions will evolve. We have, though, seen enough consistency in the early results to extract themes about what the findings imply for improving the connections between research and practice.

Why Practice? What About Policy?

In this chapter, we are focused on the research–practice connection that is not mediated by policy. Explicit in some analyses of the research–practice connection is the assumption that the path from research to practice goes through public policy. Some of it does. Policy making unquestionably influences practice through regulations and laws that manipulate incentives and allocate resources. However, policy is a blunt instrument for shaping day-to-day practice. Under law, or within a funding stream or domestic social program, practice varies widely. Some of the variation is in accord with the intentions of policy makers and some is far off. Consider, for example, people driving on the same road. Some drive much faster—a few much slower—than the speed limit. Similarly, teachers in the same school under the same policies and constraints vary widely in their practices and effectiveness (Loeb, Rouse, & Shorris, 2007). Because of this, we see changes in policy similarly to the way we view researcher-driven improvements in the conduct and dissemination of research—useful but not sufficient to improve practice.

WHO ARE THE KEY PRACTITIONERS?

At the Foundation, we are trying to understand and improve the immediate social settings that shape youth development, including classrooms, youth programs, and households. Much of the research we support is focused on the frontline practitioners—teachers, youth workers, case managers, social workers, and mentors who directly work with youth. But in studies of how practitioners acquire, interpret, and use research, we have focused on the mid-level decision makers in state and local agencies, as well as their counterparts in intermediary organizations who serve as bridges between research and practice.

Within these state and local agencies—which include departments of education, employment, health, justice, mental health, and social services—administrators and program managers shape the frontline practices of concern to many policy makers and researchers. They play a critical role in interpreting legislation, writing regulations, allocating resources, designing staff development systems, and adopting new programs. Many of these agencies lack the internal capacity to access and interpret research and seek help from intermediaries (e.g., professional associations, consultants, advocacy organizations).

Within the research community, there is insufficient understanding of these decision makers' work; their research needs; and how they acquire, interpret, and use research. In the private sector, such ignorance of clients' needs would doom a business to failure. We need to do better.

Cultural Divides

Nathan Caplan (1979) asserted that the problem of research use was due to researchers and policy makers living in "two communities" that were not well connected. Each community has distinct customs, languages, norms, and incentives—essentially creating a "cultural divide." The two communities became three, to include practitioners, in writings by Jack Shonkoff (2000) and Aletha Huston (2005, 2008).

The divide between researchers and practitioners is manifest in many ways. One example is seen in how each defines *evidence* and prioritizes its importance for practice. Although standards for evidence are contested in the research community (National Research Council, 2002), researchers rarely question the importance of using research evidence in practice. Researchers often use the words *research* and *evidence* interchangeably (Kellam & Langevin, 2003), but practitioners define evidence more broadly. In their review of more than 50 studies, Honig and Coburn (2008) found that school district staff drew on a wide array of evidence, including social science research, student achievement data, expert testimony, practitioner knowledge, and parent and community input. More recently, Asen, Gurke, and their colleagues (Asen, Gurke, Solomon, Conners, & Gumm, 2011; Asen, Gurke, Connors, Solomon, & Gumm, 2013) observed and recorded school board meetings in order to identify the types of evidence used in deliberations. They too found use of a broad array of evidence types. Specific cases or incidents were used most often to support claims made in meetings, followed by experience, data, testimony, research, and, last, law/policy. Nelson et al. (2009) interviewed and conducted focus groups with a range of education stakeholders including congressional education staffers, chief state school officers, state legislators, superintendents, curriculum coordinators, and school board members. Those policy makers and practitioners employed a broad definition of *research* that included empirical findings, data, personal experiences, the experiences of others, and constituent feedback.

In an attempt to decrease the variety in what counts as evidence, recent education, Head Start, and child welfare legislation has defined *evidence* as information relevant to practice that comes from high-quality studies. For example, the No Child Left Behind Act (2002, subpart 37 of section 9101) invokes the term *scientifically based research*, defining it as "research that involves the application of rigorous, systematic, and objective procedures to obtain reliable and valid knowledge relevant to education activities and programs." This definition is inclusive of research using "observational or experimental methods," but the practitioners and policy makers interviewed in Nelson's study often associated the term more narrowly with "gold standard," randomized controlled trials used to assess whether interventions are effective (i.e., the "what works" agenda). In an environment calling for the use of evidence-based programs and practices, these different definitions can easily create misunderstanding and confusion.

Connecting research and practice requires bridging these definitional differences. We need to acknowledge that research is only one type of evidence that matters in practice. And we need greater shared understanding of the strengths and weaknesses of different sources of evidence and the role each might play in practitioners' decisions. Researchers who develop a stronger understanding of practitioners' work are better positioned to appreciate clinical knowledge. Practitioners who better understand research will improve the inferences they draw. Both parties would learn how research and other types of evidence can be integrated to arrive at sound decisions.

Trust

Lack of trust is another byproduct of the cultural divide and takes at least two forms: differences between researchers and practitioners in what makes research evidence trustworthy and the characteristics of a trustworthy source.

TRUSTWORTHY RESEARCH EVIDENCE

For researchers, an argument about the trustworthiness of research findings often concerns the standards of evidence for research-based claims. This causes researchers to focus on the claims that can be supported by particular research designs, samples, measures, data, and analyses. Researchers also worry about making too much of a single study, and methodologically weak reviews of groups of studies (O'Connell et al., 2009).

Researchers take pride in improved rigor and standards of evidence. Many researchers and research-savvy users now understand that well-designed and -implemented field experiments are a powerful way to produce unbiased estimates of the effects of a range of policy and program interventions (Bloom, 2005; Flay et al., 2005). They know that the field still needs better analysis techniques to determine the causal mechanisms by which interventions improve youth outcomes (Hong, 2012). Researchers recognize that sampling and data analysis strategies need to account for the nesting of individuals within clusters such as programs, families, or classrooms (Raudenbush & Bryk, 2002) and that integrating quantitative and qualitative methods within a study can provide greater understanding than can one method alone (Weisner, 2005). Furthermore, many agree that it is useful to include multiple measures of the key constructs in studies (Shadish, Cook, & Campbell, 2002). Such methodological advances are supported by new, powerful, and cost-effective software programs for estimating the required sample size, as well as for managing and analyzing quantitative and qualitative data. In the eyes of researchers, these improvements combine to provide more stable and accurate information.

Social science canons also acknowledge that individual studies are usually tied to the particular people, place, and time studied, since samples are rarely drawn at random from known populations. Thus, researchers are trained to put greater faith in the synthesis of results from a number of related studies than in the results of any one study—no matter how well that single study was done. In the past 20 years, the standards and tools for synthesizing research have improved as much as those for conducting a single study (Cooper, Hedges, & Valentine, 2009; Glass, McGaw, & Smith, 1981). Groups such as the Campbell Collaboration and the What Works Clearinghouse have created protocols for how studies should be identified and synthesized, and their experiences have helped improve guidance about the design and implementation of studies of program effects (Song & Herman, 2010). As a result, recent reviews are more inclusive and transparent and produce more stable, accurate information than any single study.

In describing these advances, we do not mean to imply that they are uniformly understood or implemented. For example, researchers vary in their standards for evidence when creating lists of programs that "work." This produces confusion when a program appears on some lists as "evidence-based" but not on others (Gandhi, Murphy-Graham, Petrosino, Chrismer, & Weiss, 2007).

Agency leaders and managers tend to evaluate the trustworthiness of research evidence based on its relevance to their political and service contexts. Would the program work given the youth they serve, the capacity of their institutions, and their fiscal and political constraints? Are the findings "actionable," and is the path to adoption and implementation clear? Palinkas and colleagues (Palinkas, Finno, Fuentes, Garcia, & Holloway, 2011a), for example, found that system leaders and managers in human services evaluate research on evidence-based practices primarily on its relevance to their local circumstances and implementation concerns. This is indicated by how well the study's population matches theirs, the program's effects in counties with similar demographics, how much the program costs to implement, and how much time is required to train staff. Nelson and colleagues' (2009) study of education stakeholders found that they too valued research conducted with local data or in sites similar to theirs in size, demographics, and urban versus rural locale. School and district staff in Daly and Finnigan's (2012) study also placed a premium on local contexts and expressed doubt that what works in one place would necessarily work in others.

TRUSTWORTHY SOURCES

Considering their differing definitions of research and what constitutes trustworthy evidence, it is unsurprising that researchers and practitioners also have different ideas about the characteristics of a trustworthy source.

For researchers, trustworthy sources contain findings published after a rigorous review process, managed and implemented by competent peers. This process is followed by many research journals, certain web sites (e.g., What Works Clearinghouse), and publications of various federal agencies (e.g., Congressional Budget Office, the Government Accounting Office, the National Institutes of Health, the Institute for Education Sciences, and federal statistical agencies). Weaknesses due to method or motive are tempered by multiple peers applying accepted standards.

Practitioners usually learn about research evidence through a secondary source. This means that, in assessing trustworthiness, practitioners focus on the research purveyor, whether it is a researcher, policy maker, advocate, web site, or other practitioner. Is this a source with an axe to grind? Does the person or organization understand my needs, my work, and the constraints I am under? Are they making excessive claims to further their own agenda? Educators in Daly and Finnigan's study (2012) overwhelmingly believed that research and evidence could be, and often are, manipulated to buttress political agendas. As one practitioner stated,

> You know, you can find research to support anything. The problems we have in our society today.... People are now using research to say that all the problems are the teacher, and if you can correct the teacher, all our problems go away, which is ridiculous.... The point is research can be slanted to support many different viewpoints. It doesn't mean it's correct. (Daly, Finnigan, & Che, 2012)

Nelson and colleagues (2009, p. 24) found that some education stakeholders believed that "research could be found to support any point of view and was therefore of little valid use." Such views are reinforced when policy makers and advocates selectively compile research evidence in support of their political agendas (the tactical use of research). Another contributing factor may be when researchers publicly disagree about how to interpret findings. Recent examples include the debates among researchers about the implications of evaluations of Head Start (Besharov, 2005; National Forum on Early Childhood Policy and Programs, 2010), the 21st Century Community Learning Centers (Dynarski, 2006; Mahoney & Zigler, 2006), the Comprehensive Child Development Program (Gilliam, Ripple, Zigler, & Leiter, 2000; Goodson, Layzer, St. Pierre, Bernstein, & Lopez, 2000), and charter schools (Henig, 2008). Regardless of intent, such public disagreements can lead decision makers to say, as one school board member did to another, "at the end of the day, you're both going to be able to find studies that counter the other ones" (Asen et al., 2013, p. 57).

Given the prevalence of distrust, it is worth noting that practitioners see certain peers and intermediaries as trusted sources of evidence. When confronted with questions about a program or reform, agency administrators often ask peers working in equivalent positions, serving similar populations, and working under comparable conditions. They also turn to intermediaries whom they see as honest brokers, such as professional associations and consultants who are familiar to them. They seek sources who understand the decisions they need to make and the constraints they face.

Future efforts need to deal head-on with the issue of trust (Bryk & Schneider, 2002; Mayer, Davis, & Schoorman, 1995). Part of the remedy rests in researchers' pursuit of questions that practitioners see as relevant. These include questions about what it takes to launch and implement an innovation well and which sites can most benefit from a new program. One obstacle to the production of relevant research is the academic community's prevailing attitude that such research is not sufficiently theoretical. We disagree and follow Huston (2008), Morris (Morris, Gennetian, Duncan, & Huston, 2009), Aber (Aber, Brown, Jones, Berg, & Torrente, 2011), and others in believing that intervention studies are an opportunity to test developmental theories by attempting to induce change (William T. Grant Foundation, 2011). We also believe that if journals, funders, and review sites such as the What Works Clearinghouse required information relevant to practitioner concerns—such as cost, implementation requirements, and how context is related to effects—then researchers would start collecting, analyzing, and reporting such data.

Increasing cross-role understanding and trust is also critical. One method is to create opportunities for researchers to learn more about and from practitioners, and vice versa. At the Foundation, we have several mechanisms for doing so. One is our Distinguished Fellow grants program, which is designed to enable influential, mid-career researchers, practitioners, and policy makers to spend time embedded in each other's roles and settings. Another is convening grantees from different roles working in a shared area, which we initially did as part of our work to improve the quality of after-school programs. We commissioned an independent consultant to look into this strategy—which included advocates, practitioners, and researchers meeting over several years—and her findings suggest that participants found the cross-role convenings useful (Stevens, 2012). In subsequent "learning communities," we have continued to do this. For example, with the Spencer Foundation, we are supporting 3 years of semiannual meetings of a group of program developers, school district personnel, and evaluators working to scale up and test innovations meant to improve teaching.

Consistent with the literature on cultural exchange (Palinkas et al., & the Research Network on Youth Mental Health, 2009), our efforts have underscored the need for sustained interactions between researchers and practitioners. We know that differences will endure between culturally different groups that rarely mix. Progress will require sustained intergroup contact under circumstances that support joint understanding about the nature of problems and appropriate solutions.

Most recently, this led us to create a "learning community" of research–practice partnerships in education (Tseng, 2012b). These long-term collaborations require practitioners and researchers to work together to address persistent, practical problems (Coburn et al., 2012). In many ways, these partnerships subvert the conventional model of "research to practice" (Tseng, 2012a). Instead of asking how researchers can produce better work for practitioners, researchers and practitioners jointly define research questions. Rather than pushing researchers to better disseminate findings to practitioners, partnerships seek reciprocal interactions that support back-and-forth learning from one another. These shifts help researchers develop a stronger understanding of practitioners' views, norms, expertise, and constraints. And they help practitioners understand the strengths and limits of research for improving their work.

Access to Research Findings

Research findings are often hidden away in inaccessible journals where they are described in theory-heavy, discipline-specific jargon that can be confusing to anyone who does not share the authors' training. Shonkoff (2000), Shonkoff and Bales (2011), and Huston (2002, 2005, 2008) have written about these issues. Not only do they call for brief, jargon-free writing, they also urge the research community to frame arguments in ways that lead to policies that reflect what science shows.

Scientific writing in journals and reports often mirrors the structure of the scientific method. Authors "bury their lead." They begin with the theory they are testing, review the empirical literature on the topic, and eventually get to the study's questions or hypotheses. Next, they describe methods. Finally, they discuss the results, with an emphasis on their theoretical significance and the study's limitations. This structure gets to the point too late and loses readers. In addition, researchers are usually ill-equipped to draw implications for policy or practice. Fortunately, the clarity of scientific writing is changing for the better. Professional organizations such as the Society for Research in Child Development now create public summaries of notable scientific articles; many research firms, such as MDRC, Child Trends, the American Enterprise Institute, and the Brookings Institution, have mastered the art of the coherent executive summary and the "one-pager"; and print and Internet media such as *Education Week* make research conferences and reports accessible to wider audiences.

These improvements, however, have limitations. They do not capitalize on the strategies that most of us use when confronted with a problem—drawing advice from peers working in similar situations. They also leave practitioners to interpret and apply research evidence to the problem at hand, an unwelcome task for people who must make decisions quickly, with incomplete information and too few resources (Yohalem & Tseng, in press).

ACQUISITION OF RESEARCH EVIDENCE

How might we alleviate these limitations? One strategy is to influence practitioners' networks (Rogers, 2003). A number of our grantees are mapping social networks in order to better understand how practitioners acquire research evidence.

Finnigan, Daly, and Che (2012) found that teachers saw their principals as important sources of evidence. This was particularly true in lower performing schools. Principals, in turn, are most likely to learn about evidence and research-based ideas from district staff. This suggests that whether teachers have strong ties to principals—and principals to key district administrators—influences whether research-based ideas get into schools. Interventions to strengthen ties between districts and principals and between principals and their teachers may improve the research–practice connection.

Palinkas, Holloway, Rice, Fuentes, Wu, and Chamberlain (2011b) have been studying network influences on evidence acquisition among human service agencies. Their findings support the importance of opinion leaders whose positions in a social network enable them to influence others. Palinkas and colleagues (2011b) used social network analyses to identify those individuals who were seen as sources of information about evidence-based and/or innovative programs. Longitudinal analyses 2 years later demonstrated that these opinion leaders worked in counties that made greater progress implementing an evidence-based program. In semi-structured interviews, agency leaders and managers elaborated on their reliance on other counties and intermediary organizations for information about funding, staffing, and clients. Small, rural counties were more isolated and relied more on other counties for information and advice.

Understanding social networks could provide insights into how to promote the productive use of research evidence. Rather than pursuing broad-based dissemination efforts, there may be value in understanding the existing social system and capitalizing on it. Dearing and Kreuter (2010) describe a strategy that involves (1) clearly delineating the sector you seek to influence, (2) collecting data to map the social structure within that sector and identify its opinion leaders (e.g., the states or localities that others look to for promising ideas or the intermediaries seen as trustworthy), and (3) recruiting those opinion leaders to help with diffusion efforts.

An extension of Dearing and Kreuter's strategy is to identify opinion leaders within the research and practice communities and create opportunities for them to work together on practical problems. By mixing individuals or organizations that are influential within their respective professional communities, it becomes more likely that researchers will study practice-relevant questions, practitioners will access research, and that the new knowledge and perspectives both groups gain will diffuse through their networks.

INTERPRETING AND APPLYING EVIDENCE

Access to research evidence is not sufficient—evidence of all types must be interpreted to be used. Practitioners and policy makers face the challenge of interpreting research evidence for its implications for their specific problems and decisions because research rarely provides "facts" that can be mechanically applied.

As Kennedy (1984, p. 225) described, "evidence is not merely attached to the user's store of knowledge like barnacles are to clams…rather [it] is a formative process in which evidence is acted on by the user. It is sorted, sifted, and interpreted; it is transformed into implications and translated into inferences."

Given the central role of interpretation, more needs to be done to facilitate it. It is important to determine which people, interactions, and systems lead to the productive interpretation of research for practice. For example, as noted earlier, it is common for practitioners to draw on a network of peers for information and interpretation. However, if that network is homogeneous and has few ties to others (i.e., an isolated group of like-minded people), it could lead to limited information and potential blind spots or biases (Daly, 2010; Finnigan, Daly, & Che, in press).

One option is for intermediary organizations to serve as relationship brokers, bringing researchers and practitioners together. This approach capitalizes on the trustworthiness of intermediaries. They can help researchers and practitioners develop and debate implications from existing evidence. In this process of interpreting and extrapolating from research results, both researchers and practitioners bring their understanding of the facts and their professional judgment gleaned from experience (McDonnell & Weatherford, 2012).

Research–practice partnerships may also aid interpretation (Yohalem & Tseng, in press). Practitioners often seek help making sense of the research they see or hear about; they want to know what the best available research has to say about the decisions at hand. They often ask for more research synthesis, secondary analyses of existing local data, and faster turnaround. Providing this help, however, can challenge the pace of research. In addition, academic incentives often reward new studies, and sometimes new data collection, instead of reviews of existing work. Partnerships are innovating to try to better meet these demands. The Baltimore Education Research Consortium, for example, is a partnership between Baltimore City Public Schools, Morgan State University, Johns Hopkins University, and other civic and community partners. When the district requests it, their Rapid Response agreement is to provide data analyses and reviews in 1 month or less.

Conclusion

There are many forces shaping practice, and we do not believe research is or should be the most important. Political scientists and policy analysts have written about the various forces that shape legislation (Haskins & Sawhill, 2009; Kingdon, 1995; Rich, 2004). The list is extensive and includes the state of the economy, the prevailing political climate, and the interests and expertise of key congressional committee chairs and agency staff. In the same vein, many forces shape practice. Rather than view practitioners as targets of dissemination efforts, researchers and policy makers are wise to consider them as agents who are actively sifting, interpreting, and applying a wide range of evidence to carry out their daily work.

Moreover, practitioners' social ecologies—the features of their organizations, the political environment, and community and public demands—affect their ability to acquire, interpret, and use research. How these contextual influences shape practice is not well understood, and we hope the studies we are supporting will help fill the gap.

Policy makers at many levels support the evidence-based practice movement. As previously noted, practitioners face unprecedented demands to use research. The No Child Left Behind Act (NCLB, 2002) included more than 100 references to "scientifically based research" and required that school districts use research in their decisions about curricula, instructional programs, and professional development. The Obama administration has made program evaluation a priority across agencies and wants to use evaluations to "help the Administration determine how to spend taxpayer dollars effectively and efficiently—investing more in what works and less in what does not" (Orszag, 2009). Recent state legislative and judicial actions have also required that child welfare and mental health agencies use research to redesign systems, select evidence-based programs and practices, and implement them.

Having caught the attention of policy makers and practitioners, the research community has to deliver. Changes have been made to improve the relevance of applied developmental research for practice, but these efforts fall short by not understanding practitioners' perspectives, nor leveraging how they acquire, interpret, and use research evidence. We choose to view these shortcomings as an opportunity for scholars to work more closely with practitioners and intermediaries toward the goal of improved youth outcomes. More than 30 years ago, Nathan Caplan argued that the relationship between researchers and policy makers must be reciprocal to be productive (Caplan, 1979). We agree. The most promising approaches will go beyond the framing of "research to practice" to a bidirectional relationship in which each influences the other.

References

Aber, L., Brown, J. L., Jones, S. M., Berg, J., & Torrente, C. (2011). School-based strategies to prevent violence, trauma, and psychopathology: The challenges of going to scale. *Development and Psychopathology, 23*(2), 411–421.

Asen, R., Gurke, D., Solomon, R., Conners, P., & Gummw, E. (2011). "The research says:" Definitions and uses of a key policy term in federal law and local school board deliberations. *Argumentation and Advocacy, 47*, 195–213.

Asen, R., Gurke, D., Connors, P., Solomon, R., & Gumm, E. (2013). Research evidence and school-board deliberations: Lessons from three Wisconsin school districts. *Educational Policy, 27*, 33–63

Besharov, D. J. (2005, October). Head Start's broken promise. *On the issues*. Retrieved from: http://www.aei.org/files/2005/10/25/20051025_3419153OTIBesharov_g.pdf

Bloom, H. S. (Ed.). (2005). *Learning more from social experiments*. New York: Russell Sage Foundation.

Bryk, A. S., & Schneider, B. (2002). *Trust in schools: A core resource for improvement.* New York: Russell Sage Foundation.

Caplan, N. (1979). The two communities theory and knowledge utilization. *American Behavioral Scientist, 22,* 459–470.

Coburn, C. E., Penuel, W. R., & Geil, K. E. (2012). *Research-practice partnerships at the district level: A new strategy for leveraging research for educational improvement.* New York: William T. Grant Foundation.

Cooper, H., Hedges, L. V., & Valentine, J. C. (Eds.). (2009). *The handbook of research synthesis and meta-analysis* (2nd ed.). New York: Russell Sage Foundation.

Daly, A. (2010). *Social network theory and educational change.* Cambridge, MA: Harvard Education Press.

Daly, A., & Finnigan, K. (2012). Exploring the space between: Social networks, trust, and urban school district leaders. *Journal of School Leadership, 22: 493–530*

Davies, H. T. O., & Nutley, S. (2008). *Learning more about how research-based knowledge gets used.* New York: William T. Grant Foundation.

Dearing, J., & Kreuter, M. (2010). Designing for diffusion: How can we increase uptake of cancer communication innovations? *Patient Education and Counseling, 81,* S100–S110

Dynarski, M. (2006). Advancing the use of scientifically based research in forming policy: A response to Mahoney and Zigler. *Journal of Applied Developmental Psychology, 27*(4), 295–297.

Finnigan, K., Daly, A., & Che, J. (in press). Systemwide reform in districts under pressure: The role of social networks in defining, acquiring and diffusing research evidence. *Journal of Educational Administration, 51*(4).

Finnigan, K., Daly, A., & Che, J. (2012). *The acquisition and use of evidence district-wide.* Paper presented at the annual meeting of the American Educational Research Association, Vancouver, Canada. Retrieved from http://www.wtgrantfoundation.org/resources/studying-the-use-of-research-evidence.

Flay, B. R., Biglan, A., Boruch, R. F., Castro, F. G., Gottfredson, D., Kellam, S., et al. (2005). Standards of evidence: Criteria for efficacy, effectiveness and dissemination. *Prevention Science, 6,* 151–175.

Gandhi, A. G., Murphy-Graham, E., Petrosino, A., Chrismer, S. S., & Weiss, C. H. (2007). The devil is in the details: Examining the evidence for "proven" school-based drug abuse prevention programs. *Evaluation Review, 31*(1), 43–74.

Gilliam, W. S., Ripple, C. H., Zigler, E. F., & Leiter, V. (2000). Evaluation child and family demonstration initiatives: Lessons from the Comprehensive Child Development Program. *Early Childhood Research Quarterly, 15,* 41–59.

Glass, G. V., McGaw, B., & Smith, M. L. (1981). *Meta-analysis in social research.* Beverly Hills, CA: Sage Publications.

Goodson, B. D., Layzer, J. I., St. Pierre, R. G., Bernstein, L. S., & Lopez, M. (2000). Effectiveness of a comprehensive, five-year family support program for low-income children and their families: Findings from the Comprehensive Child Development Program. *Early Childhood Research Quarterly, 15,* 5–39.

Granger, R. G. (2011). The big why: a learning agenda for the scale-up movement. *Pathways,* Winter 2011, 28–32.

Haskins, R., & Sawhill, I. (2009). *Creating an opportunity society.* Washington, DC: Brookings Institution Press.

Henig, J. R. (2008). *Spin cycle: How research is used in policy debates: The case of charter schools.* New York: Russell Sage Foundation.

Hong, G. (Ed.). (2012). Special issue on the statistical approaches to studying mediator effects in education research. *Journal of Research on Educational Effectiveness, 5*(3).

Honig, M. I., & Coburn, C. (2008). evidence-based decision making in school district central offices. *Educational Policy, 22*(4), 578–608.

Huston, A. C. (2002). From research to policy: Choosing questions and interpreting the answers. In A. Higgins-D'Alessandro & K. R. B. Jankowski (Eds.), *Science for society: Informing policy and practice through research in developmental psychology. New Directions for Child and Adolescent Development (No. 98)* (pp. 29–42). San Francisco: Jossey-Bass.

Huston, A. C. (2005). Connecting the science of child development in public policy. *SRCD Social Policy Report, 19*(4), 3–18.

Huston, A. C. (2008). From research to policy and back. *Child Development, 79*, 1–12.

Kellam, S., & Langevin, D. (2003). A framework for understanding "evidence" in prevention research and programs. *Prevention Science, 4*, 137–153.

Kennedy, M. (1984). How evidence alters understanding and decisions. *Educational Evaluation and Policy Analysis, 3*, 207–226.

Kingdon, J. W. (1995). *Agendas, alternative, and public policies* (2nd ed.). Boston: Little, Brown.

Loeb, S., Rouse, C., & Shorris, A. (2007). Excellence in the classroom. *The Future of Children, 17*(1).

Mahoney, J. L., & Zigler, E. F. (2006). Translating science to policy under the No Child Left Behind Act of 2001: Lessons from the national evaluation of the 21st Century Community Learning Centers. *Journal of Applied Developmental Psychology, 27*(4), 282–294.

Mayer, R. C., Davis, J. H., & Schoorman, F. D. (1995). An integrative model of organizational trust. *Academy of Management Review, 20*, 709–734.

McDonnell, L. M., & Weatherford, M. S. (2012). *Evidence use and stages of the common core standards movement.* Paper presented at the Annual Meeting of the American Education Research Association, Vancouver, Canada.

Morris, P. A., Gennetian, L., Duncan, G., & Huston, A. (2009). How welfare policies affect child and adolescent school performance: Investigating pathways of influence with experimental data. In James P. Ziliak (Ed.), *Welfare reform and its long-term consequences for America's poor* (pp. 255–289). Cambridge, UK: Cambridge University Press.

National Forum on Early Childhood Policy and Programs. (2010). *Understanding the Head Start Impact Study.* Retrieved from: http://www.developingchild.harvard.edu/download_file/-/view/627/

National Research Council. (2002). *Scientific research in education.* Washington, DC: National Academy Press.

Nelson, S. R., Leffler, J. C., & Hansen, B. A. (2009). *Toward a research agenda for understanding and improving use of research evidence* Portland, OR: Northwest Regional Educational Laboratory.

No Child Left Behind (NCLB) Act of 2001, Pub. L. No. 107-110, § 115, Stat. 1425 (2002).

O'Connell, M. E., Boat, T., & Warner, K. (Eds.). (2009). *Preventing mental, emotional, and behavioral disorders among young people: Progress and possibilities* [National Research Council and Institute of Medicine]. Washington DC: The National Academic Press.

Orszag, P. (2009). *Increased emphasis on program evaluation*. Office of Management and Budget. Retrieved from http://www.whitehouse.gov/sites/default/files/omb/assets/memoranda_2010/m10-01.pdf.

Palinkas, L. A., Aarons, G. A., Chorpita, B. F., Hoagwood, K. E., Landsverk, J., Weisz, J. R., & the Research Network on Youth Mental Health. (2009). Cultural exchange and the implementation of evidence-based practice: Two case studies. *Journal of Evidence-Based Social Work, 19*, 602–612.

Palinkas, L. A., Finno, M., Fuentes, D., Garcia, A., & Holloway, I. W. (2011a). *Evaluating dissemination of research evidence in public youth-serving systems*. Paper presented at the National Child Welfare Evaluation Summit, Washington, DC.

Palinkas, L. A., Holloway, I. W., Rice, E., Fuentes, D., Wu, Q., & Chamberlain, P. (2011b). Social networks and implementation of evidence-based practices in public youth-serving systems: A mixed methods study. *Implementation Science, 6*, 113.

Raudenbush, S. W., & Bryk, A. S. (2002). *Hierarchical linear models: Applications and data analysis methods* (2nd ed.). Thousand Oaks, CA: Sage.

Rich, A. (2004). *Think tanks, public policy, and the politics of experience*. New York: Cambridge University Press.

Rogers, E. M. (2003). *Diffusion of innovations* (5th ed.). New York: Free Press.

Shadish, W. R., Cook, T. D., & Campbell, D. T. (2002). *Experimental and quasi-experimental designs for generalized causal inference*. Boston: Houghton Mifflin.

Shonkoff, J. P. (2000). Science, policy, and practice: Three cultures in search of a shared mission. *Child Development, 82*, 181–187.

Shonkoff, J. P., & Bales, S. N. (2011). Science does not speak for itself: Translating child development research for the public and its policymakers. *Child Development Special Issue: Raising Healthy Children, 82*(1), 17–32.

Song, M., & Herman, R. (2010). Critical issues and common pitfalls in designing and conducting impact studies in education: Lessons learned from the what works clearinghouse. *Educational Evaluation and Policy Analysis, 32*(3), 351–371.

Stevens, P. (2012). *The W. T. Grant Foundation: Contributions to the after-school field 2003–2011*. New York: William T. Grant Foundation.

Tseng, V. (2012a). The uses of research in policy and practice. *SRCD Social Policy Report, 26*(2), 3–16.

Tseng, V. (2012b). *Partnerships: Shifting the dynamics between research and practice*. New York: William T. Grant Foundation.

Weisner, T. S. (2005). *Discovering successful pathways in children's development: Mixed methods in the study of childhood and family life*. Chicago: University of Chicago Press.

William T. Grant Foundation. (2011). *Intervention research interests: Guidelines for applicants and reviewers*. New York: Author. Retrieved from http://www.wtgrantfdn.org/File%20Library/Funding%20Opportunities/Intervention-Guidelines.doc

Yohalem, N., & Tseng, V. (in press). Moving from practice to research and back again. *Applied Developmental Science*.

Epilogue

THE ECOLOGY OF HUMAN DEVELOPMENT IN THE 21ST CENTURY

Aletha C. Huston

It has been more than 30 years since the publication of *The Ecology of Human Development* (1979), in which Bronfenbrenner proposed the now-famous concentric circles model of human development, with the child at the center and the contexts of development radiating out from the individual child's experience in proximal to distal order. Rejecting the "family bubble" model (Neito & Yoshikawa, Chapter 6), the major thesis was that families and children live in environments that provide both opportunities and constraints—that transactions with societal contexts and institutions are central to children's experiences from infancy onward. Important contexts are not limited to those with which children have direct contact (e.g., schools), but include macrolevel economic conditions, cultural institutions and values, and public policies. Although the model was expanded and refined in subsequent years (e.g., Bronfenbrenner & Morris, 1998, 2006), its basic premises were apparent in the initial formulation. Three are particularly relevant to this volume.

First, human development is conceptualized as a transactional process, with an emphasis placed on the interplay of individual (or family) and context, as well as on the interactions between and among contexts. The systems perspective underlying this model is antithetical to unidirectional "effects" of environments on children or of children on environments. Instead, it leads us to think about how individuals' skills, motives, and values interact with the opportunities, barriers, social structures, and economic conditions that they encounter. Taking this perspective leads researchers to consider individuals and families as active agents affecting their worlds *and* to recognize the importance of variations in available opportunities. Instantiating transactional processes in empirical analysis is, however, difficult. Much of the available research is designed to understand unidirectional influences of contexts on children and families, but, as the chapters in this book illustrate, it is increasingly common for it to include transactional processes.

Second, ideology and culture affect not only children and families but also the social scientists and policy makers attempting to understand and influence development. We social scientists are embedded in culture(s) along with everyone else, and, like everyone else, we often need a contrasting culture or a major social change to get a broader perspective. Gender research provides a vivid illustration. As Liben, Bigler, and Hilliard (Chapter 1) point out, both theory and research questions were dramatically altered in the 1970s, largely as a result of the Women's Movement. Researchers shifted away from the prevailing Freudian view that traditional gender roles were "good" and desirable goals of socialization toward valuing "androgyny" for both males and females.

Third, public policy is critical to providing a comprehensive understanding of human development. Bronfenbrenner (1979) asserted that, "in the interests of advancing fundamental research on human development, *basic science needs public policy even more than public policy needs basic science*" (p. 8; italics in original). A "functional integration" of the two is needed because public policies alert the investigator to those aspects of the environment that are most critical for development and lay bare the ideological assumptions underlying, and sometimes limiting, the formulation of research problems (p. 8). To this end, the chapters of this volume are arranged in pairs; within each topic, one covers "basic" research and the second presents what we know about policy and practice. The chapters not only illustrate the usefulness of integrating the two approaches but also suggest fruitful directions for future research.

The U.S. Landscape for Children in the 21st Century

In the expansions of his theory of human development, Bronfenbrenner and Morris (1998, 2006) introduced time as a fourth dimension (along with person, context, and process), arguing for a dynamic view of development over time. Contexts are dynamic as well, and they interact with one another (Gershoff & Benner, Chapter 9). Individual development occurs within the framework of secular and historical changes and events that create different opportunities and contexts for each generation (Elder & Shanahan, 2006).

Children in the United States confront radically different environments than those that existed 50 or 100 years ago. Within the first year or two of life, the average child is exposed to a wide variety of electronic media (e.g., television, touchscreen toys, toys that talk and squeak). Many have television sets in their bedrooms (Calvert & Wartella, Chapter 11). More than half of them spend some time in the care of adults other than parents before they are a year old (O'Brien, Weaver, Burchinal, Clarke-Stewart, & Vandell, Chapter 3). Although sex-typed toys continue to prevail, both boys and girls grow up with different concepts and expectations about gendered relationships and careers than did earlier generations (Eccles, Chapter 2).

Today's children are born into a society that is increasingly diverse with respect to ethnic and nationality background as well as income levels. The percent of children who are non-Hispanic White has decreased at the same time as Hispanic, Asian, and other groups have increased. By 2023, less than half of all children in the United States are projected to be White, non-Hispanic (Federal Interagency Forum on Child and Family Statistics, 2011). At the same time, the number of children from immigrant families and the percent living in a non–English-speaking household has increased (Marks, Godoy, & García Coll, Chapter 5; Neito & Yoshikawa, Chapter 6).

Today's children also face rising levels of economic inequality. For many years, a high percent of U.S. children have lived in poverty, but, in the past 30 years, families in the high-income ranges have become much more prosperous. As a result, income inequality has become a serious national problem. Roughly 40% of American children live in "low-income" families (less than 200% of the poverty threshold)—a figure that has changed little over the past 30 years. At the same time, the percentage of children living in families with high incomes (greater than 400% of poverty) grew from 17% in 1980 to 30% in 2007, and the percentage of children in families with very high incomes (greater than 600% of poverty) rose from 4% in 1980 to 13% in 2007 (Federal Interagency Forum on Child and Family Statistics, 2011). This increasing disparity of incomes has implications for children's early care and education, media exposure, neighborhoods, schools, recreation, and social networks (Duncan & Murnane, 2011).

The chapters in this book offer thoughtful insights into understanding how the landscape of contexts outside the family contributes to children's development and family functioning. The themes running through many of them resonate with the three principles that guided Bronfenbrenner's original model of human development in context.

TRANSACTIONS OF INDIVIDUALS AND CONTEXTS

Both theorists and policy makers face questions about person–environment interactions. On the one hand, families and children live within economic and cultural conditions over which they have limited control; on the other hand, individuals and families vary greatly in how they cope with barriers and use available resources. For example, the mass media convey a constant stream of messages, but parents influence children's exposure to those messages and children themselves use media in variable ways (Calvert & Wartella, Chapter 11; Truglio & Kotler, Chapter 12). Similarly, images of gender pervade children's environments, but individuals and families construct variable patterns of gendered concepts and behavior (Liben et al., Chapter 1). Understanding the transactional relations among contexts and individuals lies at the heart of much of the research discussed in this book.

Developmental theorists have long wrestled with person–environment issues. The pendulum has swung from intrinsic maturational processes in the early 20th century to strong environmentalism in mid-century and back to genetic and temperamental bases of behavior in more recent years. A parallel dichotomy exists in discussions of policy. One of these, described by McLoyd, Mistry, and Hardaway

(Chapter 7), is the contrast between social selection and social causation models of poverty (Conger & Donnellan, 2007). According to the social selection model, adults' poverty or prosperity is largely a result of individual characteristics that include intelligence, responsibility, and moral integrity. The social causation model, by contrast, posits the social, economic, and cultural conditions surrounding an individual as major "causes" of poverty. The two models have different implications for policy and research. The social selection model suggests that policies should be designed to change individuals' abilities and personal characteristics (e.g., early childhood intervention, job training, and welfare sanctions). The social causation model leads to policies designed to change social conditions (e.g., school quality improvement, minimum wage laws, publicly supported child care). Obviously, neither extreme is accurate, but the basic assumptions underlying them are often implicit in controversies about such public policies as welfare, early care and education, and employment incentives. Conger and Donnellan (2007) proposed a hybrid "interactionist" model in which individual characteristics interact with external conditions, a model well-illustrated by the finding that families use policies and programs in ways that are consistent with their family routines and values (Weisner & Duncan, Chapter 8).

Theories that emphasize individual characteristics as determinants can be distinguished along a continuum from passive to active. For example, the proposal that genetically based abilities are major determinants of poverty (Rowe & Rodgers, 1997) suggests that individuals have little power to alter their lot in life. By contrast, a theme of individual agency (by both children and parents) runs throughout most of the chapters in this book. Some families promote ethnic identity and pride in their culture as a strategy for building resilience in their children (Marks et al., Chapter 5; Nieto & Yoshikawa, Chapter 6), and some parents promote their daughters' math performance with high expectations and confidence about their children's abilities (Eccles, Chapter 3).

Parents exercise agency by choosing environments for their children, often consciously taking advantage of promotive contexts or, at the very least, avoiding antisocial ones. They make decisions about child care, where they live, where and how much they work, where or if they worship, and what kinds of electronic media pervade their household. Of course, parents and families do not have unlimited options from which to choose, particularly if they are poor or are part of an ethnic group that faces discrimination, but even the very poor can exercise agency. One mother in the New Hope study completed a GED while working full time and raising four children because she wanted to be able to help her son with his homework (Duncan, Huston, & Weisner, 2007). As another example, immigrant families use and choose institutions in the United States to teach their children the language and customs of the new culture (Neito & Yoshikawa, Chapter 6).

As children grow into middle childhood and adolescence, they exercise agency by selecting the environments in which they spend time (Scarr & McCartney, 1983). Children are actors in their own development of gender identity and roles

(Liben et al., Chapter 1). They also make choices about media use, extracurricular activities, and friends. Even in contexts about which they have little choice, such as school, they can be engaged or disengaged and, ultimately, decide whether or not to attend (Gershoff & Benner, Chapter 9).

Public policies are often designed on the implicit assumption that individuals respond passively to the social forces around them; hence, policy makers (and policy researchers) do not involve recipients as active participants in change. Viewing recipients as people to be acted upon rather than as participants may reduce the effectiveness of many policies. The chapters in this book offer several examples of exceptions—policies that came about partly through advocacy and grassroots organizing. For example, the New Hope Project was originated by a coalition of labor organizers, political leaders, and community groups. It operated on the philosophy that the program and the participant each brought something to the table. The program offered a set of benefits in return for full-time employment; the participant could choose to fulfill the contract or not (Duncan et al., 2007).

Policies can be designed to assist parents and families in advocacy. The chapter by Nieto and Yoshikawa in this volume provides a number of examples, focusing "on participation in schools, working conditions and political incorporation as three specific pathways through which immigrant parents' experiences outside of the home context may impact their children" (p. 102). Activities of parents and families were promoted using social networks, advocacy organizations, and other mechanisms arising from immigrants and others who advocate for their own needs and interests.

In summary, a transactional approach is consistent with the fact that parents and children exercise agency to affect their environments and ultimately their development. Their choices are limited by available options, but public policies can broaden those opportunities. For example, parents can take advantage of the educational value of such television programs as *Sesame Street* only if the programs are produced and disseminated—a decision over which individual parents have little control. The Children's Television Act of 1990, requiring broadcasters to offer educational and informational programs for children, is designed to assure that these options are available to children and families (Calvert & Wartella, Chapter 11; Truglio & Kotler, Chapter 12). Likewise, not all young girls will participate in sports, but regulations (e.g., Title IX passed as part of the Higher Education Amendments Act of 1972) prohibiting gender discrimination can assure that the opportunities are available.

CULTURE AND IDEOLOGY

Ideology and culture are macrosystems that affect not only children and families but also the social scientists and policy makers attempting to understand and influence development. A clear example is early child care (O'Brien et al., Chapter 3). Until the late 1980s, virtually all of the research was guided by the assumption that child care might be harmful; hence, both advocates and opponents of child care framed their research questions around possible negative effects (e.g., Does child care reduce secure attachment to mothers?). As maternal employment and nonparental care for very young children became more common and socially acceptable, researchers began to ask about positive as well as negative consequences (e.g., Can quality child care enhance language acquisition?). It is not a coincidence that professionals and advocates have striven to shift the associated label from "day care" to "child care" and recently to "early care and education" as a way of reducing negative connotations (Rhodes & Huston, 2012).

Despite the recognition that individual characteristics and environmental opportunities interact, the ideology of individualism, social mobility, and individual initiative underlies most policy proposals and decisions. Implicitly or explicitly, it is assumed that individuals' fates are largely a function of their own characteristics and actions (i.e., social selection with agency) rather than social conditions or characteristics beyond their control. Policy makers' language conveys assumptions about the social values associated with policies. For example, prolonged use of welfare is typically called "dependency," and the goal of welfare policy is "self-sufficiency." The changes in the welfare system in 1996 carry the label "welfare reform," with the clear implication that they improved the system. The underlying premise of this language is that individual parents, who are predominantly single mothers, can or should be able to make it on their own. Policy researchers often adopt the same vocabulary, either because they do not consider it important or because it enables them to communicate with policy makers, but we should work harder to examine the consequences of the values implied by language for our conceptions of processes and research questions.

POLICY AND DEVELOPMENT

Bronfenbrenner argued for a functional integration of basic science and public policy, not simply to infuse scientific information into policy, but also to promote a comprehensive understanding of basic developmental processes. Several chapters in this book contain excellent examples. Large-scale studies of policies designed to move families into better neighborhoods have brought about a better understanding of adolescent development, as well as highlighting the limitations of policy makers' conceptualizations. Discussing the failure of the Moving to Opportunity experiment to improve most aspects of adolescent functioning, Crosnoe and Leventhal (Chapter 10, p. 168) point out, "Lack of consideration of social and emotional functioning is a major oversight, one that may account for the mixed results across setting-level policy efforts. Without more attention to children's developmental needs across interrelated domains—social, emotional, and cognitive—future policies and programs are not likely to achieve their full potential."

Developmentalists have garnered basic knowledge from examining how early childhood education and care influences social and cognitive development and how the effects of care environments vary depending on family conditions, ethnic group, gender, and family income. Information about which interventions are most effective builds scientific knowledge about the malleability of developmental trajectories and interactions of temperament with environment. Bronfenbrenner once criticized developmental psychology for being the study of children's reactions to strange people in strange settings (i.e., laboratories). Studying children and families in complex natural environments has enabled scientists to answer questions about development in situ that enrich science and permit extrapolation to policy and practice. Policy experiments have provided unique opportunities to test the impacts of changes in family income, child care settings, educational media, and neighborhoods on children and families.

Policy issues influence research topics and questions because they generate funding programs. Seminal research on almost every topic covered in this book occurred partly as a consequence of federal agency programs and priorities that arose from social issues under public debate. Eccles' original work on gender was conducted as part of a federal program inspired by public controversy about females' underperformance in math. My research on children's television began with funding from a National Institute of Mental Health (NIMH) program that was launched in response to the Surgeon General's Advisory Committee on Social Behavior (1971), which in turn had been created because of alarm about urban riots and violence in the late 1960s. The Study of Early Child Care and Youth Development (SECCYD) was initiated and funded by the National Institute of Child Health and Human Development (NICHD) because of public concern about the effects of child care on very young children. Moving to Opportunity was initiated and funded by federal agencies to test ideas that grew out of the Gatreaux Project, a study resulting from court-ordered desegregation of public housing in Chicago (Crosnoe & Leventhal, Chapter 10). The federal agency in charge of welfare programs mandated and funded numerous experiments to test policy variations in the 1980s and 1990s (Morris, Gennetian, Duncan, & Huston, 2009). The coalition that organized New Hope included evaluation in their plan because they hoped that it would become a model for policy. The program provided a platform on which an interdisciplinary team attracted funding to carry out an extensive multimethod investigation of child development and family processes (Weisner & Duncan, Chapter 8). Federal agencies have recently increased funding for research on immigrant children. Although researchers can and do follow their own interests, funding is critical for generating the kinds of information presented in this book—and funding is inextricably intertwined with policy questions.

Research, Policy, and Practice

Integration of research with policy and practice is an overriding theme of this book, but merely conducting the research does not assure that it will affect policy and practice. Granger, Tseng, and Wilcox (Chapter 13) examine how research does or does not get used. They turn our attention from policy to practice, making the excellent point that practitioners make decisions about how, when, and under what circumstances policies are implemented. Five years ago, when I did the research for my Society for Research in Child Development (SRCD) presidential address on uses of child development knowledge (Huston, 2008), the dearth of information about translation of evidence to policy and practice was startling. The small amount of good empirical work had been done in the 1980s. The research described by Granger et al., in this volume is beginning to fill that gap. Why has it taken so long? Because it is not only complex, but requires methods and conceptual frameworks representing an integration of disciplines that usually do not work together. Policy makers' and practitioners' decision making often appears to be idiosyncratic and highly dependent on personalities. Finally, it is likely that the relevant processes are specific to particular policy domains—for example, decision making in education may occur differently than decision making in welfare policy (Prewitt, Schwandt, & Straf, 2012).

Nevertheless, the results of the research reported here suggest some principles for communicating research, as well as for the methods by which it is conducted and the questions that might be fruitful to ask. For example, child development policy studies could benefit from more attention to program costs and to sources of funding (e.g., public, private, partnerships), including benefit–cost analyses. When small demonstration programs are effective, additional research is needed to take them to scale. A great deal of public money has been invested in early education on the strength of treatment–control differences in the Perry Preschool study (Schweinhart, Barnes, & Weikart, 1993), but that seminal work does not inform many of critical questions about implementing large-scale high-quality early education. Researchers should also consider the extent to which results are specific to time, place, and population, and therefore need replicating across locations, historical periods, and groups.

Investigators could be more attentive to the political and community processes involved in creating and implementing programs. For example, well-intentioned efforts to integrate schools by race or by economic status have repeatedly fallen victim to public opposition, especially from parents (Crosnoe & Leventhal, Chapter 10). The New Hope Project came to fruition only after the Greater Milwaukee Committee, a group of powerful business and professional leaders in the city, supported it and after it received crucial support from both the Democratic mayor and the Republican governor, as well as a number of religious leaders and private foundations. One reason for the business leaders' support was its possibility of improving the economic climate of the city by helping people to get and keep employment; that is, it appealed to their goals and values (Duncan et al., 2007).

Research to understand the uses of science is best served by multiple methods, including qualitative ethnographic data as well as large-scale quantitative information. The rich information obtained by multiple methods is illustrated in the chapters on interventions affecting minority group children (Neito & Yoshikawa,

Chapter 6) and on poverty programs (Weisner & Duncan, Chapter 8). Effective use of multiple methods is difficult, however; it requires true collaboration and respect among investigators, not just parallel but separate qualitative and quantitative tracks (Duncan, 2012; Huston, 2011).

In conclusion, the chapters in this book offer important insights and new knowledge that build on the framework of Bronfenbrenner's model of human ecology. They testify to the "village" needed to raise a child by providing new understanding of children's and families' transactions with the social, physical, and cultural environments in which they live. They provide perspectives on the social and cultural assumptions that affect the scholars' research questions, as well as on policy makers' and practitioners' actions. They confirm the premises that (a) policy is critical to basic science, offering unique opportunities to understand developmental processes, and (b) developmental science offers important tools for policy and practice that may be exploited more extensively as our understanding of knowledge use expands.

References

Bronfenbrenner, U. (1979). *The ecology of human development: Experiments by nature and design.* Cambridge MA: Harvard University Press.

Bronfenbrenner, U., & Morris, P. A. (1998). The ecology of developmental processes. In W. Damon (Series Ed.) & R. M. Lerner (Volume Ed.), *Handbook of child psychology: Vol. 1. Theoretical models of human development* (5th ed., pp. 993–1028). New York: Wiley.

Bronfenbrenner, U., & Morris, P. (2006). The bioecological model of human development. In R. M. Lerner and W. Damon (Series Eds.) & W. Damon & R. M. Lerner (Volume Eds.) *Handbook of child psychology: Vol. 1. Theoretical models of human development:* (6th ed., pp. 793–828). New York: Wiley.

Conger, R. D., & Donnellan, M. B. (2007). An interactionist perspective on the socioeconomic context of human development. *Annual Review of Psychology, 58,* 175–199.

Duncan, G. J. (2012) Give us this day our daily breadth *Child Development, 83,* 6–15.

Duncan, G. J., Huston, A. C., & Weisner, T. S. (2007). *Higher ground: New Hope for the working poor and their children.* New York: Russell Sage.

Duncan, G. J., & Murnane, R. J. (Eds.) (2011). *Whither opportunity? Rising inequality, schools, and children's life chances.* New York: Russell Sage Foundation.

Elder, G. H., Jr., & Shanahan, M. J. (2006). The life course and human development. In W. Damon & R. M. Lerner (Series Eds.) & W. Damon & R. M. Lerner (Volume Eds.), *Handbook of child psychology: Vol. 1. Theoretical models of human development* (6th ed., pp. 665–715). New York: Wiley.

Federal Interagency Forum on Child and Family Statistics. (2011). *America's children: Key national indicators of well-being* Washington, DC: U.S. Government Printing Office.

Huston, A. C. (2008). From research to policy and back. *Child Development, 79,* 1–12.

Huston, A. C. (2011). A path to interdisciplinary scholarship. In L. Campbell & T. Loving (Eds.), *Close relationships.* Washington DC: American Psychological Association Press.

Morris, P. A., Gennetian, L. A., Duncan, G. J., & Huston, A. C. (2009). How welfare policies affect child and adolescent school performance: Investigating pathways of influence with experimental data. In J. Ziliak (Ed.), *Welfare reform and its long-term consequences for America's poor* (pp. 255–289). New York: Cambridge University Press.

Prewitt, K., Schwandt, T. A., & Straf, M. L. (2012). *Using science as evidence in public policy.* Washington DC: National Research Council.

Rhodes, H., & Huston, A. C. (2012). Building the workforce our youngest children deserve. *SRCD Social Policy Report, 26*(1), 1–26.

Rowe, D., & Rodgers, J. (1997). Poverty and behavior: Are environmental measures nature and nurture? *Developmental Review, 17,* 358–375.

Scarr, S., & McCartney, K. (1983). How people make their own environments: A theory of genotype-environment effects. *Child Development, 54,* 424–435.

Schweinhart, L. J., Barnes, H. V., & Weikart, D. P. (1993). *Significant benefits: The High/Scope Perry Preschool Study through age 27.* Ypsilanti, MI: High/Scope Educational Research Foundation.

Surgeon General's Scientific Advisory Committee on Television and Social Behavior. (1971). *Television and growing up: The impact of televised violence.* Washington DC: U.S. Department of Health, Education, and Welfare.

{ INDEX }

Figures are indicated by an italic *f* following the page number.